Exchange-Traded F
For Dummies®

Asking a Financial Professional about Working ETFs into Your Portfolio

If you think that you want a professional to help you construct an ETF portfolio, here are some questions to ask:

- Given my personal economics, how much risk should I be taking with my money? Specifically, what percent of my portfolio should be in stock ETFs and what percent in bond ETFs? (Most portfolios should have 50 to 80 percent stock.)

- Given the size of my portfolio, how many individual ETFs would you suggest?

- Which brokerage house do you recommend for housing my ETF portfolio?

- What is the historical rate of return on the ETF portfolio that you are suggesting, and just how volatile can it be?

- Given my age, my tax bracket, and my employment, what kind of account — IRA, Roth IRA, taxable brokerage account — do you suggest for my ETFs?

- What selection of ETFs would you advise for an optimally diversified portfolio?

- Do I keep my present investments, or sell them? If I keep them, how are you going to choose ETFs that best complement those investments?

- Can you help me jiggle the investments in my 401(k) plan to complement my new ETF portfolio?

Choosing the Best ETFs

With more than 300 ETFs available as of this writing, where do you start to shop?

- **Mix and match your holdings appropriately.** You not only want a well-diversified portfolio; you want one that includes various asset classes that tend to go up and down in value at different times. There's no point to holding four different ETFs that all invest in large cap stocks. Hold a large cap ETF *and* a small cap, a U.S. stock ETF *and* an international stock ETF. See sample portfolios in Chapter 16.

- **Go for lowest cost.** As with any other investment vehicle, be careful of paying more than you need to. Although most ETFs are very economical, some are more economical than others. You may not always want to pick the cheapest, but certainly aim in that direction. Parts II and III help steer you to the best ETF options.

- **Don't sweat the small stuff.** Two ETFs that track similar indexes (such as, say, large value stocks) are not going to be all that different from one another. Spend some time researching your options, but don't agonize over your selection. Much more important — perhaps worth *a little* agony — is choosing ETFs that track dissimilar indexes so your eggs are in different baskets.

- **Go passive.** A handful of ETFs promise "active management." Know that active management has an awfully spotty track record. The bulk, if not all, of your ETF portfolio should be in passively managed (indexed) ETFs. Part II helps you tell which ETFs are active and which are passive.

- **Look for breadth.** Examine the holdings of the ETF. As a rule, no one security (such as, for example, Microsoft or General Electric stock) should represent more than 10 percent of the ETF's total assets.

For Dummies: Bestselling Book Series for Beginners

Exchange-Traded Funds For Dummies®

Cheat Sheet

Web Sites for Up-to-Date ETF Information

The world of ETFs is forever changing. Keep updated by checking in on the following Web sites. (These are some of my faves, but I provide others in Appendix B.)

- ✔ **etfguide.com**: A good, quick summary of the entire ETF industry and the *raison d'etre* behind it. Contains an entire listing of all ETFs available, along with their trading symbols. (The same list appears in Appendix A of this book, although the Web site's, naturally, will be more up-to-date.)

- ✔ **etftrends.com**: The closest thing that ETF enthusiasts have to a gossip column. There's chatter about new ETFs on the market, proposed ETFs, and behind-the-scenes industry workings.

- ✔ **etfconnect.com**: A great place for quick quotes, yields, and ETF nuts-'n'-bolts information (expense ratios, performance records). A search function allows you to winnow through the world of ETFs to find one that fits whatever criteria.

- ✔ **finance.yahoo.com/etf**: Also boasts a search function, intimate details on individual funds, an ETF glossary, and regularly updated news and commentary.

- ✔ **morningstar.com (click the ETF icon on the blue bar at the top of the screen)**: Extensive information on individual funds, along with Morningstar's exclusive, trademarked rating system. (One star is bad; five stars is grand.)

How ETFs Differ from Mutual Funds

They are similar in that they both represent "baskets" of securities (usually stocks or bonds), but mutual funds and ETFs differ in a number of ways:

- ✔ **ETFs trade differently.** They can be bought and sold, and their price changes, throughout the day. In contrast, mutual fund orders can be made during the day, but the actual trading (and any resulting price change) doesn't occur until after the markets close.

- ✔ **ETFs are cheaper.** They require you to pay small trading commissions, but ETFs usually wind up costing you much less than a mutual fund because the ongoing operating expenses are usually much less. Most ETFs charge no more than one-half of 1 percent a year, some less than one-tenth of 1 percent.

- ✔ **ETFs tend to track indexes.** Managers of ETFs tend to do very little trading of securities in the ETF. The vast majority of mutual fund managers spend a lot of their time trading.

- ✔ **ETFs result in less tax.** Because of low portfolio turnover and also the way they are structured, ETFs' investment gains usually are more gingerly taxed than the gains on mutual funds.

For Dummies: Bestselling Book Series for Beginners

Exchange-Traded Funds

FOR DUMMIES®

by Russell Wild, MBA

Wiley Publishing, Inc.

Exchange-Traded Funds For Dummies®

Published by
Wiley Publishing, Inc.
111 River St.
Hoboken, NJ 07030-5774
www.wiley.com

Copyright © 2007 by Wiley Publishing, Inc., Indianapolis, Indiana

Published by Wiley Publishing, Inc., Indianapolis, Indiana

Published simultaneously in Canada

For general information on our other products and services, please contact our Customer Care Department within the U.S. at 800-762-2974, outside the U.S. at 317-572-3993, or fax 317-572-4002.

For technical support, please visit www.wiley.com/techsupport.

Wiley also publishes its books in a variety of electronic formats. Some content that appears in print may not be available in electronic books.

Library of Congress Control Number: 2006932693

ISBN-13: 978-0-470-04580-0

ISBN-10: 0-470-04580-9

Manufactured in the United States of America

10 9 8 7 6 5 4 3 2

1B/RW/RQ/QW/IN

WILEY

About the Author

Russell Wild is a Certified Financial Planner and a Registered Investment Advisor. He is one of only a handful of wealth managers in the nation who is both fee-only (takes no commissions) and welcomes clients of both substantial *and* modest means. He calls his firm Global Portfolios to reflect his ardent belief in international diversification — using exchange-traded funds to build well-diversified, low-expense, tax-efficient portfolios.

Wild, in addition to the fun he has with his financial calculator, is also an accomplished writer who helps readers understand and make wise choices about their money. His articles have appeared in many national publications, including *AARP The Magazine, Consumer Reports, Details, Maxim, Men's Journal, Cosmopolitan, Reader's Digest,* and *Real Simple.* He also contributes regularly to professional financial journals, such as *Wealth Manager* and *Financial Planning.*

The author or coauthor of two dozen nonfiction books, Wild's last work (prior to the one you're holding in your hand) was *The Unofficial Guide to Getting a Divorce,* coauthored with attorney Susan Ellis Wild, his ex-wife — yeah, you read that right — and published by Wiley. No stranger to the mass media, Wild has shared his wit and wisdom on such shows as *Oprah, The View, CBS Morning News,* and *Good Day New York,* and in hundreds of radio interviews.

Wild holds a Master of Business Administration (MBA) degree in international management and finance from Thunderbird, the Garvin School of International Management, in Glendale, Arizona (consistently ranked the #1 school for international business by both *U.S. News and World Report* and the *Wall Street Journal*); a Bachelor of Science (BS) degree in business/economics *magna cum laude* from American University in Washington, D.C.; and a graduate certificate in personal financial planning from Moravian College in Bethlehem, Pennsylvania (America's sixth oldest college). A member of the National Association of Personal Financial Advisors (NAPFA) since 2002, Wild is also a long-time member and board member of the American Society of Journalists and Authors (ASJA).

The author grew up on Long Island and now lives in Allentown, Pennsylvania, with his two children, Adrienne and Clayton, along with Norman, the killer poodle. His Web site is www.globalportfolios.net.

Dedication

To the small investor, who has been bamboozled, bullied, and beaten up long enough.

Author's Acknowledgments

Although I've written many books, this is my first *Dummies* book, and writing a first *Dummies* book is a bit like learning to ride a bicycle — on a very windy day. If it weren't for Joan Friedman, project editor, who kept a steady hand on the back of my seat, I would surely have fallen off a curb and been run over by a pickup truck flying a Confederate flag. Joan, hands down, is one of the best editors I've ever worked with. She's a very nice person, too.

Other nice people that I'd also like to tip my bicycle helmet to include Marilyn Allen of Allen O'Shea Literary Agency (she calls me "babe," just like agents do in movies; I love that) and Stacy Kennedy, acquisitions editor at Wiley. If these two gals hadn't gotten together, I wouldn't have had a bicycle to ride.

Thanks, too, to Noel Jameson, technical editor, for making sure that this remained strictly a work of nonfiction. And to Michael Pace, who double checked.

I'd like to thank Morningstar, and particularly Sumita Ghosh, for extreme generosity in providing fund industry data and analysis.

I'd also like to thank Donald Bowles, my old professor of economics at American University, for showing me that supply curves can be fun. Sorry we lost touch, but I haven't forgotten you.

I am indebted to Brenda Lange, my sage partner, for convincing me that I should write this book. Truth is, when Brenda tries, she could convince me to do just about anything.

And finally, I'd like to thank my old man, Lawrence Wild, both my most beloved and most difficult client, who, if he told me once, told me a thousand times: "Rich or poor, it's good to have money." It took me years to discover the profound wisdom in that statement.

Publisher's Acknowledgments

We're proud of this book; please send us your comments through our Dummies online registration form located at www.dummies.com/register/.

Some of the people who helped bring this book to market include the following:

Acquisitions, Editorial, and Media Development

Project Editor: Joan Friedman

Acquisitions Editor: Stacy Kennedy

Technical Editor: Noel M. Jameson

Editorial Supervisor: Carmen Krikorian

Editorial Manager: Michelle Hacker

Editorial Assistants: Erin Calligan, David Lutton

Cartoons: Rich Tennant (www.the5thwave.com)

Composition Services

Project Coordinator: Patrick Redmond

Layout and Graphics: Claudia Bell, Lavonne Cook, Lauren Goddard, Denny Hager, Stephanie D. Jumper, Barbara Moore, Shelley Norris, Barry Offringa

Anniversary Logo Design: Richard Pacifico

Proofreaders: Laura Albert, Techbooks

Indexer: Techbooks

Publishing and Editorial for Consumer Dummies

   Diane Graves Steele, Vice President and Publisher, Consumer Dummies

   Joyce Pepple, Acquisitions Director, Consumer Dummies

   Kristin A. Cocks, Product Development Director, Consumer Dummies

   Michael Spring, Vice President and Publisher, Travel

   Kelly Regan, Editorial Director, Travel

Publishing for Technology Dummies

   Andy Cummings, Vice President and Publisher, Dummies Technology/General User

Composition Services

   Gerry Fahey, Vice President of Production Services

   Debbie Stailey, Director of Composition Services

Contents at a Glance

Table of Contents

Introduction

. . . .

*E*very month, it seems, Wall Street comes up with some newfangled investment idea. The array of financial products (replete with 164-page prospectuses) is now so dizzying that the old lumpy mattress is starting to look like a more comfortable place to stash the cash. But there is one relatively new product out there definitely worth looking at. It's something of a cross between an index mutual fund and a stock, and it's called an *exchange-traded fund,* or ETF.

Just as computers, fax machines, and Humvees were used by big institutions before they caught on with individual consumers, so it was with ETFs. They were first embraced by institutional traders — investment banks, hedge funds, and insurance firms — because, among other things, they allow for the quick juggling of massive holdings. Big traders like that sort of thing. Personally, playing hot potato with my money is not my idea of fun. But all the same, over the past several years, I've invested most of my own savings in ETFs, and I've suggested to many of my clients that they do the same.

I'm not alone in my appreciation of ETFs. They have grown exponentially in the past few years — nearly 50 percent in 2005 — and they will surely continue to grow and gain influence. While I can't claim that my purchases and my recommendations of ETFs account for much of the growing $300 billion ETF market, I'm happy to be a (very) small part of it. After you've read *Exchange-Traded Funds For Dummies,* you may decide to become part of it as well, if you haven't already.

About This Book

As with any other investment, you're looking for a certain payoff in reading this book that you've just purchased. In an abstract sense, the payoff will come in your achieving a thorough understanding and appreciation of a powerful financial tool called an exchange-traded fund. In a more concrete sense, this book — by explaining how to use this powerful financial tool — can help you make money.

What makes me think ETFs can help you make money?

- ✔ **ETFs are intelligent.** Most financial experts agree that playing with individual stocks can be hazardous to one's wealth. Anything from an accounting scandal to the CEO's sudden angina attack can send a single stock spiraling downward. That's why it makes sense for the average investor to own lots of stocks — or bonds — through ETFs or mutual funds.

- ✔ **ETFs are cheap.** Many ETFs carry total management expenses under 0.20 percent a year. Some of the larger ETFs carry management fees as low as 0.07 percent a year. The average mutual fund, in contrast, charges 1.67 percent a year. Such differences, while appearing small on paper, can make a huge impact on your take-home. I crunch some appropriate numbers in Chapter 2.

- ✔ **ETFs are tax-smart.** Because of the very clever way ETFs are structured, the taxes you pay on any growth are minimal. I crunch some of those numbers in Chapter 2, as well.

- ✔ **ETFs are open books.** Quite unlike mutual funds, an ETF's holdings are readily visible. If this afternoon, for example, I were to buy 100 shares of the ETF called the SPDR (pronounced "spider") 500, I would know that exactly 3.54 percent of my money was invested in General Electric, another 3.52 percent was in Exxon Mobil Corp., and 2.26 percent was in Microsoft. You don't get that kind of detail when you buy most mutual funds. Mutual fund managers, like stage magicians, are often reluctant to reveal their secrets. In the investment game, the more you know, the less the odds of you getting sawed in half.

And speaking of open books, if this open book — the one you're now reading — were like some (but certainly not all) mutual funds, it would be largely unintelligible and expensive. (It might be doubly expensive if you tried to resell the book within 90 days!) Luckily, this book is more like an ETF. Here's how:

- ✔ *Exchange-Traded Funds For Dummies* **is intelligent.** I don't try to convince you that ETFs are your best investment choice, and I certainly don't tell you that ETFs will make you rich. Instead, I lay out facts and figures and summarize some hard academic findings, and I let you draw your own conclusions.

- ✔ *Exchange-Traded Funds For Dummies* **is cheap.** Hey, top-notch investment advice for only $24.99 (plus or minus any discounts, shipping, and tax) . . . Where else are you going to get that kind of deal? *And* should you come to the conclusion after reading this book that ETFs belong in your portfolio, you'll likely get your $24.99 (plus any shipping costs and tax) back in no time at all.

> ✔ *Exchange-Traded Funds For Dummies* **is tax-smart.** Yes, the money you spent for this book, as all other outlays you make for investment advice, may be deducted from your federal income taxes (provided you itemize your deductions). Go for it!

> ✔ *Exchange-Traded Funds For Dummies* **is an open book.** We've already established that!

If you've ever read a book *For Dummies* before, you have an idea what you're about to embark on. This is not a book you need to read from front to back. Feel free to jump about and glean whatever information you think will be of most use. There is no quiz at the end. You don't have to put it all to memory.

Conventions Used in This Book

To help you navigate this text as easily as possible, I use the following conventions:

> ✔ Whenever I introduce a new term, it appears in *italics*. You can rest assured that I provide a definition or explanation nearby.

> ✔ If I want to share some interesting information that isn't crucial to your understanding of the topic at hand, I place it in a *sidebar,* a gray box with its own heading that is set apart from the rest of the text. (See how this whole italics/definition thing works?)

> ✔ All Web addresses appear in `monofont` so they're easy to pick out if you need to go back and find them.

Keep in mind that when this book was printed, some Web addresses may have needed to break across two lines of text. If that happened, rest assured that we haven't put in any extra characters (such as hyphens) to indicate the break. So, when using one of these Web addresses, just type in exactly what you see in this book, pretending as though the line break doesn't exist.

What You're Not to Read

When my computer is ill, and I call "Tom" (Dell's man somewhere in the Far East), all I want is for Tom to fix my problem, whatever that is. I'm not in the market for explanations. On the ETF front, however, I really like knowing all the technical ins and outs. That may not be your thing. You may be like me with my computer problems: "Just tell me how to make money with these things, and keep the technical stuff to yourself, Russ." Okay, I do that. Sort of.

Throughout this book, you usually find the heavy technical matter tucked neatly into sidebars. But if any technicalities make it into the main text, I give you a heads up with a Technical Stuff icon so you can skip over that section, or just speed-read it if you wish.

Foolish Assumptions

I assume that most of the people reading this sentence know a fair amount about the financial world. I think that's a fairly safe assumption. Why else would you have bought an entire book about exchange-traded funds?

If you think that convertible bonds are bonds with removable tops and that the futures market is a place where fortunetellers purchase crystal balls, I help you along the best I can in this book by letting you know how to find out more about certain topics. However, you may be better off picking up and reading a copy of the basic nuts-n-bolts *Investing For Dummies* by Eric Tyson (published by Wiley). After you spend some time with that title, c'mon back to this book. You'll be more than welcome!

How This Book is Organized

Here's a down-and-dirty look at what's in store in the next 320 or so pages.

Part I: The ABCs of ETFs

Just what *is* an ETF, after all? The beginning of the book would seem like a logical place to cover that topic, and I do. You also find out what makes an ETF different — more sleek and economical — than a mutual fund. (Think Prius versus Humvee.) This section of the book also begins the discussion of how to actually buy ETFs — the very best of them — hold them, and, when necessary, cash them out.

Part II: Building the Stock (Equity) Side of Your Portfolio

You wouldn't want a closet filled with nothing but black slacks or red sweaters, and similarly, you don't want a portfolio filled with, say, nothing but tech stocks (remember 2000–2003 when your tech portfolio suddenly went poof?). ETFs are wonderful diversification tools, if used right. In Part II, I show you how to mix and match your stock ETFs to build a portfolio that will serve you well in both good times and bad.

Part III: Adding Bonds, REITs, and Other ETFs to Your Portfolio

In this part, I walk you through the construction of a portfolio beyond its stock components. I introduce you to a bevy of bond, real estate (otherwise known as *REIT*), and commodity ETFs, and I show you how to massage those into your portfolio for maximum diversification. (Oh, have I not mentioned that diversification is all-important?) Afterward, I discuss non-ETF investments (such as mutual funds and individual stocks) and how to determine if those are appropriate and desirable additions to your portfolio.

Part IV: Putting It All Together

Here, you find sample portfolios. You may find one that fits you like a glove. Or you may find one that you can tinker with to make it your own. After that business is done with, you enter a section of this book that I almost titled "Zen and the Art of ETF Portfolio Maintenance." After all, after you have your ETF portfolio, you need to know how to maintain it, tweak it from time to time, and use it to serve both your material and spiritual needs — preferably with a cool head and calm spirit. Part IV helps you to address those needs.

Part V: The Part of Tens

A classic feature in the *For Dummies* series, The Part of Tens offers concise advice and food for extra thought, all in handy dandy list form.

Part VI: Appendixes

Here's where you find a complete list of ETFs available as of this writing, Web sites you can visit to get even more information about this investment tool, and a glossary to help you navigate any ETF resource.

Icons Used in This Book

Throughout the book, you find little globular pieces of art in the margins called *icons.* These admittedly cutesy but handy tools give you a heads up that certain types of information are in the neighborhood.

Although this is a how-to book, you also find plenty of whys and wherefores. Any paragraph accompanied by this icon, however, is guaranteed pure, 100 percent, unadulterated how-to.

The world of investments offers pitfalls galore. Wherever you see the bomb, know that there is a risk of your losing money — maybe even Big Money — if you skip the passage.

Read twice! This icon indicates that something important is being said and is really worth putting to memory.

If you don't really care about the difference between standard deviation and beta, or the historical correlation between U.S. value stocks and REITs, feel free to skip or skim the paragraphs with this icon.

The world of Wall Street is full of people who make money at other people's expense. Where you see the pig face, know that I'm about to point out an instance where someone will likely be sticking a hand deep in your pocket.

Where to Go from Here

Where would you like to go from here? If you wish, start at the beginning. If you're interested only in stock ETFs, hey, no one says that you can't jump right to Part II. Bond ETFs? Go ahead and jump to Part III. It's entirely your call.

Part I
The ABCs of ETFs

The 5th Wave · By Rich Tennant

Looks like another new exotic investment strategy to me.

WALL ST

In this part . . .

In these first few ground-laying chapters, you find out what makes exchange-traded funds different from other investment vehicles. You discover the rationale for their being, why they are popular with institutional investors, why they are rapidly becoming so popular with noninstitutional folk, and why the author of this book likes them almost as much as he does milk chocolate.

Although the art and science of building an ETF portfolio come later in the book, this first part introduces you to how ETFs are bought and sold and helps you ponder whether you should even be thinking about buying them.

Chapter 1

The New Kid on the Block

*T*here are, no doubt, a good number of pinstriped ladies and gentlemen in and around Wall Street who froth heavily at the mouth when they hear the words *exchange-traded fund.* In a world of very pricey investment products and very lucratively paid investment-product salespeople, ETFs are the ultimate killjoys.

Since their arrival on the investment scene in the early 1990s, more than 300 ETFs have been created, and they have grown faster in asset accumulation than any other investment product. And that is a good thing. ETFs have allowed the average American investment opportunities that do not involve shelling out fat commissions or paying layers of ongoing, unnecessary fees. And they've saved investors oodles and oodles in taxes.

Hallelujah.

SPDRs, DIAMONDS, Qubes . . . Why the plurals?

Many ETFs have names that end in an *s.* That can be confusing. After all, you would never refer to the Fidelity Magellan Fund as *Magellans.* So why the plural when talking about a single ETF? The convention is to refer not just to the fund but to the components of the fund. Thus, *DIAMONDS* refers to the 30 companies that make up the Dow Jones Industrial Average index. *Qubes* refers to the 100 companies that make up the NASDAQ-100 Index. But rest assured that when brokers talk about DIAMONDS and Qubes, they are talking about a single ETF.

In the Beginning

When I was a lad growing up in the 'burbs of New York City, my public school educators taught me how to read, write, and learn the capitals of the 50 states. I also learned that anything and everything of any importance in this world was, ahem, invented in the United States of America. I've since learned that, well, that isn't entirely true. Take ETFs. The first ETF was introduced in Canada. It was a creation of the Toronto Stock Exchange — no Wall Streeters were anywhere in sight!

I'm afraid that the story of the development of ETFs isn't quite as exciting as, say, the story behind penicillin or the atom bomb. As one Toronto Stock Exchange insider once explained to me, "We saw it as a way of making money by generating more trading." And so, thus was born the original ETF known as TIP, which stood for Toronto Index Participation Unit. It tracked an index of large Canadian companies (Bell Canada, Royal Bank of Canada, Nortel, and 32 others) known as the Toronto 35. That index was then the closest thing that Canada had to the Dow Jones Industrial Average index that exists in the United States.

Enter the traders

TIP was an instant success with large institutional stock traders, who saw that they could now trade an entire index in a flash. The Toronto Stock Exchange got what it wanted — more trading. And the world of ETFs got its start.

TIP has since morphed to track a larger index, the so-called S&P/TSX 60 Index, which — you probably guessed — tracks 60 of Canada's largest and most liquid companies. The fund also has a new name, the iUnits S&P/TSX 60 Index Fund, and it trades under the ticker XIU. It is now managed by Barclays, the British financial powerhouse that has come to be the biggest player in ETFs in Europe, Canada, and the United States. (Barclays has since introduced another ETF in the United States that uses the ticker TIP, but it has nothing to do with the original TIP. The present-day TIP invests in U.S. Treasury Inflation-Protected Securities.)

Moving south of the border

The first ETF didn't come to the United States (oh, how my public school teachers would cringe!) for three or so more years after its Canadian birth.

On January 29, 1993, the Mother of All U.S. ETFs was born on the American Stock Exchange. It was called the S&P Depository Receipts Trust Series 1, commonly known as the SPDR (or Spider) 500, and it traded (and still does) under the ticker symbol SPY.

The SPDR 500, which tracks the S&P 500 index, an index of the 500 largest U.S. companies, was an instant darling of institutional traders. It continues to be one of their darlings, but it is also a major holding in the portfolios of many individuals.

Fulfilling a Dream

ETFs were first embraced by institutions, and those institutions very much continue to this day to use ETFs for institutional use. They are constantly buying and selling ETFs and options on ETFs for various institutional purposes, which I touch on in Chapter 18. For us noninstitutional types, the creation and expansion of ETFs has allowed for the construction of portfolios of institutional-like sleekness.

Goodbye, ridiculously high mutual fund fees

A mutual fund investor with a $150,000 portfolio filled with actively-managed funds will likely spend $2,505 (1.67 percent) or more in annual expenses. By switching to an ETF portfolio, that investor will incur trading costs (because trading ETFs costs the same as trading stocks) of, oh, perhaps $100 or so. But he can then lower his ongoing annual expenses to about $600 (0.4 percent). That's a difference, ladies and gentlemen of the jury, of $1,905, which is compounded every year his money is invested.

Loads, those odious fees that some mutual funds charge for getting into or out of the fund, simply don't exist in the world of ETFs.

Capital gains taxes, the blow that comes on April 15th to many mutual fund holders with taxable accounts, hardly exist. In fact, here's what my clients and I have paid in capital gains taxes in the past three years: $00.00.

In Chapter 2, I delve much deeper into both the cost savings and the tax efficiency of ETFs.

Hello, building blocks for a better portfolio

In terms of diversification, my own portfolio and those of my clients include large stocks; small stocks; micro cap stocks; English, French, Swiss, Japanese, and Korean stocks; long-term bonds; short-term bonds; and real estate investment trusts (REITs) — all held in low-cost ETFs. I talk all about diversification, and how to use ETFs as building blocks for a class A portfolio, in Part II.

Yes, you could use other investment vehicles, such as mutual funds, to create a well-diversified portfolio. But ETFs make it much easier because they tend to track very specific indexes. They are, by and large, much more pure than mutual funds. An ETF that bills itself as an investment in, say, small growth stocks is going to give you an investment in small growth stocks, plain and simple. A mutual fund that bills itself as an investment vehicle for small growth stocks may include everything from cash to bonds to shares of General Electric. (No, I'm not exaggerating, and I give a specific example or two in the next chapter.)

Will you miss the court papers?

While scandals of various sorts — hidden fees, "soft-money" arrangements, after-hours sweetheart deals, and executive kickbacks — have plagued the world of mutual fund and hedge fund investments, here are the number of scandals that have touched my life or the lives and fortunes of any of my clients: 0. That's because ETFs' managers, forced to follow existing indexes, have very little leeway in the investments they choose or the proportions in which they choose them. ETFs are closely regulated by the Securities and Exchange Commission, which not all investment vehicles are. And ETFs trade during the day, in plain view of millions of traders — not after hours, as mutual funds do, which can allow for sweetheart deals when no one is looking.

I talk much more about the transparency and cleanliness of ETFs in Chapter 2.

Not Quite as Popular as the Beatles, But Getting There

With all that ETFs have going for them, I'm not surprised that they have lately begun to sell like wildfire. The Investment Company Institute, an organization that obsessively tracks the whims of investors, tells us that from the beginning of 2000, when there were only 80 ETFs on the U.S. market, to the end of 2005, when there were over 200, the total assets invested in ETFs rose from $52 billion to $300 billion. At the time of this writing — several months into 2006 — the total is $320 billion.

Certainly, $320 billion pales in comparison to the amount of money invested in mutual funds: $9+ trillion. But if current trends continue, ETFs may indeed become as popular as were John, Paul, George, and Ringo.

Part of ETFs' popularity stems from the growly bear market of 2000–2003. Investors who had been riding the double-digit-yearly gravy train of the 1990s suddenly realized that their portfolios weren't going to keep growing in leaps and bounds, and perhaps it was time to start watching investment costs. There has also been a greater awareness of the triumph of *indexing* — investing in entire markets or market segments — rather than trying to cherry-pick stocks. Much more on that topic in Chapter 2.

The little kid is growing fast: ETFs' phenomenal growth

Following are a few facts and figures that indicate how the ETF market compares with the mutual fund market and how rapidly ETFs are gaining in popularity.

The amount of money invested in ETFs and mutual funds as of March 2006:

- ETFs: $320 billion
- Mutual funds: $9.2 trillion

The total number of ETFs and mutual funds available to U.S. investors as of March 2006:

- ETFs: 203
- Mutual funds: 7,800

The number of ETFs available to U.S. investors in recent years:

- 2000: 80
- 2001: 102
- 2002: 113
- 2003: 119
- 2004: 151
- 2005: 201

The amount of money invested in ETFs in recent years:

- 2000: $52 billion
- 2001: $75 billion
- 2002: $100 billion
- 2003: $150 billion
- 2004: $220 billion
- 2005: $300 billion

Moving from Wall Street to Main Street

Investment trends work sort of like fashion trends. In the world of fashion, trendsetters — movie stars, British royals, or Paris Hilton (wherever she came from) — wander out into public wearing something that most people consider ridiculous, and the next thing you know, everyone is wearing that same item. It took from 1993 until about, oh, 2001 or so (around the time I bought my first ETF) for this newfangled investment vehicle to really start moving. By about 2003, insiders say, the majority of ETFs were being purchased by individual investors, not institutions or investment professionals.

Today, Barclays, which controls about 55 percent of the U.S. market for ETFs, estimates that approximately 60 percent of all the trading in ETFs is done by individual investors. The other 40 percent is being done by both institutions and by fee-only financial advisors, like me.

(*Fee-only,* by the way, signifies that a financial advisor takes no commissions of any sort. It's a very confusing term because *fee-based* is often used to mean the opposite. Check out Chapter 20, where I talk about whether you need a financial professional to build and manage an ETF portfolio.)

Actually, individual investors — especially the buy-and-hold kind of investors — benefit much more from ETFs than do institutional traders. That's because institutional traders have always gotten, and continue to get, the very best deals on investment vehicles. They often pay much less in management fees than do individual investors for shares in the same mutual fund. (Fund companies often refer to *institutional class* versus *investor class* shares. All that really means is "wholesale/low price" versus "retail/higher price.")

Keeping up with the Vanguards

It may sound like I'm pushing ETFs as not only the best thing since white bread but as a replacement for white bread. Well, not quite. As much as I like ETFs, good old white-bread mutual funds still have their place in the sun. And that's especially true of inexpensive index mutual funds, such as Vanguard's and Fidelity's. They still have very much to offer. Mutual funds, for example, are clearly the better option when you're investing in dribs and drabs and don't want to have to pay for each trade you make.

One of the largest purveyors of ETFs is The Vanguard Group, the very same people who pioneered index mutual funds. In the case of Vanguard (and only Vanguard at this point), shares in the company's ETFs are the equivalent of shares in one of the company's index mutual funds. In other words, they are different class shares in the same fund — the same representation of companies, but a different structure and slightly lower costs for the ETFs.

The ripple effect: Forcing down prices on other investment vehicles

You don't need to invest in ETFs to profit from them. They are doing to the world of investing what Chinese labor has done to manufacturing wages in the United States. In other words, they are driving prices down. Thanks to the competition that ETFs are giving index mutual funds (already ETFs have claimed one-third of the $800 or so billion invested in such funds), mutual fund providers have been lowering their charges. Fidelity Investments, for example, in 2005 lowered the expense ratio on some of its index funds from as much as 0.47 percent down to 0.10 percent. With many mutual funds, however, you must keep a minimum balance. Fidelity's minimum for its lowest-cost index funds is $10,000

Because Vanguard funds allow for an apples-to-apples comparison of ETFs and index mutual funds, and because the company presumably has no great stake in which you choose, Vanguard may be a good place to turn for objective advice on which investment is better for you. But rest assured — a point that I'll make again in this book — we're not talking rocket science. For most buy-and-hold investors, especially in taxable accounts of more than $50,000 or so, ETFs will almost always be the winners, at least in the long-run.

I look much more closely at the ETFs versus mutual funds question when I design specific portfolios and give actual portfolio examples in Chapters 15 and 16.

Ready for Prime Time: Becoming Household Words

One survey in the summer of 2005 found that only about one-third of investors with at least $50,000 in investable assets said that they were very or somewhat familiar with ETFs. My guess is that by the time *Exchange-Traded Funds For Dummies* appears on bookshelves, at least half of U.S. investors will be familiar with ETFs. And I believe that in a couple of years, the vast majority of investors will be at least somewhat familiar with ETFs. But will ETFs surpass mutual funds as the nation's favorite investment vehicle? They should. But they won't.

People just aren't that logical.

Can you pick next year's winners?

Okay, study after study shows that most actively managed mutual funds don't do as well in the long-run as the indexes, but certainly some do much, much better, at least for a few years. And any number of magazine articles will tell you how to pick next year's winners.

If only it were that easy. Alas, studies show rather conclusively that it is anything but easy. Morningstar, on a great number of occasions, has earmarked the top-performing mutual funds and mutual fund managers over a given period of time and tracked their performance moving forward. In one representative study, the top 30 mutual funds for sequential five-year periods from 1971 to 2002 were evaluated for their performance moving forward. In each and every five-year period, the "30 top funds," as a group, did worse than the S&P 500 in subsequent years.

Index mutual funds, which most resemble ETFs, have been in existence since Vanguard rolled out the First Index Investment Trust fund in 1976. Since that time, Vanguard and other mutual fund companies have created literally hundreds of index funds, tracking every conceivable index. Yet index funds remain relatively obscure. According to figures from Vanguard, index mutual funds hold only a scant 3 percent of all money invested in stock mutual funds; bond index funds represent less than 1 percent of all money invested in bond mutual funds.

Why would anyone want to invest in index funds or ETFs? After all, the financial professionals who run actively-managed mutual funds spend many years and tens of thousands of dollars educating themselves at places with real ivy on the walls, like Harvard and Wharton. They know all about the economy, the stock market, business trends, and so on. Shouldn't we cash in on their knowledge by letting them pick the best basket of investments for us?

Good question! Here's the problem with hiring these financial whizzes, and the reason that index funds or ETFs generally kick their ivy-league butts: When these whizzes from Harvard and Wharton go to market to buy and sell stocks, they are usually buying and selling stock (not directly, but through the markets) from *other* whizzes who graduated from Harvard and Wharton. One whiz bets that ABC stock is going down, so he sells. His former classmate bets that ABC stock is going up, so he buys. Which whiz is right? Half the time, it's the buyer. Half the time, it's the seller. Meanwhile, you pay for all the trading, not to mention the whiz's handsome salary while all this buying and selling is going on.

Economists have a name for such a market; they call it "efficient." It means, in general, that there are soooo many smart people analyzing and dissecting and studying the market that the chances are slim that any one whiz — no matter how whizzical, no matter how thick his Cambridge accent — is going to be able to beat the pack.

That, in a nutshell, is why actively managed mutual funds tend to lag the indexes, usually by a considerable margin. If you want to read more about why stock-pickers and market-timers almost never beat the indexes, I suggest picking up a copy of the seminal *A Random Walk Through Wall Street* by Princeton economist Burton G. Malkiel. The book, now in something like its 200th edition, is available in paperback from W. W. Norton & Company. There's also a Web site — www.indexfunds.com — run by something of an indexing fanatic (hey, there are worse things to be) that is literally choked with articles and studies on the subject. You could spend days reading!

The proof of the pudding

According to Morningstar analysis, the average annual return of all index funds over the past 15 years has been 10.08 percent. Compare that number with the average annual return for all actively managed mutual funds: 8.70 percent. That difference — 1.38 percent — is largely due to differences in fees. It may not seem like a big number, but compounded over time, it is *huge*.

Let's plug in a few numbers. An initial investment of $100,000 earning 10.08 percent for 15 years will be worth $422,305 at the end of the day. An investment of $100,000 earning 8.70 percent for 15 years will be worth $349,497. That's $72,808 extra in your pocket if you invest in index funds. And in fact, that figure would likely be much higher after you account for taxes. (Taxes on actively managed funds can be considerably higher than those on index funds.)

You may be thinking, "Well bully for index funds, but what does this have to do with ETFs?" Index funds are the investment vehicles that most closely resemble ETFs, and because index funds have been around a lot longer, we have better data on them. I can't yet tell you how ETFs perform over a 15-year period. However, I do have some long-term data on the earliest ETFs to be created:

- **SPY:** The very first ETF to enter the U.S. market, the SPDR 500 (SPY), has seen an annualized return of 8.86 percent in the past 10 years. Over the same period, the average return for actively managed large cap mutual funds has been 7.94 percent. (I discuss large cap funds in Chapters 5 and 6.)

- **MDY:** The Midcap SPDR Trust Series 1 (MDY) has enjoyed a 10-year annualized average return of 14.41 percent versus 12.11 percent for all actively managed mid cap stock funds. In the case of the mid caps, $100,000 invested 10 years ago would now be worth $384,273. That same money invested in an average actively managed fund would now be worth $313,649. That's a difference of $70,624. And, depending on your tax bracket over the years, the tax difference beyond that would be even more substantial. You may easily have scored an extra $75,000 going with the ETF over the actively managed mutual fund.

By the way, the very first ETF — SPY — is still by far the largest ETF on the market, with total assets of $54 billion. (In contrast, the largest mutual fund, American Funds Growth A, has total assets of $78 billion.)

The major players

In Parts II and III of this book, I provide details about many of the ETFs that are on the market. Here, I want to introduce you to just a handful of the biggies. You will likely recognize a few of the names.

In Table 1-1, I list the six largest ETFs on the market today, as calculated by the number of shares traded.

Table 1-1	The Six Largest ETFs by Number of Shares Traded	
Name	*Ticker*	*Average daily trading volume*
NASDAQ-100 Trust Series 1	QQQQ	95 million shares
SPDR 500	SPY	68 million shares
iShares Russell 2000	IWM	30 million shares
iShares MSCI Japan Index	EWJ	25 million shares
Energy Select Sector SPDR	XLE	21 million shares
Semiconductor HOLDRS	SMH	18 million shares

In Table 1-2, I list the six largest ETFs based on their assets. You'll notice some overlap with the funds listed in Table 1-1.

Table 1-2	The Six Largest ETFs by Assets	
Name	*Ticker*	*Assets (in billions)*
SPDR 500	SPY	$53.7
iShares MSCI EAFE Index Fund	EFA	$25.0
NASDAQ-100 Trust Series 1	QQQQ	$18.0
iShares S&P 500	IVV	$15.9
iShares MSCI Japan Index	EWJ	$13.8
iShares MSCI Emerging Markets Index	EEM	$12.5

Twist and shout: Commercialization could ruin a good thing

Innovation is a great thing. Usually. In the world of ETFs, a few big players (Barclays, Vanguard) jumped in when the going was hot. Now, in order to get their share of the pie, a number of new players have entered the fray with some pretty wild ETFs. ("Let's invest in all companies whose CEO is named Fred!") Okay, I'm just kidding about the Fred portfolio, but if things keep going the way they are going . . . I dunno.

I tend to like my ETFs vanilla plain, maybe with a few sprinkles. I like them to follow indexes that make sense. And, above all, I like their expense ratios looooow. At present, the average ETF carries an expense ratio of 0.40 percent. Some of the newer ETFs have expense ratios edging up into the ballpark of what you usually see for mutual funds.

I'm not saying that ETFs must follow traditional indexes. There may be room for improvement. (Actually, when I think about it, some of the traditional indexes, like the Dow, are darn dumb. I explain why in Chapter 3) But I do hope the ETF industry can maintain its integrity and not go too far astray into the field of high expenses and silly investment schemes. Future editions of this book will tell the tale.

Chapter 2

What the Heck Is an ETF, Anyway?

*B*anking your retirement on stocks is risky enough; banking your retirement on any individual stock, or even a handful of stocks, is Evil Knievel-jumping-Snake-River investing. Banking on individual bonds is typically less risky (maybe Evil Knievel jumping a creek), but the same general principle holds. There is safety in numbers. That's why teenage boys and girls huddle together in corners at school dances. That's why gnus graze in groups. That's why smart stock and bond investors grab onto ETFs.

The Nature of the Beast

Just as a deed shows that you have ownership of a house, and a share of common stock certifies ownership in a company, a share of an ETF represents ownership (most typically) in a basket of company stocks. To buy or sell an ETF, you place an order with a broker, either by phone or online. The price of an ETF changes throughout the trading day, which is to say from 9:30 a.m. to 4:00 p.m. Wall Street time, going up or going down with the market value of the securities it holds. (Sometimes there can be a little sway, but rarely anything serious.)

Originally, ETFs were developed to mirror various indices:

✔ The SPDR 500 (ticker SPY) represents stocks from the S&P (Standard and Poors) 500, an index of the 500 largest companies in the United States.

✔ The DIAMONDS Trust Series 1 (ticker DIA) represents the 30 underlying stocks of the Dow Jones Industrial Average index.

✔ The NASDAQ-100 Trust Series 1, otherwise known as *Qubes* (ticker QQQQ), represents the 100 stocks of the NASDAQ-100 Index.

Since ETFs were first introduced, many others, tracking all kinds of things, have emerged.

Knowing that not all ETFs are created equal

Depending on the ETF, the component companies in the ETF portfolio usually represent a certain index or segment of the market. That segment may be, say, large U.S. value stocks, small growth stocks, or micro cap stocks. (If you're not 100 percent clear on the difference between *value* and *growth,* or what a micro cap is, rest assured that I discuss each in Part II.)

Sometimes, the stock market is broken up into industry sectors, such as technology, industrials, or consumer discretionary, and there are ETFs that mirror those sectors, as well as many others.

Choosing between the classic and the new

Some of the ETF providers (Vanguard, Barclays) tend to use traditional indexes, such as those I mention earlier in the chapter. Others (PowerShares, Rydex) tend to develop their own indexes.

For example, if you were to buy 100 shares of an ETF called the iShares S&P 500 Growth Index Fund (IVW), you'd be buying into a traditional index (large U.S. growth companies). At about $61 a share, you'd plunk down $6,100 for a portfolio of stocks that would include shares of Microsoft, Exxon Mobil Corp., Procter & Gamble, Johnson & Johnson, and General Electric. If you wanted to know exactly how your money was being spent, the iShares prospectus (or any number of financial Web sites, such as `http://finance.yahoo.com`) would tell you specific percentages: Microsoft, 4.19 percent; Exxon Mobil Corp., 3.92 percent; Procter & Gamble, 3.4 percent; and so on.

Many ETFs represent shares in foreign indexes. If, for example, you were to own 100 shares of the iShares MSCI Japan Index Fund (EWJ), with a current market value of about $13.50 share, your $1,350 would buy you a stake in large Japanese companies such as Mitsubishi, Toyota, Sony, and Honda Motors. I devote an entire chapter — Chapter 10 — to international ETFs.

Both IVW and EWJ mirror standard indexes: IVW mirrors the S&P 500 Growth Index, and EWJ mirrors the MSCI Japan Index. If, however, you purchase 100 shares of the PowerShares Dynamic Large Cap Growth Portfolio, you'll buy roughly $1,600 of a portfolio of stocks that mirror a very unconventional index — one created by the PowerShares family of exchange-traded funds. The large U.S. growth companies in the index don't include Microsoft or Exxon Mobil Corp., but rather companies like UnitedHealth Group, Dell, and American Express. PowerShares refers to their custom indexes as "enhanced."

The single largest controversy in the world of ETFs is whether the newfangled, customized indexes of companies like PowerShares make any sense. Most financial professionals are, frankly, nauseated by newness. We are a conservative lot. But I'm trying to keep an open mind. For now, let me continue with my introduction to ETFs, but rest assured that I address this raging controversy later in the book (in Chapter 3 and throughout Part II).

Other ETFs — a distinct but growing minority — represent holdings in valuables other than stocks, notably U.S. Treasury Bonds, corporate bonds, gold, or silver. I discuss these in Part III of this book.

Recognizing common elements

Regardless of what securities an ETF represents, regardless of what index those securities are a part of, your fortunes as an ETF holder are directly tied to the value of the underlying securities. If the price of Exxon Mobil Corp. stock, U.S. Treasury Bonds, or gold goes up, so does the value of your ETF. If GE stock pays a dividend, you are due a certain amount of that dividend. If the price of gold tumbles, your portfolio (if you hold a gold ETF) may lose some glitter.

ETFs are Preferable to Individual Stocks

Okay, why buy a basket of stocks rather than individual stock? Quick answer: You'll sleep better.

You may recall that in March 2004, the always fashionable Martha Stewart was convicted of obstructing justice and lying in an insider-trading case involving a small company called ImClone. Within hours, shares in Stewart's namesake firm, Martha Stewart Living Omnimedia, tumbled 23 percent.

Those sorts of things — sometimes much worse — happen every day in the world of stocks.

A company I'll call ABC Pharmaceutical sees its stock shoot up by 68 percent because the firm just earned an important patent for a new diet pill; a month later, the stock falls by 84 percent because a study in the *New England Journal of Medicine* found that the new diet pill causes people to hallucinate and think they are Genghis Khan.

Compared to the world of individual stocks, the stock market as a whole is as smooth as a morning lake. Heck, a daily rise or fall in the Dow of more than a percent or two is generally considered a pretty big deal.

If you, like me, are not especially keen on roller coasters, then you are advised to put your nest egg into not one stock, not two, but many. If you have a few million sitting around, hey, no problem diversifying. Maybe individual stocks are for you. But for most of us commoners, the only way to effectively diversify is with ETFs or mutual funds.

ETFs Are Not Mutual

So what is the difference between an ETF and a mutual fund? After all, mutual funds also represent baskets of stocks or bonds. The two, however, are not twins. They're not even siblings. Cousins are more like it. Here are some of the big differences between ETFs and mutual funds:

✔ ETFs are bought and sold just like stocks (through a brokerage house, either by phone or online), and their price can change from second to second. Mutual fund orders can be made during the day, but the actual trading doesn't occur until after the markets close.

✔ ETFs tend to represent indexes — market segments — and the managers of the ETFs tend to do very little trading of securities in the ETF. (The ETFs are *passively* managed.)

✔ Although they require you to pay small trading fees, ETFs usually wind up costing you much less than a mutual fund because the ongoing management fees are typically much less, and there is never a *load* (an entrance or exit fee, sometime an exorbitant one) as there is with many mutual funds.

✔ Because of low portfolio turnover and also the way they are structured, ETFs' investment gains usually are more gingerly taxed than the gains on mutual funds.

Table 2-1 provides a quick look at some ways that investing in ETFs differs from investing in mutual funds and individual stocks.

Table 2-1   ETFs Versus Mutual Funds Versus Individual Stocks

	ETFs	Mutual Funds	Individual Stocks
Priced, bought, and sold throughout the day?	Yes	No	Yes
Offer some investment diversification?	Yes	Yes	No
Is there a minimum investment?	No	Yes	No
Purchased through a broker or online brokerage?	Yes	Yes	Yes
Do you pay a fee or commission to make a trade?	Yes	Sometimes	Yes
Can you buy/sell options?	Yes	No	Sometimes
Indexed (passively managed)?	Typically	Atypically	No
Can you make money or lose money?	Yes	Yes	You bet

Why the Big Boys Prefer ETFs

When ETFs were first introduced, they were primarily of interest to institutional traders — insurance companies, hedge fund people, banks — who often have investment needs considerably more complicated than yours and mine.

Trading in large lots

Prior to the introduction of ETFs, there was no way for a trader to instantaneously buy or sell, in one fell swoop, hundreds of stocks or bonds. Because they trade both during market hours and, in some cases, after market hours, ETFs made that possible.

Institutional investors also found other things to like about ETFs. For example, ETFs are often used to quickly put cash to productive use or to fill gaps in a portfolio by allowing immediate exposure to an industry sector or geographic region.

Your basic trading choices (for ETFs or stocks)

Buying and selling an ETF is just like buying and selling a stock. There is really no difference. Although there are all sorts of ways to trade, the vast majority of trades fall into these categories:

✓ **Market order:** This is as simple as it gets. You place an order with your broker or online to buy, say, 100 shares of a certain ETF. Your order goes to the stock exchange, and you get the best available price.

✓ **Limit order:** More exact than a market order, you place an order to buy, say, 100 shares of an ETF at $23 a share. That is the price you will pay. If no sellers are willing to sell at $23 a share, your order will not go through. If you place a limit order to sell at $23, you'll get your sale if someone is willing to pay that price. If not, there will be no sale.

✓ **Stop-loss (or stop) order:** Designed to protect you should the price of your ETF or stock take a tumble, a stop-loss order goes into effect when your ETF falls beneath a certain point. At that point (say 10 percent below the current price), your order automatically turns into a market order. Stop-loss orders can serve to limit your exposure to a falling market.

✓ **Short sale:** You sell shares of an ETF that have been borrowed from the broker. If the price of the ETF then falls, you can buy replacement shares at a lower price and pocket the spread. If, however, the price rises, you are stuck holding a security that is worth less than its market price, so you lose.

Savoring the versatility

ETFs, unlike mutual funds, can also be purchased with limit, market, or stop-loss orders, taking away the uncertainty involved with placing a buy order for a mutual fund and not knowing what price you're going to get until several hours after market close. See the sidebar "Your basic trading choices (for ETFs or stocks)" if you're not certain what limit, market, and stop-loss orders are.

And because ETFs can be sold short, they provide an important means of risk management. If, for example, the stock market takes a dive, *shorting* ETFs — selling them now at a locked-in price with an agreement to purchase them back (cheaper) later on — may help keep a portfolio afloat. For that reason, ETFs have become a darling of hedge fund managers who offer the promise of investments that won't tank should the stock market tank. See Chapter 18 for more information on this topic.

Why Individual Investors are Learning to Love ETFs

Clients I've worked with are often amazed that I can put them into a financial product that will cost them a fraction in expenses compared to what they are currently paying. Low cost is probably the thing I love most about ETFs. But I also love their tax efficiency, their transparency (you know what you're buying), and a long track record of success for indexed investments.

The cost advantage: How low can you go?

In the world of mutual funds, the average management fee at present, according to Morningstar, is 1.67 percent (of the account balance) annually. That may not sound like a lot of money, but it is a very substantial sum. A well-balanced portfolio with both stocks and bonds may return, say, 8 percent over time. In that case, paying 1.67 percent to a third party means that you've just lowered your total investment returns by about 20 percent. On a bad year, where your investments earn, say, 1.67 percent, you've just lowered your investment returns to *zero*. And on a *very* bad year . . . You don't need me to do the math.

I'm astounded at what some mutual funds charge. Whereas the average is 1.67 percent, I've seen charges 10 times that amount. Crazy. Investing in such a fund is tossing money to the wind. Yet people do it. The chances of your winding up ahead after paying such high fees are next to nil. Paying a *load* (either an entrance or exit fee) that can total as much as 8.50 percent is just as nutty. Yet people do it.

In the world of ETFs, the expenses are much, much lower, averaging 0.40 percent, and many of the more traditional domestic indexed ETFs cost no more than 0.20 percent a year in management fees. A handful are under 0.10 percent.

Some fees, as you can see in Table 2-2, are so low as to be negligible. Each ETF in this table has a yearly management expense of 0.12 percent or less.

Table 2-2	The Rock Bottom ETFs	
ETF	*Ticker*	*Total annual management expense*
Vanguard Total Stock Market ETF	VTI	0.07%
Vanguard Extended Market ETF	VXF	0.08%
iShares S&P 500	IVV	0.09%
Vanguard Small Cap ETF	VB	0.10%
Vanguard Growth ETF	VUG	0.11%
Vanguard Value ETF	VTV	0.11%
Vanguard Small Cap Growth ETF	VBK	0.12%
Vanguard Small Cap Value ETF	VBR	0.12%
Vanguard REIT ETF	VNQ	0.12%

Numerous studies have shown that low-cost funds have a huge advantage over higher-cost funds. One study by Morningstar looked at stock returns over the five-year period ended December 2001. In almost every category of stock mutual fund, low-cost funds beat the pants off high-cost funds. You think that by paying high fees you're getting better fund management? Hardly. The Morningstar study found, for example, that among mutual funds that hold large blend stocks (*blend* meaning a combination of value and growth), the annualized gain was 8.75 percent for those funds in the costliest quartile of funds; the gain for the least costly quartile was 9.89 percent.

The reasons ETFs are cheaper

The management companies that bring us ETFs, such as Barclays and PowerShares, are presumably not doing so for their health. No, they're making a good profit. One reason they can offer ETFs so cheap compared to mutual funds is that their expenses are much less. When you buy an ETF, you go through a brokerage house, not Barclays or PowerShares. That brokerage house (Charles Schwab, Merrill Lynch, Fidelity, TD AMERITRADE) does all the necessary paperwork and bookkeeping on the purchase. If you have any questions about your money, you'll likely call Schwab, not Barclays. So unlike a mutual fund company, which must maintain telephone operators, bookkeepers, and a mailroom, the providers of ETFs can operate almost entirely in cyberspace.

To boot, ETFs are linked to indexes, which means they have to pay some kind of fee to Dow Jones or Morgan Stanley or whoever created the index. But that fee is *nothing* compared to the exorbitant salaries that mutual funds pay their stock pickers, er, market analysts.

An unfair race

Active mutual funds really don't have much chance of beating passive index funds — whether mutual funds or ETFs — over the long run. Someone once described the contest as a race in which the active mutual funds are "running with lead boots." Why? In addition to the management fees that eat up much of any gains, there are also the trading costs. Yes, when mutual funds trade stocks or bonds, they pay a spread and a small cut to the stock exchange, just like you and I do.

It's been estimated that turnover costs for active mutual funds typically run about 0.8 percent. And active mutual fund managers must constantly keep some cash on hand for all those trades. Having cash on hand costs money, too: There's an opportunity cost, estimated to be in the ballpark of 0.4 percent.

So you take the 1.67 percent average management fee, and the 0.8 percent hidden trading costs, and the 0.4 percent opportunity cost, and you can see where the lead boots come in. Add taxes to the equation, and while some actively managed mutual funds may do better than ETFs for a few years, over the long haul I wouldn't bank on many of them coming out ahead.

Uncle Sam's loss, your gain

Alas, unless your money is in a tax-advantaged retirement account, making money in the markets means that you have to fork something over to Uncle Sam at year's end. That's true, of course, whether you invest in individual securities or funds. But before there were ETFs, individual securities had a big advantage over funds in that you were only required to pay capital gains taxes when you actually enjoyed a capital gain. With mutual funds, that isn't so. The fund itself may enjoy a capital gain by selling off an appreciated stock. You pay the capital gains tax regardless of whether you sell and regardless of whether the share price of the mutual fund increased or decreased since the time you bought it.

There have been times (such as the year 2000) when many mutual fund investors lost considerable amounts of money in the market yet had to pay whopping capital gains tax at the end of the year. Talk about adding insult to injury! One study found that over the course of time, taxes have wiped out approximately 2 full percentage points for investors in the highest tax brackets.

In the world of ETFs, such losses are very unlikely to happen. Because ETFs are index-based, there is generally little turnover to create capital gains. To boot, ETFs are structured in a way that insulate shareholders from having to pay capital gains tax, as mutual fund shareholders must often do, when other shareholders cash in their chips.

Capital gains, investor pains

If you hold a mutual fund, and that fund sells shares for more than the purchase price of the shares, you, as an existing shareholder, will likely get slapped with a capital gains tax. How much that tax will be depends on several factors:

✔ **The 5 percent rate.** *Eligibility:* You are in the 10 percent and 15 percent federal income tax brackets, and the capital gains you've incurred come from selling investment securities held for more than one year.

✔ **The 15 percent rate.** *Eligibility:* You are in the 25 percent federal income tax bracket or higher, and the capital gains you've incurred come from selling investment securities held for more than one year.

✔ **Rates as high as 35 percent.** *Suckerability:* The capital gains come from selling investment securities held for less than one year, in which case you will be taxed at the same rate you are taxed for regular (job) income.

No tax calories

The structure of ETFs makes them different than mutual funds. Actually, ETFs are legally structured in three different ways: as exchange-traded open-end mutual funds, exchange-traded unit investment trusts, and exchange-traded grantor trusts. The differences are subtle, and I elaborate on them somewhat in Chapter 3 and throughout Part II. For now, I want to focus on one seminal difference between ETFs and mutual funds, which boils down to an extremely clever setup whereby ETF shares, which represent stock holdings, can be traded without any actual trading of stocks. In a way it's like those Olestra potato chips that have no fat calories because the fat just passes through your body.

Perhaps a better analogy is to the poker player who can play hands all night and, thanks to the miracle of chips, not have to touch any cash.

Market makers and croupiers

In the world of ETFs, we don't have croupiers, but we have market makers. *Market makers* are people who work at the stock exchanges and create (like magic!) ETF shares. ETF shares each represent a portion of a portfolio of stocks, sort of like poker chips represent a pile of cash. As an ETF grows, so does the number of shares. Concurrently (once a day), new stocks are added to a portfolio that mirrors the ETF. See Figure 2-1, which may help you envision the structure of ETFs and what makes them such tax wonders.

When a shareholder of an ETF sells shares, those shares are sold, through the market markers, to other ETF investors. By contrast, with mutual funds, if one person sells, the mutual fund must sell off shares of stock. If those stocks sold in the mutual fund are being sold for more than the original purchase price, the shareholders left behind are stuck paying a capital gains tax. In some years, that amount can be substantial. In 2000, for example, when lots of people were cashing out of mutual funds, the average mutual fund holder paid almost $7 in tax for every $100 invested.

In the world of ETFs, no such thing has happened or is likely to happen. Because of ETFs' poker-chip structure, Barclays, the biggest player in the ETF arena, just claimed four years straight in which none of its 110 ETFs — domestic or international — issued a single dollar in capital gains. That's not a guarantee that there will never be capital gains, but if there ever are, they are sure to be minor.

Tax efficient does not mean tax-free. Although you won't pay capital gains taxes, you will pay taxes on any dividends issued by your ETFs, and ETFs are just as likely to issue dividends as are mutual funds. In addition, if you sell your ETFs and they are in a taxable account, you have to pay capital gains tax (15 percent for most folks) if the ETFs have appreciated in value since the time you bought them.

Taxes on earnings, of course, aren't an issue if your money is held in a tax-advantaged account, such as a Roth IRA. I love Roth IRAs! Much more on that when I get into retirement accounts in Chapter 19.

Traditional Mutual Fund

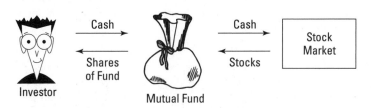

Exchange-Traded Fund

Figure 2-1: The secret to ETFs' tax friendliness lies in their very structure.

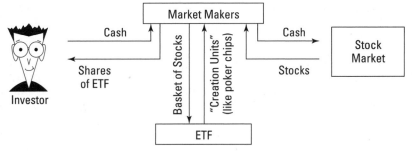

What you see is what you get

A key to building a successful portfolio, right up there with low costs and tax efficiency, is diversification, a subject I discuss more in Chapter 4. You cannot diversify optimally unless you know exactly what's in your portfolio. In a rather infamous example, when tech stocks (some more than others) started to go belly up in 2000, holders of Janus mutual funds got clobbered especially badly. That's because they learned after the fact that their three or four Janus mutual funds, which gave the illusion of diversification, were actually holding many of the same stocks.

With a mutual fund, you often have little idea of what stocks the fund manager is holding. In fact, you may not even know what *kinds* of stocks he is holding. Or even if he is holding stocks! I'm talking here about *style drift,* the mutual fund manager who portends to be aggressive and is conservative, or portends to be conservative and is aggressive. I'm talking about the mutual fund manager who says he loves large value but invests in large growth or small value.

One classic case of style drift cost investors in the all-popular Fidelity Magellan Fund a bundle. The year was 1996, and fund manager Jeffrey Vinik reduced the stock holdings in his "stock" mutual fund to 70 percent. He had 30 percent of the fund's assets in either bonds or short-term securities. He was betting that the market was going to sour, and he was planning to fully invest in stocks after that happened. He was dead wrong. Instead, the market continued to soar, bonds took a dive, Fidelity Magellan seriously underperformed, and Vinik was out.

Style drift: An epidemic

One study by the Association of Investment Management concluded that a full 40 percent of actively managed mutual funds are not what they say they are. Some funds bounce around in style so much that an investor would have almost no idea where her money was. The Parnassus Fund, for example, was once placed by Morningstar in the small cap blend category. Then it moved to small cap value. Later it moved to mid cap blend. Later yet, the fund was reclassified as mid cap growth.

ETFs are the cure

When you buy an ETF, you get complete transparency. You know exactly what you are buying. No matter what the ETF, you can see on the prospectus or on the ETF provider's Web site (or on any number of independent financial Web sites) a complete picture of the ETF's holdings. See, for example, either `www.etfconnect.com` or `http://finance.yahoo.com`. If I go to either Web site and type the letters *IYE* (the ticker for the iShares Dow Jones U.S Energy sector ETF) in the box in the upper right of screen, I can see in an instant what my holdings are. You can see too, in Table 2-3.

Table 2-3	Holdings of the iShares Dow Jones U.S. Energy Sector ETF as of 12/31/2005	
Stock	*Holding Dollar Value*	*% of Total Portfolio*
Exxon Mobil Corp.	$167,033,740.00	20.56
Chevron Corp.	$136,682,745.00	16.82
ConocoPhillips	$44,121,501.00	5.43
Schlumberger Ltd.	$42,752,315.00	5.26
Burlington Resources Inc.	$38,154,620.00	4.7
Occidental Petroleum Corp.	$37,790,190.00	4.65
Devon Energy Corp.	$23,770,829.00	2.93
Baker Hughes Inc.	$21,151,318.00	2.6
Halliburton Co.	$21,031,640.00	2.59
Anadarko Petroleum Corp.	$20,920,705.00	2.58

You simply can't get that information on most actively managed mutual funds.

Transparency also discourages dishonesty

The scandals that have rocked the mutual fund world have left the world of ETFs untouched. There's not a whole lot of manipulation that a fund manager can do when his picks are tied to an index. And because ETFs trade throughout the day, with the price flashing across thousands of computer screens worldwide, there is no room to take advantage of the "stale" pricing that occurs when the markets close and mutual fund orders are settled. All in all, ETF investors are much, much less likely to ever get bamboozled than are investors in active mutual funds.

The index advantage

The triumph of indexed mutual funds and ETFs over actively managed funds is also leading people to ETFs. Index funds (which buy and hold a fixed collection of stocks or bonds) consistently outperform actively managed funds. One study done by Fulcrum Financial tracked mutual fund performance over 10 years and found that 81 percent of value funds underperformed the indexes, as did 63 percent of growth funds.

Here are some reasons that index funds (both mutual funds and ETFs) are hard to beat:

- ✔ They typically carry much lower management fees, sales loads, or redemption charges.

- ✔ Hidden costs — trading costs and spread costs — are much lower when little trading is done.

- ✔ They don't have cash sitting around idle (as the manager waits for what he thinks is the right time to enter the market).

Perhaps the greatest testament to the success of index funds is how many allegedly actively managed funds are actually index funds in (expensive) disguise. I'm talking about closet index funds. According to a recent report in *Investment News,* a newspaper for financial advisers, the number of actively managed stock funds that are closet index funds has tripled over the past four years. As a result, many investors are paying high (active) management fees for investment results that could be achieved with low-cost ETFs.

R squared is a measurement of how closely a fund's performance correlates with an index. It can range from 0.00 to 1.00. An R squared of 1.00 indicates *perfect correlation*: When the index goes up x percent, the fund goes up x percent; when the index falls y percent, the fund falls y percent. An R squared of 0.00 indicates no correlation. This measurement is used to assess tracking error or closet index funds.

According to Morningstar data as interpreted by *Investment News,* nearly 28 percent of all large cap funds carry a three-year R squared of 0.95 or higher relative to the S&P 500 stock index. That kind of R squared makes them closet index funds. And if you look at the entire mutual fund industry, it is apparent that the triumph of indexing is becoming well known. At year end 2004, the average large cap fund had an R squared of almost 0.90. That number is up from 0.74 only four years earlier.

Getting the Professional Edge

I don't know about you, but when I take the kids bowling and — as happens on very rare occasion — I bowl a strike, I feel as if a miracle of Biblical proportions has occurred. And then I turn on the television, stumble upon a professional bowling tournament, and see guys for whom *not* bowling a strike is a rare occurrence. The difference between amateur and professional bowlers is huge. The difference between investment amateurs and investment professionals can be just as huge. But you can close much of that gap by using ETFs.

Consider a few impressive numbers

By investment professionals, Lord knows I'm not talking about stockbrokers or insurance salesmen. I'm talking about the managers of foundations and endowments with $1 billion or greater in invested assets. By amateurs, I'm talking about the average U.S. investor with a few assorted and sundry mutual funds in his 401(k).

Let's compare the two: During the period 1984–2002, the U.S. stock market, as measured by the S&P 500 Index, provided an annual rate of return of 12.2 percent. Yet the average mutual fund investor, according to a study by Dalbar, earned an annual rate of 2.6 percent over that same period, barely keeping up with inflation. Why the pitiful returns? There are several reasons, but two main ones:

- Mutual fund investors pay too much for their investments.

- They jump into hot funds in hot sectors when they're hot and jump out when those funds or sectors turn cold. (In other words, they are constantly buying high and selling low.)

To give you an idea of the difference between amateurs and professionals, consider this: For the period 2003–2005, during which the S&P provided an annual rate of return of 14.38 percent, the average return of managers of foundations and endowments with assets greater than $1 billion was 14.75 percent.

You can do what they do!

Professional managers, you see, don't pay high expenses. They don't jump in and out of funds. They know that they need to diversify. They tend to buy indexes. They know exactly what they own. And they know that asset allocation, not stock picking, is what drives long-term investment results. In short, they do all the things that an ETF portfolio can do for you. So do it. Well, maybe. . . . First read the rest of this chapter!

Do ETFs Belong in Your Life?

Okay, so on the plus side of ETFs we have ultra-low management expenses, super tax efficiency, transparency, and a lot of fancy trading opportunities, such as shorting, if you are so inclined. What about the negatives? In the sections that follow, I walk you through some other facts about ETFs that you should consider before parting with your precious dollars.

Calculating commissions

I talk a lot more about commissions when I compare and contrast various brokerage houses in Chapter 3, but I want to give you a heads up here: You have to pay a commission every time you buy and sell an ETF.

Here's the good news: Trading commissions for stocks and ETFs (it's the same commission for either) have been dropping faster than the price of desktop computers. What once would have cost you a bundle, now — if you trade online, which you definitely should — is really pin money, perhaps as low as $4 a trade. However, you can't simply ignore trading commissions. They aren't always that low, and even $4 a pop can add up. In most cases, you shouldn't agonize over the cost of trading ETFs; merely keep an eye on them.

Moving money in a flash

The fact that ETFs can be traded throughout the day like stocks makes them, unlike mutual funds, fair game for day-traders and institutional wheeler-dealers. For the rest of us common folk, there isn't much about the way that ETFs are bought and sold that makes them especially valuable. Indeed, the ability to trade throughout the day may make you more apt to do so, perhaps selling or buying on impulse. As I discuss in detail in Chapter 17, impulsive investing, although it can get your endorphins pumping, is generally not the most profitable investing.

Making a sometimes tricky choice

In Parts II, III, and IV of this book, I give you lots of detailed information about how to construct a portfolio that contains ETFs to meet your needs. Here, I want to just whet your appetite with a couple very basic examples of decisions you may be facing.

Say you have a choice between investing in an index mutual fund that charges 0.15 percent a year and an ETF that tracks the same index and charges the same amount. What should you invest in?

If your money is in a taxable account, go with the ETF, provided you are investing at least a few thousand dollars and you plan to keep your money invested for at least several years. If you're investing less, and/or if you think you may need to tap the money anytime soon, you are likely better off with the index mutual fund.

The index mutual fund trap

Some brokerage houses, such as Vanguard and Fidelity, offer wonderful low-cost index mutual funds. But a problem with them is that you either can't buy them at other financial "supermarkets" (such as Charles Schwab or T. Rowe Price), or you have to pay a substantial fee to get into them. So building an entire portfolio of index mutual funds can be tough. If you want both Fidelity and Vanguard, you may be forced to pay high fees or to open up separate accounts at different supermarkets, which means extra paperwork and hassle. With ETFs, you can buy them anywhere, sell them anywhere, and keep them — even if they are ETFs from several different providers — all parked in the same brokerage house.

But say you have, oh, $5,000 to invest in your IRA. (All IRA money is taxed as income when you withdraw it in retirement, and therefore the tax efficiency of securities held within an IRA isn't an issue.) An ETF charges you a management fee of 0.15 percent a year, and a comparable index mutual fund charges 0.35, but buying and selling the ETF will cost you $10 at either end. Now what should you do?

The math isn't difficult. The difference between 0.15 and 0.35 (0.20 percent) of $5,000 is $10. It will take you one year to recoup your trading fee of $10. If you factor in the cost of selling (another $10), it will take you about two years to recoup your trading costs. At that point, the ETF will be your lower-cost turtle, and the mutual fund your higher-cost hare.

In general, building an entire portfolio out of ETFs usually makes sense starting in the ballpark of $50,000. Anything less than that, and you are most likely better off with mutual funds or a mix of mutual funds and ETFs.

Chapter 3

Getting to Know the Players

I love to shop on Christmas Eve. It's the only time the entire year when men — husbands and boyfriends who finally realize that they need to buy a gift, quick — outnumber women at the mall. I see these hulking figures, some in bright orange hunting jackets, walking the halls of the Lehigh Valley Mall, looking themselves like scared prey. "Where's the lingerie?" they ask, eyes to the ground.

Sometimes, when I suggest to a client that he buy a few ETFs for his portfolio, I see the same look of dire trepidation. I need to reassure him that buying ETFs isn't all that difficult. In this chapter, I want to do the same thing for you.

This chapter is something of a shopper's guide to ETFs — a mall directory, if you will. I don't suggest which ETFs to buy specifically (I will, I will — but that's for later chapters), but I show you where to find the good shops and locate the best lingerie. I talk about the brokerage houses that allow you to buy and sell ETFs; the financial institutions that create ETFs; the indexes that the financial institutions model their ETFs after; and the exchanges where millions of ETF shares are bought, sold, and borrowed each day.

Creating an Account for Your ETFs

You — you personally — can't just buy a share of an ETF as you would buy, say, a negligee. You need someone to actually buy it for you and hold it for you. That someone is a broker, sometimes referred to as a *brokerage house* or a *broker-dealer*. Some broker-dealers, the really big ones, are sort of like financial department stores or supermarkets where you can buy ETFs, mutual funds, individual stocks and bonds, or fancier investment tools like puts and calls. You'll recognize, I'm sure, the names of such financial department stores: Fidelity, Vanguard, TD AMERITRADE, and T. Rowe Price.

ETFs are usually traded just as stocks are traded. Same commissions. Mostly the same rules. Same hours (generally 9:30 a.m. to 4:00 p.m., Manhattan Island time). Through your brokerage house, you can buy 1 share, 2 shares, or 10,000 shares. Here's one difference between ETFs and stocks: Although people today rarely do it, you can sometimes purchase stocks directly from a company, and you may even get a pretty certificate saying you own the stock. (I *think* some companies still do that!) Not so with ETFs. Call Barclays or State Street and ask to buy a share of an ETF, and they will tell you to go find yourself a broker. Ask for a certificate, and . . . well, don't even bother.

The first step then, prior to beginning your ETF shopping expedition, is to find a brokerage house, preferably a financial department store where you can keep all your various investments. It makes life a lot easier to have everything in one place, to get one statement every month, and to see all your investments on one computer screen.

Answering a zillion questions

The first question you have to answer when opening an account is whether the account will be a retirement account or non-retirement account. If you want a retirement account, you need to specify what kind (IRA? Roth IRA? SEP?). I cover the ins and outs of retirement accounts — and how ETFs can fit snuggly in the picture — in Chapter 19. A non-retirement account is a simpler animal. You don't need to know any special tax rules, and your money isn't committed for any time period unless you happen to stick something like a CD into the account.

The next question you have to answer is whether you want to open a *margin* account or a *cash* account. A margin account is somewhat similar to a checking account with overdraw protection. It means that you can borrow from the account or make purchases of securities (such as ETFs, but generally not mutual funds) without actually having any cash to pay for them on the spot. Cool, huh?

Unless you have a gambling addiction, go with margin. You never know when you may need a quick (and, compared to credit cards, inexpensive) and potentially tax-deductible loan. If you think you may have a gambling addiction, read the sidebar "Don't margin your house away!"

Don't margin your house away!

I once had a client whose husband handled all the finances. Then they divorced. Divorcing couples usually split the family assets, but they also split the liabilities. This woman had no idea, until she divorced, that her hubbie had been playing with stocks and ETFs, buying them on margin. Suddenly, she inherited a rather enormous debt. "Buying on margin" means that the brokerage house is lending you money, and charging you interest, so you can purchase securities. Ouch. One of the often touted "advantages" of ETFs is that you can buy them on margin — something you often can't do with mutual funds. Margin buying is very dangerous business. The fact that you can buy an ETF on margin is *not* an advantage as I see it. The stock market is risky enough. Don't ever compound

that risk by borrowing money to invest. You may wind up losing not only your nest egg but your home. My client was able to save hers; not everyone is so lucky.

Two things about margin you should know:

- ✔ The brokerage house can usually change the rate of interest you're paying without notice.

- ✔ If your investments dip below a certain percentage of your margin loan, the brokerage house can sell your stocks and bonds from right under you.

It can be dangerous business. Margin only with great caution.

You're also asked questions about beneficiaries and titling (or registration), such as whether you want your joint account set up with rights of survivorship. I'll just say one quick word about naming your beneficiaries: Be certain that who you name is who you want to receive your money if you die. Beneficiary designations supercede your will. In other words, if your will says that all your ETFs go to your spouse, and your beneficiary designation on your account names someone else, your spouse loses; all the ETFs in your account will go to someone else.

For more information on what happens to your assets when you die, I recommend *Estate Planning For Dummies* by N. Brian Caverly, Esq. and Jordan S. Simon (Wiley).

Finally, you're asked all kinds of personal questions about your employment, your wealth, and your risk tolerance. Don't sweat them! Federal securities regulations require brokerage houses to know something about their clients. Honestly, I don't think anyone ever looks at the personal section of the forms. I've never heard any representative of any brokerage house so much as whisper any of the information included in those personal questions.

Placing an order to buy

After your account is in place, which should take only a few days, you're ready to buy your first ETF. Most brokerage houses give you a choice: Call in your order, or do it yourself online. Calling is typically much more expensive. Being the savvy investor that you are, you're not going to throw money away, so place all your orders online! If you need help, a representative of the brokerage house will walk you through the process step-by-step — at no expense to you.

Keep in mind when trading ETFs that the cost of the trades, if substantial enough, can nibble seriously into your holdings. Here's how to avoid such nibbling:

✔ **Don't trade often.** Buy and hold, buy and hold, buy and hold! (See Chapter 17.)

✔ **Know your percentages.** In general, don't bother with ETFs if the trade is going to cost you anything more than half of 1 percent. In other words, if making the trade is going to cost you $10 (an average amount for an online trade), you want to invest at least $2,000 at a pop. If you have only $1,000 to invest, or less, you are often better off purchasing a no-load mutual fund, preferably an index fund, or waiting until you've accumulated enough cash to make a larger investment.

✔ **Be a savvy shopper.** Keep the cost of your individual trades to a minimum by shopping brokerage houses for the lowest fees, placing all your orders online, and arguing for the best deals. Yes, you can often negotiate with these people for better deals, especially if you have substantial bucks. Also know that many brokerage houses offer special incentives for new clients: Move more than $50,000 in assets and get your first 20 trades for free, or that sort of thing. Always ask.

But wait just a moment!

Please don't be so enthralled by anything you read in this book that you rush out, open a brokerage account, and sell your existing mutual funds or stocks and bonds to buy ETFs. Rash investment decisions almost always wind up to be mistakes. Remember that whenever you sell a security, you may face serious tax consequences. (Vanguard offers a unique advantage here; see the sidebar "The Vanguard edge" later in this chapter.) If you decide to sell certain mutual funds, annuities, or life insurance policies, there may also be nasty surrender charges. If you're unsure whether selling your present holdings would make for a financial hit on the chin, talk to your accountant or financial planner.

Introducing the Shops

I've read that the motorcycle industry boasts the highest level of consumer loyalty in the United States. A Harley man would *never* be caught dead on a Yamaha. Not being a motorcyclist, I have no idea why that is. In the world of brokerage houses, after someone has a portfolio in place at a house such as Fidelity, Vanguard, or Schwab, that client is often very hesitant to switch. I know *exactly* why that is: Moving your account can sometimes be a big, costly, and time-consuming pain in the ass. So, whether you're a Harley man or a Yamaha mama with money to invest, it behooves you to spend some serious time researching brokerage houses and to choose the one that will work best for you. Perhaps I can help.

What to look for

Here are the some things you want from any broker who is going to be holding your ETFs:

- Reasonable prices
- Good service, meaning they pick up the phone without putting you through voicemail hell
- A user-friendly Web site
- Good advice, if you think you're going to need advice
- A service center near you, if you like doing business with real human beings
- Incentives for opening an account, which can run the gamut from a certain number of free trades to laptop computers
- Financial strength

Financial strength really isn't as important as the others because all brokerage houses carry insurance. Still, a brokerage house that collapses under you can be a hassle, and it may take time to recoup your money. See the sidebar "Can you lose your ETFs if your brokerage house collapses?"

I give you my take on some of the major brokerage houses in just a moment, but I first want to talk a bit about prices, which can be downright devilish to compare and contrast.

Can you lose your ETFs if your brokerage house collapses?

Brokerage houses, as part of their registration process with the federal government, are automatically insured through the Securities Investor Protection Corporation (SIPC). Each individual investor's securities are protected up to $500,000 should the brokerage house go belly up. Larger brokerage houses generally carry supplemental insurance that protects customers' account balances beyond the half-million that SIPC covers. TD AMERITRADE, for example, has insurance through Lloyd's of London that protects each customer's account up to $150 million.

Note: Neither SIPC coverage nor any kind of supplemental insurance will protect the value of your account from a market downfall! For additional information on SIPC, you can order the free brochure by calling 1-800-934-4448 or checking out its Web site at www.sipc.org.

A price structure like none other

Shopping for shoes? Beer? Pickled herring? Go to one store. Go to another store. Or open up an issue of *Consumer Reports.* Compare the prices. Easy business.

Comparing the prices at brokerage houses is anything but easy. Charles Schwab, for example, may charge you $19.95 for an online trade, or it may charge you $9.95 for the very same online trade, depending on how much money you have in your account and how many trades you make per quarter. At Fidelity, different criteria apply, including not only your portfolio balance and number of quarterly trades but sometimes the number of shares you're trading at any particular point. At ShareBuilder, you can pay only $4 a trade, but you need to commit to a schedule of regular trades that occur only on Tuesdays. (That's right, only on Tuesdays.) This is *not* easy business.

It would take me many pages to relay to you the complicated price structures of the various brokerage houses. I'll pass. Instead, in the following sections, I give you a short summary of the pricing and then leave you to do some leg work. Always look at the entire brokerage package. That includes not only the price of trades but total account fees. You need to do some comparing and contrasting on your own, but with the tools I give you in the following sections, it shouldn't take an eternity.

The Vanguard Group

I mention Vanguard frequently in this book for a number of reasons. For one, I like Vanguard because of its leadership role in the world of index investing. Vanguard is also the only investment house that serves as both custodian of ETFs and is itself a provider of ETFs. (Okay, Fidelity has one ETF, but one hardly counts.) There's also "The Vanguard edge" (which I discuss in a side-bar of that name later in this chapter). And — perhaps most important to the theme of this book — Vanguard's lineup of ETFs are top-notch products. But more on that in a few pages. Right now, I'm here to discuss Vanguard as a shop where you can buy and hold your ETFs.

Incidentally, buying and holding Vanguard ETFs at Vanguard offers no particular advantage over buying and holding those ETFs elsewhere. Vanguard the shop and Vanguard the supplier should be assessed separately.

As for Vanguard the shop, the trading commissions are middle of the road, and the service is middle of the road. What really shines about Vanguard is its broad array of top-rate index mutual funds. I know, I know, this is a book about ETFs. But index mutual funds and ETFs are close cousins, and sometimes it makes a lot of sense to have both in a portfolio. (More on that in Chapter 15.) If you do wish to hold Vanguard index mutual funds alongside your ETFs, Vanguard is an awfully logical place to hold them because you can buy and sell Vanguard funds, provided you don't do it often, at no charge. At Fidelity, in contrast, buying any Vanguard mutual fund will typically cost you $75.

Address:

The Vanguard Group

P.O. Box 1110

Valley Forge, PA 19482-1110

Telephone: 800-992-8327

Web site: www.vanguard.com

Fidelity Investments

I like this brokerage house as well. In fact, I house my own ETFs at Fidelity. The service, at least for me, is fabulous. (Okay, I admit it, I have a fair amount of money there.) The price of trades at Fidelity is competitive. Like Vanguard, Fidelity also has some excellent low-cost index funds of its own, which you may wish to keep alongside your ETF portfolio. And the Fidelity Web site has some really good tools — some of the best available — for analyzing your portfolio and researching new investments.

The last I heard, Fidelity was offering 25,000 miles on United Airlines to any new customer opening a brokerage account with the company. By the time this book appears in print, the company may be offering a year's supply of parsley, or Peter Lynch will come to your house and give you a leg wax, or whatever.

Here's a bit of insider information: The cost of Fidelity's trades is based on how much your *household* has invested at Fidelity. I have found Fidelity to be quite liberal in its interpretation of household. If, for example, your parents, your in-laws, your siblings, or your adult children have money at Fidelity, and you ask a rep real nicely to include you under the same household, you may be successful at saving some serious money. If he says no, call back the next day, and hope to get another rep.

Address:

Fidelity Investments

P.O. Box 770001

Cincinnati, OH 45277-0001

Telephone: 800-343-3548

Web site: www.fidelity.com

T. Rowe Price

This Baltimore-based shop has several claims to fame, including its bend-over-backward friendliness to small investors and its plethora of really fine financial tools, especially for retirement planning, available to all customers at no cost. The price of trading is a wee bit higher than average. The service is excellent (reps tend to be very chummy). If you decide that part of your portfolio should be in mutual funds, you can do a lot worse than going with T. Rowe Price's lineup of entirely load-free funds.

Address:

T. Rowe Price

P.O. Box 17630

Baltimore, MD 21297-1630

Telephone: 800-225-5132

Web site: www.troweprice.com

TD AMERITRADE

For a number of years, TD Waterhouse and Ameritrade were known as the discount kings of the brokerage biz. They recently merged into one company called TD AMERITRADE. The trading prices at TD are just about middle of the pack. Although I've never had occasion to work with TD, the service is reputedly quite high. The Web site has a very clean and crisp feel to it. On the down side (in my opinion, of course), the TD culture and many of the articles on the Web site promote frequent trading, as opposed to, say, Vanguard, where the culture is decidedly more buy-and-hold. (The same two philosophies exist among providers of ETFs, as I discuss shortly.)

At the moment I'm writing this sentence, if you invest $25,000 or more with TD as a new customer, you qualify for a free Palm Treo 650 Smartphone and 25 free trades. I'm sure the freebies will come and go, but always be sure to ask!

> **Addresses:**
>
> TD AMERITRADE
>
> P.O. Box 2630
>
> Jersey City, NJ 07303-2630
>
> or
>
> P.O. Box 919091
>
> San Diego, CA 92191-9091
>
> **Telephone:** 800-454-9272
>
> **Web site:** www.tdameritrade.com

ShareBuilder

At an unheard-of $4 a trade, or even less if you're willing to pay a monthly fee, you can't beat ShareBuilder for price. The catch is that you have to commit to regular trades. You need to make trades (investing as little as $25) once a week or once a month. And therein lies the problem.

If you're putting in money once a week or once a month, chances are you're not putting in a whole lot. You're a drib-and-drab investor, and drib-and-drab investors, although certainly better off with ShareBuilder than most other brokers, should be investing in mutual funds, not ETFs. Do the math. Even if you are saving a very impressive $200 every week out of your paycheck, at $4 a trade, you're losing 2 percent right off the top. That's a chunk.

ShareBuilder, at the time of this writing, is offering seven free trades with each new IRA account opened. As with the other brokerage houses, this deal is subject to change, and probably will by the time you read this chapter. So ask for the special deal of the day, whatever that may be.

Address:

ShareBuilder

1445 120th Avenue Northeast

Bellevue, WA 98005

Telephone: 800-747-2537

Web site: www.sharebuilder.com

Other major brokerage houses

The five houses I discuss in the previous sections aren't the only players in town. Here are a few more to consider:

- **Charles Schwab:** 866-232-9890; www.schwab.com. I've never liked Schwab because of its high trading costs, but just as I was writing this chapter, the firm lowered its fees across the board.

- **eTrade:** 800-387-2331; www.etrade.com. Not only can you house your ETFs with eTrade, but you can refinance the mortgage on your house, as well.

- **TIAA-CREF:** 800-842-2776; www.tiaa-cref.org. I've heard pretty good things about TIAA, but I can't work with them directly because I'm not a teacher. This brokerage house works only with people who have chalk under their nails. (If you're married to someone with chalk under the nails, you qualify, too.)

Presenting the Suppliers

There are dozens and dozens of mutual fund providers. Some of the firms may offer just one fund, and they sometimes give the feeling that the entire business is run out of someone's garage. Not so with ETFs. There are only a few providers, and they tend to be large companies. Why is that? In part because the operating expenses are so low that a company can't profit unless it has the economies of scale and the multiple incomes that offering a bevy of ETFs provides. Like your favorite professional sports team, clothing store, or political party, each supplier of ETFs has its own personality.

It's okay to mix and match

I want to emphasize that while picking a single brokerage house to manage your accounts makes enormous sense, there is no reason that you can't own ETFs from different sources. A portfolio with a combination of Barclays, Vanguard, and State Street ETFs can work just fine. In fact, I would recommend *not* wedding yourself to a single ETF supplier but being flexible and picking the best ETFs to meet your needs in each area of your portfolio.

(Note that brokerage houses typically do not sell all mutual funds. But I've never heard of a brokerage house being picky and choosy about what ETFs it will sell. The reason is simple: When you buy or sell an ETF, you pay a trading fee directly to the brokerage house. Because brokerage houses are in the business of making money, the more ETFs they can offer, the merrier.)

Table 3-1 offers a handy reference to the largest ETF providers, which I introduce you to in a moment.

Table 3-1	Providers of ETFs		
Company	*Number of ETFs*	*Average expense ratio*	*Claim to fame*
Barclays iShares	116	0.45	Biggest variety
State Street Global Advisors	42	0.27	Oldest ETF
PowerShares	37	0.63	Active indexes
Vanguard	24	0.22	Cost leader
WisdomTree Investments	20	0.50	Dividend mania
ProShares	12	0.95	High volatility
Rydex	9	0.30	Artsy indexes

Check your passport

Just a quick word for you readers who live outside the United States: All ETFs (and mutual funds) sold in the United States must be approved by the Securities and Exchange Commission. Other countries have their equivalent governmental regulatory authorities. None of the ETFs listed in this section or in Part II of this book are sold beyond the borders of the United States.

Some of the ETF providers mentioned — particularly Barclays — do sell ETFs in other countries, but they go by different names (*iShares* in Canada are known as *iUnits*), and they likely have different structures.

Barclays iShares

When I was a very young man traveling the world with my backpack and sleeping bag, I always carried a packet of beautiful baby-blue Barclays Traveller's Cheques. When I returned home to the States, and for many years thereafter, I hardly came across the Barclays name. Then along came ETFs, and now Barclays is, once again, a part of my life.

With 116 ETFs for sale and $150 billion in ETF assets, Barclays Global Investors is not only one of the largest investment banks in the world ($1.3 trillion in assets under management); it is far and away the largest player in the ETF game. Barclays ETFs, known as *iShares,* offer the broadest selection. You can buy iShares that track the major S&P indexes for growth and value, large and small cap stocks. Other equity ETFs track the major Russell and Morningstar indexes. You can also find industry sector ETFs from technology and healthcare to financial services and software.

In the international arena, you can buy an ETF to track either an intercontinental index, such as the MSCI EAFE (*E*urope, *A*ustralia, *F*ar *E*ast), or much narrower markets, such as the Malaysian or Brazilian stock market. To date, Barclays is the only supplier of fixed-income (bond) ETFs, with six offerings ranging from long-term Treasury bonds to inflation-protected bonds (TIPS) to corporate bonds.

Management fees vary from a low of 0.09 percent for the iShares S&P 500 (IVV) to a high of 0.75 percent for the MSCI Emerging Markets fund (EEM), with an average of 0.30 percent.

Russell's review: You can't go too wrong with Barclays. My only beef is with the price of some of the international funds where Barclays has thus far had a monopoly. On the other hand, the firm has done an outstanding job of tracking indexes and offering variety. It has done a good job of maintaining tax efficiency. I caution you, however, not to get sucked into the iShares candy store. Some of the ETFs track very small markets and market segments and clearly don't belong in most people's portfolios. I do not suggest, for example, that you stock up on the MSCI Malaysia fund.

For more information, call 800-474-2737 or visit www.ishares.com.

State Street Global Advisers (SSgA) streetTRACKS, SPDRs, and Dow Industrial DIAMONDS

State Street's flagship ETF, the first ETF on the U.S. market, is the SPDR 500 (SPY). Traded on the American Stock Exchange, it boasts almost $60 billion in net assets, well more than twice the assets of any other ETF on the market. I suspect that will change over time, but for now, SSgA's pet spider gives it a firm perch as the second-largest provider of ETFs. State Street's ETFs follow traditional indexes, carry reasonable fees, and are varied enough to allow for a very well diversified portfolio, at least on the domestic equity side. All told, SSgA's 42 U.S.-based ETFs hold about $70 billion in assets.

Russell's review: The management expenses — 0.27 percent on average — are extremely reasonable, and I like the variety of funds except for the lack of international and fixed income. The Select Sector SPDRs offer a very efficient way of investing in various industry sectors (if that's your kind of thing). The Web sites are topnotch, and the SPDRs Web site in particular — www.spdr index.com — offers some fabulous portfolio-construction tools, such as the *Correlation Tracker,* which allows you to find ETFs that best compliment your existing portfolio.

One drawback to SSgA's offerings, however, is the legal structure of some of its ETFs. The oldest ETFs, such as the SPDRs and DIAMONDS, are set up as unit investment trusts rather than as open-end mutual funds as most ETFs are. That means they can't reinvest dividends on a regular basis, which can create a cash drag, bringing down long-term total returns by a smidgen and a half. (It's hard to actually measure the impact.)

For more information, call 866-787-2257 or visit www.streettracks.net or www.spdrindex.com.

PowerShares

PowerShares hesitates to call its 37 ETFs "actively managed" and instead calls them ETFs with "enhanced indexes" or "strategy indexes." Or, to use the company's own jargon, it calls them "Intellidexes." The Intellidexes, custom-made indexes produced jointly by PowerShares and the American Stock Exchange, represent "a modified equal weight portfolio" that is "rebalanced and reconstituted quarterly."

Reconstituted. Hmmm. That means considerable turnover and some added trading expenses. It also means that if you choose PowerShares ETFs to build your portfolio, you are no longer an index investor, which (judging by wads and wads of historical data) puts you at something of a disadvantage.

The company has been quite innovative in its offering of market sectors. Several are offered by no one else. The Water Resources ETF (PHO), for example, allows you to invest in a "group of companies that focus on the provision of potable water." And the WilderHill Clean Energy Fund (PBW) allows you to invest in "companies that focus on greener and generally renewable sources of energy."

Russell's review: I'm not a big fan of active management, but if you insist on going there, PowerShares ETFs may be a good option. Thus far, the firm has been very good at avoiding capital gains taxes, and with average management expenses of 0.60 percent, the funds are still cheap when compared to actively managed mutual funds. Some of the market segments created by PowerShares, such as the two mentioned in the previous paragraph, are intriguing, especially if they prove over time to show limited correlation to the rest of the stock market. Still, Water Resources should not make up the lion's share of anyone's portfolio.

For more information, call 800-843-2639 or visit www.powershares.com.

Vanguard ETFs

It goes without saying that these people know something about index investing. In 1976, Vanguard launched the first consumer index mutual fund, the Vanguard Index Trust–500 Portfolio. (Wells Fargo already had an index fund, but it was available only to endowments and other such institutions.) In 2001, Vanguard launched its first ETF. Why Vanguard wasn't exactly in the vanguard is anyone's guess, but by the time Vanguard ETFs (which they used to call *VIPERs*) were introduced to the market, Barclays had already taken a solid lead. But Vanguard ETFs, largely due to their incredibly low costs, are quickly moving up. As of this writing, the 24 ETFs hold $14 billion in assets — an increase of 22 percent over the previous year.

How low is low? The lowest-cost Vanguard ETF — the Vanguard Total Stock Market ETF (VTI) — sets you back 0.07 percent in total management expenses a year. (That's 70 cents per $1,000 invested.) As far as I know, that may be the lowest cost noninstitutional investment vehicle anywhere in the world.

TIP

The Vanguard edge

If you own a Vanguard mutual fund and you want to convert to the Vanguard ETF that tracks the same index, you can do so without any tax ramifications. The conversion is tax-free because you will actually be exchanging one class of shares for another class of shares, all within the same fund. You can do this *only* with Vanguard ETFs. Vanguard actually has a U.S. patent that gives it a monopoly on this share structure.

For example, if you own shares in the Vanguard Total Stock Market Index Fund (VTSMX), and you decide that you want to exchange them for the Vanguard Total Stock Market ETF (VTI), you can do so and not worry about having to take any tax hit. You will, however, need to pay the Vanguard conversion fee of $50. (This fee is waived for Vanguard "Flagship" clients, those with $1 million or more invested with Vanguard.)

So should you do it? The expense ratio on the mutual fund is 0.19. The expense ratio on the ETF is 0.07. If you have, say, $20,000 in the account, moving from the mutual fund to the ETF will save you $24 a year in management fees. And the conversion may also possibly save you a dollar or two a year in taxes. It would be worth your trouble to make the exchange only if you were looking to keep your investment for more than a couple of years.

Note that the tax-free transfer works only the one way. If you have ETF shares that have appreciated in value, you can't convert those shares to mutual fund shares without incurring a capital gains tax (unless you have them in a retirement account).

Russell's review: I *love* Vanguard's low costs. (Who wouldn't?) And their lineup of ETFs, in line with Vanguard's personality, is sensible and direct. They use reasonable indexes, track them well, and take the utmost care to avoid capital gains taxes and make certain that all dividends paid are qualified dividends so they are taxed at a lower rate. My only problem with Vanguard is the firm's long-standing reluctance to do anything more than dabble in overseas markets. But the few Vanguard international ETFs you can choose from are excellent choices, and if that isn't enough, there's no reason you can't choose Vanguard ETFs for the domestic side of your portfolio and Barclays for the international. (More on investing overseas in Chapter 10.)

For more information, call 800-992-8327 or visit www.vanguard.com.

WisdomTree

WisdomTree Investments out of New York, with some fairly big-gun backers, issued 20 ETFs in June 2006. Rumor has it that the company has filed applications with the Securities and Exchange Commission to produce at least six more. All 20 WisdomTree ETFs have the word *dividend* in them. You can buy the WisdomTree LargeCap Dividend Fund (DLN), the WisdomTree SmallCap Dividend Fund (DES), or the WisdomTree International Dividend Top 100 Fund (DOO).

Russell's review: DOO? WisdomTree? It sounds like a remedial reading course for middle-school students. And where does this dividend fetish come from? I hope for this company's sake that dividend investing proves profitable moving forward, but I have my doubts. More on that subject in Chapter 11. My favorite WisdomTree ETF is the WisdomTree International SmallCap Dividend Fund (DLS) because it opens up an entirely new asset class (small international) to the world of ETFs. I haven't used it in any portfolios yet, but I well may. But would I ever build an entire portfolio of WisdomTree dividend ETFs? Not likely. It would be a little like taking a remedial reading class and studying only the vowels.

For more information, call 866-909-9473 or visit www.wisdomtree.com.

ProShares

ProShares offers 12 ETFs. The Short QQQ ProShares (PSQ) allows you to *short* the NASDAQ-100: If the NASDAQ goes down 10 percent, your ETF goes up (more or less) 10 percent. Of course, the inverse is true, as well. Other ProShares offerings allow you to short the Dow, the S&P 500, or the S&P MidCap 400. The Ultra ProShares are four ETFs that allow you to move with the market at double the speed. Ultra QQQ ProShares (QLD), for example, tends to rise 20 percent when the NASDAQ-100 goes up 10 percent and to fall 20 percent when the NASDAQ-100 goes down 10 percent. All these percentages are rough approximations. In the real world, you're going to get less money than you bargain for and more risk than you hoped for.

Russell's review: I'm not too hot on the strategies these ETFs employ, to say the least. In short, selling short is akin to market timing, and market timing, while loads of fun, isn't often profitable. As for the less-than-double-your-money, more-than-double-your-risk ProShares Ultra ETFs, well . . . excuse me while I take a minute to scratch my head and try to figure out the logic in that. See my discussion of both strategies in Chapter 11.

For more information, call 866-776-5125 or visit www.proshares.com.

Rydex

With nine ETFs and a bunch more awaiting approval from the Securities and Exchange Commission, Rydex is an interesting company with an unusual mix of products. One company spokesperson describes his company as "oriented toward tactical investors." In other words, Rydex's ETFs, which total about $2.1 billion in net assets, are largely designed for people who are unhappy buying the usual indexes and want to take something of a gamble on a particular equity style, such as large growth stocks. For such an investor, Rydex offers its customized S&P 500/Citigroup Pure Growth ETF. Using a proprietary seven factors to determine which stocks among the S&P 500 are the most "growthy," Rydex bundles them into a package that promises purity for the gung-ho growth investor. They'll do the same for you on the other side if you are a gung-ho value investor. Heeeeyaaaaa!

If you want to gamble that the Euro is about to go on a tear, you can buy Rydex's Euro Currency Trust exchange-traded *product* — not quite an ETF, but almost. And perhaps most intriguing of all Rydex's investment products, the firm offers an innovative Rydex S&P 500 Equal Weight ETF (RSP), which, just like it sounds, offers you an opportunity to invest in the S&P 500 with all company stocks represented in equal allocations (as opposed to the more traditional value-weighted method of allocation).

Russell's review: At 0.30 percent as the average management expense, Rydex funds aren't all that pricey. So far, they've been relatively tax efficient, despite fairly high turnover for ETFs. And the performance record has been impressive for the short time that Rydex funds have been around. Nonetheless, I do not like currency gambling, and gambling is what it is. There is simply no way to know which way the Euro is going vis-à-vis the dollar. As for the "pure" funds, I find them intriguing, but at the time of this writing, they've been in existence only for several months, and I'd like to see some kind of track record before recommending them. Even though Rydex caters to the "tactical investor," its pure funds may wind up being a good vehicle for long-term buy-and-hold types like me. Time will tell. The S&P 500 Equal Weight ETF is definitely worth some serious consideration, especially for smaller investors, and I look at that much more closely in Chapter 5.

For more information, call 800-820-0888 or visit `www.rydexfunds.com`.

Other suppliers

Brokerage biggie Merrill Lynch produces Holding Company Depository Receipts (HOLDRS). They aren't ETFs per se, but they are so much like ETFs that they may as well be. HOLDRS are baskets of stocks that Merrill says represent a certain industry, like pharmaceuticals or telecommunications. HOLDRS are strange beasts that must be bought and sold in lots of 100 shares. They can also be very concentrated; in some cases, two or three companies make up 50 percent or more of the net assets. For those reasons, I don't generally recommend HOLDRS for most investors. For more information, visit www.holdrs.com.

HOLDRS shouldn't be confused with BLDRS, which are true ETFs administered by the Bank of New York. BLDRS — there are four of them — are collections of American Depository Receipts (ADRs), foreign companies whose stock trades on U.S. exchanges. BLDRS are rather *thinly traded* (that's industry jargon for "they aren't all that popular"), but, in fact, they should be considered as viable alternatives for the international equity side of your portfolio. BLDRS trade on the NASDAQ, whereas most ETFs trade on either the American Stock Exchange or the New York Stock Exchange. For more information, visit www.bldrsfunds.com.

Fidelity Investments is the number one or number two U.S. brokerage house, neck-in-neck with Vanguard the past couple of years. However, it produces only one ETF, the Fidelity NASDAQ Composite ETF (ONEQ), which tracks companies listed on the NASDAQ Stock Market. For more information, visit www.fidelity.com.

Familiarizing Yourself with the Indexers

At the core of every ETF is an index. The index is the blueprint upon which the ETF is built. Some ETF providers use old, established indexes. Others create their own, often in conjunction with seasoned indexers. (That association helps them get approval from the Securities and Exchange Commission.) As a rule, for an ETF to be any good, it has to be based on a good index. On the other hand, a good index doesn't guarantee a good ETF because other things, like costs and tax efficiency, matter as well. That being said, I turn now to the five indexers that create and recreate the indexes upon which about 95 percent of all ETFs are based.

Standard & Poors

Owned by publishing powerhouse McGraw-Hill, Standard & Poors is perhaps best known for its credit rating services. The company also maintains hundreds of indexes, including the S&P 500 (the one you're most likely to see flashed across your television screen at any hour of the day). Over $1 trillion in investors' assets are directly tied to S&P indexes — more than all other index providers combined.

More ETFs are based on S&P indexes than any other. Those include the Barclays broad-based international ETFs, the Select Sector SPDRs that track various market segments, and the iShares S&P Growth and Value series of ETFs.

For more information, visit `www.standardandpoors.com`.

Dow Jones

If there were an index for the price of peanuts in Portugal, Dow Jones would do it. The company, aside from publishing *The Wall Street Journal* and *Barron's,* develops, maintains, and licenses over 3,000 market indexes. Those indexes include the world's best known stock indicator, the Dow Jones Industrial Average, which, in my opinion, should have long ago gone the way of the Edsel. (I explain why in Chapter 5.)

The iShares industry and sector ETFs are based on Dow Jones indexes, as are the streetTRACKS large, mid, and small cap ETFs.

For more information, visit `www.djindexes.com`.

Morgan Stanley Capital International

With indexes of all kinds — stocks, bonds, hedge funds, U.S. and international securities — Morgan Stanley Capital International (MSCI), although not quite a household name, has been gaining ground as the indexer of choice for many ETF providers.

MSCI indexes are the backbone of both the domestic and international Vanguard ETFs, as well as the Barclays iShares individual country ETFs.

For more information, visit `www.msci.com`.

Russell

The largest 1,000 U.S. stocks are in the Russell 1000, although that index remains relatively obscure because the Dow Industrial and the S&P 500 hog the spotlight when it comes to measuring large cap performance. The next 2,000 largest stocks on the U.S. market are in the Russell 2000. And the Russell 1000 plus the Russell 2000 make up the Russell 3000. Those are Russell's more popular indexes, but there are plenty of others as well.

A dozen of the iShares domestic ETFs are based on Russell indexes. So, too, is the Rydex Russell Top 50 Index.

For more information, visit www.russell.com.

Lehman Brothers

Yeah, I know it sounds like a clothing shop in Brooklyn, but Lehman Brothers is actually the world's leading provider of fixed income benchmarks.

Barclays iShares uses Lehman Brothers indexes for five of its six fixed-income ETFs.

For more information, visit www.lehman.com.

Meeting the Middlemen

In the beginning, most ETFs were traded on the American Stock Exchange. In July 2005, however, Barclays decided to move its primary listings for 81 of its iShares to the New York Stock Exchange, citing superior technology. As a result, about half of all ETFs today are listed on each of the two major exchanges, with a small handful listed on the NASDAQ.

Does it matter to you on which exchange your ETF is listed? No, not really, except to the extent that the stock exchanges love ETFs, and if you are an ETF investor, they will love *you*. The reason is fairly obvious: The stock exchanges make their money whenever there's an exchange. Mutual funds, per se, don't exchange. ETFs do. And in order to promote ETFs, the stock exchanges have some fairly cool stuff on their Web sites that you should know about.

American Stock Exchange

The AMEX lists roughly 1,350 securities and has a daily trading volume of about 83 million shares. This is the exchange that pioneered the creation and sale of ETFs in the United States, and ETFs remain a big part of the exchange's business today. Even though in raw numbers the AMEX and the New York Stock Exchange list about equal numbers of ETFs (about 100), the AMEX is a much smaller exchange, and some of its ETFs — especially the SPDR 500 (SPY) — are much bigger. As a result, the future of the American Stock Exchange and the future of ETFs may be somewhat intertwined.

"Listed" versus "traded"

Note that there is a difference between an ETF being *listed* on, say, the American Stock Exchange, and an ETF being *traded* on the American Stock Exchange. In the very old days, the terms were more or less synonymous. Today, an ETF or stock that is listed on the American Stock Exchange can — and usually does — trade on any number of exchanges simultaneously. In fact, the Securities Exchange Act of 1934 permits securities listed on any national securities exchange to be traded by all the other such exchanges.

ETFs currently listed on the AMEX include the iShares Russell and S&P Global ETFs, as well as all the iShares fixed income ETFs. Nearly all offerings by Vanguard, Rydex, and PowerShares are also listed on the AMEX, as well as Merrill Lynch's HOLDRS.

The Web site is www.amex.com. If you click on the ETF icon and then on Research and Tools, it takes you to an ETF screener and several other potentially helpful tools.

New York Stock Exchange

Tracing its origins to 1792, the New York Stock Exchange today lists nearly 2,700 securities and trades about 1.5 billion shares a day. Many of the member companies are among the largest in the United States. All together, New York Stock Exchange companies represent over three-quarters of the total market capitalization in the nation.

ETFs listed on the New York Stock Exchange include all the Barclays iShares sector funds and many of the broad domestic and individual country funds. You'll also find the streetTRACKS Gold Trust fund and the Rydex Euro Currency Shares fund.

The Web site for the New York Stock Exchange is www.nyse.com. Unlike the Web sites for the American Stock Exchange and the NASDAQ, there isn't a whole lot on it specifically about ETFs, but you will get the general scoop on what's happening in the financial world.

NASDAQ

No bricks and mortar here. The NASDAQ, which lists over 3,200 securities and trades about 2 billion shares a day, is a uniquely electronic exchange. ETFs listed on the NASDAQ include the four international ETFs known as BLDRS and two ETFs that track the stocks of the NASDAQ itself, the Fidelity NASDAQ Composite Index (ONEQ) and the NASDAQ-100 Trust Series 1 (QQQQ). The QQQQ, on a typical day, is the greatest volume ETF and often the greatest volume security traded in the world.

The acronym NASDAQ, by the way, stands for National Association of Securities Dealers Automatic Quotation. Go to www.nasdaq.com, click on ETFs, and you'll find a number of very useful tools, including the ETF screener and (awesome, indeed) the ETF "Heat Map," which allows you to see how 100 of the largest ETFs are faring on a particular day. I wouldn't say that feature has great practical value, but for an investment-world junkie like me, it offers a good rush.

Meeting the Wannabe Middlemen

On January 24, 1848, James Marshall found gold at Sutter's Mill, touching off the California gold rush. About 150 years later, ETFs were the hottest investment product in the land, and so began the ETF rush. Everyone wants in on the game. So we have our ETF providers, and the brokerage houses where ETFs are bought and sold, and the exchanges where they are listed, and the indexes upon which they are based. What else is there? Ah, we have our wannabe middlemen: In the whole scope of things, they are as necessary as forks in a soup kitchen, but rest assured that they will continue to try to muscle in on the money.

Commissioned brokers

Most often, they call themselves "financial planners," and some may actually do financial planning. Many, however, are merely salesmen in poor disguise, selling inferior investment products and living off the "load." The *load* — or entrance free — to buying certain investment products, such as some mutual funds, most annuities, and life insurance products, can be ridiculously high. Thank goodness they don't exist in the world of ETFs — yet.

When first introduced, the PowerShares lineup of ETFs were originally designed to be sold through commissioned brokers at 2 percent a pop. The Securities and Exchange Commission killed the idea. But give it time: The commissioned brokers will be back, lobbying in force.

Separately managed accounts

Otherwise known as SMAs, separately managed accounts have traditionally been aimed at the well-to-do. Instead of buying into mutual funds, the wealthy hire a private manager with Persian rugs in his lobby to do essentially what a mutual fund manager does: pick stocks. But now many SMAs are billing themselves as "ETF SMAs." Instead of picking stocks, they pick ETFs — at a price.

I don't suspect that ETF SMAs that promise to beat the market through exceptional ETF choices or market timing are going to do any better than stock SMAs. That is to say that you should not hold your breath waiting for these guys to usher you into billionairehood. Some SMA managers may be very good at what they do. But much of what they do can be learned in this book. If you want to hire someone to manage your ETFs, that's fine, but if they start talking about skimming 2 percent a year off your assets to buy more Persian rugs, heck, you'll do better on your own. Trust me.

Annuities and life insurance products

I've seen advertisements lately from a variable annuity company that features ETFs in its portfolio. Great! That's better than high-priced mutual funds. But still, most variable annuities are way overpriced, carry nasty penalties for early withdrawal, and prove to be lousy investments. Same for many life insurance products other than simple term life. Investments in ETFs can make these products better, but that's a relative thing. As a very good rule, it is best to keep your investment products apart from your insurance products. And never buy an annuity unless you are absolutely sure you know what you are buying.

Mutual funds of ETFs

The term is "closet index funds," and there's an increasing number of them out there, just eager to take your money and invest it in "hand-picked" portfolios of stocks that strangely resemble the entire stock market. In the old days, closet index-fund managers would actually have to wake up on Monday morning to make sure their high-priced portfolios were in line with the indexes. Today, they can sleep late because they've socked an indexed ETF or two into their portfolios. You, the investor, get to invest in the ETF or two, and the alleged manager of the mutual fund gets to milk you for all you're worth.

Any mutual fund that features ETFs among its top holdings isn't worth holding. Any mutual fund — such as the Seligman TargETFund (cute, eh?) Core A (SHVAX) — that charges a 4.75 percent load along with a gross expense ratio of 1.93 percent to hold a bunch of ETFs for you is worthy of . . . well, I'll control myself. But please don't be a dummy.

Part II

Building the Stock (Equity) Side of Your Portfolio

The 5th Wave   By Rich Tennant

"Choosing the right ETF is like choosing the right hat. You find one that fits you best and then you stick with it."

In this part . . .

The S&P 500 (an index of large stocks) has enjoyed a 10 percent annualized return over the past 75 years — a substantially greater return rate than bonds, CDs, gold, silver, or even real estate. Small stocks have done even better. Although history doesn't always repeat, it does often echo. And for that reason, most investment advisors, including me, would recommend that a good parcel of your long-term investments be put into stocks.

As fate would have it, about 95 percent of ETFs represent stock holdings. So it's appropriate that I now ask you to turn your attention to how to use ETFs to invest in the stock market. In the first chapter of this section, I look at some basic concepts of equity investing, most notably diversification and risk control. In the seven chapters that follow, I guide you through a step-by-step exploration of the world of stock ETFs. We examine which ETFs may belong in your portfolio and how to best mix and match them.

Chapter 4

Risk Control, Diversification, and Some Other Things You Need to Know

In This Chapter

▶ Understanding the relationship between risk and return

▶ Measuring risk

▶ Introducing Modern Portfolio Theory

▶ Seeking a balanced portfolio

October. This is one of the peculiarly dangerous months to speculate in stocks. The others are July, January, September, April, November, May, March, June, December, August, and February.

Mark Twain

A peculiarly good writer, but also a peculiarly bad money manager, Twain sent his entire fortune down river on a few bad investments. A century and a half later, investing, especially in stocks, can still be a peculiarly dangerous game. But today we have low-cost indexed ETFs and a lot more knowledge about the power of diversification. Together, these two things can help lessen the dangers and heighten the rewards of the stock market. In this chapter, I hope to make you a better stock investor — at least better than Mark Twain.

Risk Is Not Just a Board Game

Well, okay, actually Risk *is* a board game, but I'm not talking here about *that* Risk. Rather, I'm talking about investment risk. And in the world of investments, risk means but one thing: volatility. Volatility is what takes people's nest eggs, scrambles them, and serves them with humble pie. Volatility is what causes investors insomnia and heartburn. Volatility is the potential for financially crippling losses.

Ask people (such as a good number of my present-day clients) who had most of their money invested in tech stocks during the 1990s. For years prior, during the heady years of the stock market's longest bull run, they saw their holdings grow and grow and grow. Pennies turned into dimes and then dollars. Retirement was but a stone's throw away. But then in April 2000 (yes, April is one of those dangerous months), the bottom started to fall out of tech stocks, and for three years the market continued its sad descent. Those investors in formerly high-flying dot-coms saw their portfolios drop faster than a barrel over Niagara Falls. Many lost 80 percent of everything they had — money they won't see again for a very long time.

So is risk to be avoided at all costs? Well, no. Not at all. Risk is to be mitigated, for sure, but risk within reason can actually be *a good thing.* That is because risk and return, much like Romeo and Juliet or Corona and lime, go hand in hand. Volatility means that an investment can go way down or way up . . . hopefully way up. Without some volatility, you resign yourself to a portfolio that isn't poised for any great growth.

In fact, if you are ever offered the opportunity to partake in any investment scheme that promises you oodles and oodles of money with "absolutely no risk," run! You are in the presence of a con artist. Such investments do not exist.

The trade-off of all trade-offs (safety versus return)

To get to the Holy Grail — to get a big, fat payoff from our investments — you and I need to take on the Black Knight and the fire-breathing dragon. There simply is no way that either of us is going to make money off our investments without a willingness to deal with some volatility. The Holy Grail is not handed out to people who stuff money in their mattresses or carry their pennies to the local savings bank.

If you look at different investments over the course of time, you find an uncanny correlation between risk and return. Safe investments — those that really do carry genuine guarantees, such as U.S. Treasury Bills, FDIC-insured savings accounts, and CDs — tend to offer very modest returns (often negative returns after accounting for inflation). Volatile investments — stocks, "junk" bonds, and hedge funds, the kinds of investments that cause people to lose sleep — tend to offer handsome returns if you give them enough time.

Time, then, is an essential ingredient in determining appropriate levels of risk. If you are going to need cash within the next six months to a year, you would be wise to keep that portion of your money you anticipate needing soon either in a savings bank or possibly in an ETF such as the iShares Lehman 1–3 Year Treasury (SHY), a short-term bond fund that yields a modest return but is very unlikely to lose value. You should *not* invest that portion of your money in any ETF that is made up of company stocks, such as the popular SPY or QQQQ. True, SPY or QQQQ can (and should), over time, yield much more than SHY, but they are also much more volatile. Unless you are not going to need your cash for at least a couple of years (and preferably not for five or more years), you are best off avoiding any investment in the stock market, whether it be through ETFs or otherwise.

So just how risky are ETFs?

Asking how risky, or how lucrative, ETFs are is like trying to judge a soup knowing nothing about the soup itself, only that it is served in a blue china bowl. The bowl — or the ETF — doesn't create the risk; what's inside it does. Thus stock and real estate ETFs tend to be more volatile than bond ETFs. Short-term bond ETFs are less volatile than long-term bond ETFs (I explain why in Part III). Small-stock ETFs are more volatile than large-stock ETFs. And international ETFs often see more volatility than U.S. ETFs.

Figure 4-1 shows some examples of various ETFs and where they fit on the risk–return continuum. Note that it starts with bond ETFs at the bottom (maximum safety, minimum volatility) and nearer the top features the EAFE (Europe, Australia, Far East) Index and the South Korea Index Fund. (An investment in South Korean stocks involves not only all the normal risks of business but also includes currency risk, as well as the risk that some deranged North Korean dictator may decide he wants to pick a fight. Buyer beware.)

Keep in mind when looking at Figure 4-1 that I am segregating these ETFs — treating them as stand-alone assets — for the point of illustration. As I discuss later in this chapter (when I discuss something called Modern Portfolio Theory), stand-alone risk measurements are of limited value. The true risk of adding any particular ETF to your portfolio depends on what is already in the portfolio. (That statement will make sense by the end of this chapter. I promise!)

High Risk (and highest return potential)

100 90 iShares MSCI South Korea Index Fund (EWY)

80 70 iShares MSCI EAFE Index (EFA)

60 50 Vanguard Mid Cap ETF (VO)

40 SPDR 500 (SPY)

30 iShares Lehman 7-10 Year Treasury Bond Fund (IEF)

20 iShares Lehman 1-3 Year Treasury Bond Fund (SHY)

10

Low Risk (with more modest return potential)

Figure 4-1:
The risk
levels of
a sampling
of ETFs.

Smart Risk, Foolish Risk

There is safety in numbers, which is why teenage boys and girls huddle together in corners at school dances. In the case of the teenagers, the safety is afforded by anonymity and distance. In the case of indexed ETFs and mutual funds, safety is provided by (limited) diversification in that they represent ownership in many different securities. Owning many stocks, rather than a few, provides some safety by eliminating something that investment professionals, when they're trying to impress, call *non-systemic risk.*

Non-systemic risk is the kind of risk involved when you invest in any individual security, such as shares of Martha Stewart Omnimedia, ImClone, (remember Martha and ImClone?), Enron, or General Motors. It's the risk that the CEO of the company will be strangled by his pet python, that the national headquarters will be destroyed by a falling asteroid, or that the company's stock will take a sudden nosedive simply because of some Internet rumor started by an 11th-grader in the suburbs of Des Moines. Those kinds of risks (and more serious ones) can be effectually eliminated by investing not in individual securities but in ETFs or mutual funds.

Non-systemic risk contrasts with *systemic risk,* which, unfortunately, ETFs and mutual funds cannot eliminate. Systemic risks simply can't be avoided, not even by keeping your portfolio in cash. Examples of systemic risk include the following:

✔ **Market risk.** The market goes up, the market goes down, and whatever stocks or stock ETFs you own will generally (though not always) move in the same direction.

✔ **Interest rate risk.** If interest rates go up, the value of your bonds or bond ETFs (especially long-term bond ETFs such as TLT, the iShares 20-year Treasury ETF) will fall.

✔ **Inflation risk.** When inflation picks up, any money you have in fixed income investments (such as any of the bond ETFs) will suffer. Anything you have in cash will start to dwindle in value.

✔ **Political risk.** If you invest your money in the United States, England, France, or Japan, there's little chance that guerillas will overtake the government anytime soon. When you invest in the stocks or bonds or stock or bond ETFs of certain other countries (or when you hold currency from those countries), you'd better keep a sharp eye on the nightly news.

Although ETFs cannot eliminate systemic risks, you shouldn't despair. For while non-systemic risks are a bad thing, systemic risks are decidedly a mixed bag. Non-systemic risks, you see, offer no compensation. A company is not bound to pay higher dividends, nor is its stock price bound to rise simply because the CEO has taken up mountain climbing or hang gliding.

Systemic risks, on the other hand, do offer compensation. Invest in small stocks (which are more volatile and therefore incorporate more market risk), and you can expect (over the very long term) higher returns. Invest in a country with political instability, and (especially if that instability doesn't occur) you'll probably be rewarded with high returns in compensation for taking added risk.

In other words,

Higher systemic risk = higher historical return

Higher non-systemic risk = zilch

That's the way markets tend to work. Segments of the market with higher risks *must* offer higher returns or else they wouldn't be able to attract capital. If the potential returns on emerging market stocks (or ETFs) were no higher than the potential returns on short-term bond ETFs or FDIC-insured savings accounts, would anyone but a complete nutcase invest in emerging market stocks?

How Risk Is Measured

In the world of investments, risk means volatility, and volatility (unlike angels or love) can be seen, measured, and plotted. People in the investment world use different tools to measure volatility, such as standard deviation, beta, and certain ratios such as the Sharpe ratio. Most of these tools are not very hard to get a handle on, and they can help you better follow discussions on portfolio building that come later in this book. Ready to dig in?

Standard deviation: The king of all risk measurement tools

So, you want to know how much an investment is likely to bounce? The first thing you do is look to see how much it has bounced in the past. Standard deviation measures the degree of past bounce and, from that measurement, gives us some notion of future bounce. To put it another way, standard deviation shows the degree to which a stock/bond/mutual fund/ETF's actual returns vary from the average return over a certain time period.

In Table 4-1, consider two hypothetical ETFs and their returns over the last six years. Note that both portfolios start with $1,000 and end with $1,101. But note, too, the great difference in how much they bounce. ETF A's yearly returns range from –3 percent to 5 percent while ETF B's range from –15 percent to 15 percent. The standard deviation of the six years for ETF A is 3.09. For ETF B, the standard deviation is 10.38.

Table 4-1	Standard Deviation of Two Hypothetical ETFs	
Balance, beginning of year	*Return (% increase or decrease)*	*Balance, end of year*
ETF A		
1,000	5	1,050
1,050	–2	1,029
1,029	4	1,070
1,070	–3	1,038
1,038	2	1,059
1,059	4	1,101

Balance, beginning of year	Return (% increase or decrease)	Balance, end of year
ETF B		
1,000	10	1,100
1,100	6	1,166
1,166	−15	991
991	−8	912
912	15	1,048
1,048	5	1,101

Predicting a range of returns

What does the standard deviation number tell us? Let's take ETF A as an example. The standard deviation of 3.09 tells us that in about 68 percent of the months to come, we should expect the return of ETF A to fall within 3.09 percentage points of the mean return, which was 1.66. In other words, in about 68 percent of the months to come, we should expect a return that falls somewhere between (1.66 + 3.09) 4.75 percent and (1.66 − 3.09) −1.43 percent.

It also tells us that in about 95 percent of the months to come, the returns should fall within two standard deviations of the mean. In other words, in 95 percent of the months to come, you should see a return of between [1.66 + (3.09 × 2)] 7.84 percent and [1.66 − (3.09 × 2)] −4.52. The other 5 percent of the time is anybody's guess.

Making side-by-side comparisons

The ultimate purpose of standard deviation, the reason I'm describing it, is that it gives you a way to judge the relative risk of two ETFs. If one ETF has a 3-year standard deviation of 12, we know that it is roughly twice as volatile as another ETF with a standard deviation of 6 and half as risky as an ETF with a standard deviation of 24. A real world example: The standard deviation for most short-term bond funds falls somewhere around 0.7. The standard deviation for most precious metal funds falls somewhere around 26.0.

Important caveat: Don't assume that combining one ETF with a standard deviation of 10 with another that has a standard deviation of 20 will give you a portfolio with an average standard deviation of 15. It doesn't work that way at all, as you will see in a few pages when I introduce Modern Portfolio Theory. The combined standard deviation will not be any greater than 15, but it could (if you do your homework and put together two of the right ETFs) be much less.

Beta: Assessing price swings in relation to the market

Unlike standard deviation, which gives you a stand-alone picture of volatility, beta is a relative measure. It is used to measure the volatility of something in relation to something else. Most commonly that "something else" is the S&P 500. Very simply, beta tells us that if the S&P rises by x percent, then our investment, whatever that investment is, will likely rise by y percent. If the S&P were to fall by x percent, beta tells us that our investment is likely to fall by y percent.

The S&P is considered our baseline, and it is assigned a beta of 1. So if we know that Humongous Software Corporation has a beta of 2, and the S&P shoots up 10 percent, Jimmy the Greek would bet that shares of Humongous are going to rise 20 percent. If we know that the Sedate Utility Company has a beta of 0.5, and the S&P shoots up 10 percent, Jimmy would bet that shares of Sedate are going to rise by 5 percent. Conversely, shares of Humongous would likely fall four times harder than shares of Sedate in response to a fall in the S&P.

In a way, beta is easier to understand than standard deviation; it's also easier to misinterpret. Beta's usefulness is greater for individual stocks than it is for ETFs, but nonetheless it can be helpful, especially when gauging the volatility of U.S. industry sector ETFs. It is much less useful for any ETF that has international holdings. For example, an ETF that holds stocks of emerging market nations is going to be volatile, trust me, yet it may have a low beta. How so? Because its movements, no matter how swooping, don't generally happen in response to movement in the U.S. market. (Emerging market stocks tend to be more tied to currency flux, commodity prices, interest rates, and political climate.)

The Sharpe and Treynor ratios: Measures of what you get for your risk

Back in 1966, a goateed Stanford professor named Bill Sharpe developed a formula that has since become as common in investmentspeak as RBIs are in baseballspeak. The formula looks like this:

(Total portfolio return – Risk-free rate of return) / Portfolio standard deviation = Sharpe measure (or Sharpe ratio)

Real-life examples of standard deviation and beta

Following are the (three-year) standard deviations and the betas of several diverse ETFs. Note that iShares MSCI Hong Kong (EWH) is more volatile than iShares MSCI U.K. Index (EWU) as measured by its standard deviation, but EWH has a lower beta. That tells us that the volatility of the Hong Kong market, however great it is, seems to be less tied to the fortunes of the S&P 500 than is the volatility of the U.K. market.

ETF	Ticker	Standard deviation	Beta
SPDR 500	SPY	8.0	1.0
Consumer Staples Select Sector SPDR	XLP	7.66	0.58
Health Care Select Sector SPDR	XLV	9.34	0.54
iShares MSCI U.K. Index	EWU	10.87	0.87
NASDAQ-100 Trust Series 1	QQQQ	15.11	1.43
iShares MSCI Hong Kong	EWH	15.68	0.65

The risk-free rate of return generally refers to the return you could get on a short-term U.S. Treasury bill. If we subtract that from the total portfolio return, it tells us how much our portfolio earned above the rate we could have achieved without risking our principal. We take that number and divide it by the standard deviation (discussed earlier in this section). And what *that* result gives us is the Sharpe measure, which essentially gives an indication of how much money has been made in relation to how much risk was taken to make that money.

Suppose Portfolio A, under manager Bubba Bucks, returned 7 percent last year, and during that year Treasury bills were paying 5 percent. Portfolio A also had a standard deviation of 8 percent. Okay, applying the formula,

$$\frac{7\% - 5\%}{8\%} = \frac{2\%}{8\%} = 0.25$$

That result wasn't good enough for Bubba's manager, so he fired Bubba and hired Donny Dollar. Donny, who just read *Exchange-Traded Funds For Dummies,* takes the portfolio and dumps all its high-cost active mutual funds. In their place, he buys ETFs. In his first year managing the portfolio, Donny achieves a total return of 10 percent with a standard deviation of 7.5. But the interest rate on Treasury bills has gone up to 7 percent. Applying the formula,

$$\frac{10\% - 7\%}{7.5\%} = \frac{3\%}{7.5\%} = 0.40$$

The higher the Sharpe measure, the better. Donny Dollar did his job much better than Bubba Bucks.

The Treynor approach was first used by — you guessed it — a guy named Jack Treynor in 1965. Instead of using standard deviation in the denominator, it uses beta. What the Treynor measure shows is the amount of money that a portfolio is making in relation to the risk it carries relative to the market. To put that another way, the Treynor measure uses only systemic risk, or beta, while the Sharpe ratio uses total risk.

Suppose that Donny Dollar's portfolio, with its 10 percent return, had a beta of 0.9. In that case, the Treynor measure would be

$$\frac{10\% - 7\%}{0.9} = \frac{3\%}{0.9} = \frac{.03}{0.9} = 0.033$$

Is 0.033 good? That depends. It's a relative number. Suppose that the market, as measured by the S&P 500, also returned 10 percent that same year. It may seem like Donny isn't a very good manager. But when we apply the Treynor measure (recalling that the beta for the market is always 1.0),

$$\frac{10\% - 7\%}{1.0} = \frac{3\%}{1.0} = \frac{.03}{1.0} = 0.03$$

We get a lower number. That result indicates that although Donny earned a similar return as the market, he did so by taking less risk. To put that another way, he got more return per unit of risk. Donny's boss will likely keep him.

A newfangled measure of risk

I'm sometimes astounded what some people give away for free on the Web. A group called RiskMetrics has a free Web site called www.riskgrades.com. Go there! You can plug in either a single ETF, mutual fund, stock, or bond, or a combination thereof, and RiskGrades will spit out a darned good assessment of just how much risk you are taking. Like moving from Fahrenheit to Celsius,

RiskGrades provides a scale that just looks so much cleaner than what you've ever seen before. The risk rating starts at 0 for an investment with no volatility (cash) and moves higher with added risk.

I plugged in several ETFs (and one individual stock, just for fun), and RiskGrades provided the following risk grades:

iShares Lehman 1–3 Year Treasury (SHY): 9

iShares Lehman 7–10 Year Treasury (IEF): 22

SPDR 500 (SPY): 48

iShares MSCI EAFE Index Fund (EFA): 62

NASDAQ-100 Trust Series 1 (QQQQ): 73

Google (Goog) 236

RiskGrades' rating are similar to standard deviation, but they are much more intuitive. An ETF with a standard deviation of 17.5 is obviously more volatile than an ETF with a standard deviation of 8.4, but how much more volatile, only a doctorate-level statistician can tell you. On the other hand, an ETF with a RiskGrade of 30 has twice the volatility of an ETF with a RiskGrade of 15.

RiskGrades even allows you to build an entire portfolio online, and it will show you how diversification helps to lower the volatility of the portfolio. (That's the subject we turn to in the next section.) Even though I found a few bugs in the system (which I hope will be corrected before this book is published), RiskGrades is a great tool, and I hope it remains free.

Meet Modern Portfolio Theory

For simplicity's sake, I've talked so far of choosing one ETF over another (SHY or SPY?) based on risk and potential return. In the real world, few people, if any, come to me or to any financial planner asking for a recommendation of one single ETF. More commonly, I'm asked to help build a portfolio of ETFs. And when looking at an entire portfolio, the riskiness of each individual ETF, although important, takes a back seat to the riskiness of the entire portfolio.

In other words, I would rarely recommend or rule out any specific ETF because it is too volatile. How well any specific ETF fits into a portfolio — and to what degree it affects the risk of a portfolio — depends on what else is in the portfolio. What I'm alluding to here is something called *Modern Portfolio*

Theory: the tool I use to help determine a proper ETF mix for my clients' portfolios. You and I will use this tool throughout this book to help you determine a proper mix for your portfolio.

Tasting the extreme positiveness of negative correlation

Modern Portfolio Theory is to investing what the discovery of gravity was to physics. Almost. What the theory says is that the volatility/risk of a portfolio may differ dramatically from the volatility/risk of the portfolio's components. In other words, you can have two assets with high standard deviations (and high potential returns), and combined they give you a portfolio with modest standard deviation but the same high potential return. Modern Portfolio Theory says that you can have a whole slew of risky investments, but if you throw them together into a big bowl, the entire soup may actually splash around very little.

The key to whipping up such pleasant combinations is to find two or more holdings that do not move in synch; one tends to go up while the other goes down (although both holdings, in the long run, will see an upward trajectory). In the figures that follow, I show how you'd create the fantasy ETF portfolio consisting of two high-risk/high-return ETFs with perfect negative correlation. It is a fantasy portfolio because perfect negative correlations don't exist; they simply serve as a target.

Figure 4-2 represents hypothetical ETF A and hypothetical ETF B, each of which has high return and high volatility. Notice that even though both are volatile assets, they move up and down at different times. This fact is crucial because combining them can give you a non-volatile portfolio.

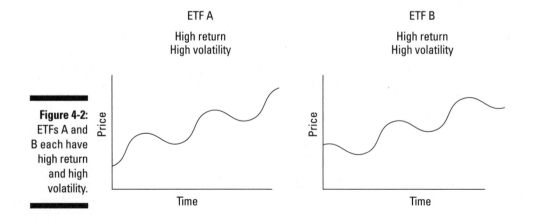

ETF A

High return
High volatility

ETF B

High return
High volatility

Figure 4-2:
ETFs A and
B each have
high return
and high
volatility.

Figure 4-3 shows what happens when you invest in both ETF A and ETF B. You end up with the perfect ETF portfolio — one made up of two ETFs with perfect negative correlation. (If only such a portfolio existed in the real world!)

The Perfect Portfolio

High return
Low volatility

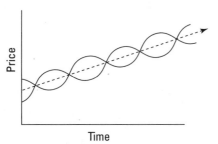

Figure 4-3: The perfect ETF portfolio, with high return and no volatility.

Reaching for the elusive Efficient Frontier

When the U.S. stock market takes a punch, which happens on average about one in every three years, most stocks fall. When the market flies, most stocks fly. Not many investments regularly move in opposite directions. We do, however, find investments that tend to move independently of each other much of the time, or at least they don't move in the same direction all the time. In investmentspeak, I'm talking about investments that have *low correlation*. The best example is stocks and bonds.

Say, for example, you had a basket of large U.S. stocks in 1929, at the onset of the Great Depression. You would have seen your portfolio lose nearly a quarter of its value every year for the next four years. Needless to say, you would not have been a very happy camper. If, however, you were holding high-quality, long-term bonds during that same period, at least that side of your portfolio would have grown by a respectable 5 percent a year. A portfolio of long-term bonds held throughout the growling bear market in stocks of 2000 through 2003 would have returned a hale and hearty 13 percent a year. (That's an unusually high return for bonds, but all the stars were seemingly in perfect alignment.)

Correlation is a measurable thing, represented in the world of investments by something called the *correlation coefficient*. This number indicates the degree to which two investments move in the same direction or move apart. A correlation coefficient can range from –1 to 1.

A correlation of 1 indicates that the two securities are like the Rockettes: When one kicks a leg, so does the other. Having both in your portfolio offers no diversification benefit. On the other hand, if investment A and investment B have a correlation coefficient of –1, that means they have a perfect negative relationship: They always move in the opposite directions. Having both in your portfolio is a wonderful diversifier. Such polar-opposite investments are, alas, very hard to find.

A correlation coefficient of zero means that the two investments have no relationship to each other. When one moves, the other may move in the same direction, the opposite direction, or not at all.

As a whole, stocks and bonds (not junk bonds, but high-quality bonds) tend to have little to negative correlation. Finding the perfect mix of stocks and bonds, as well as other investments with low correlation, is known among financial people as looking for the *Efficient Frontier*. The Frontier represents the mix of investments that offer the greatest promise of return for the least amount of risk.

The correlation of various ETFs

The following correlations of several of Barclays iShares show to what degree different ETFs moved in the same direction over a recent three-year period. The lower the correlation, the better from a portfolio-building point of view.

Low correlations reduce portfolio risk. High correlations do not. Negative correlations are, alas, not that easy to find in the real world, and portfolio managers are forever looking.

ETF	ETF	Correlation Coefficient	Rating
iShares S&P Small Cap 600 Growth (small growth)	iShares S&P 500 Value (large value)	0.73	Medium to high correlation
iShares S&P 500 Growth (large growth)	iShares Lehman 7–10 Treasury (bonds)	–0.17	Negative correlation
iShares MSCI Japan Index (Japanese stocks)	iShares S&P Small Cap 600 Value (small value)	0.25	Very modest correlation
iShares S&P Small Cap 600 Growth (small growth)	iShares S&P Small Cap 600 Value (small value)	0.95	High correlation

Fortunately, ETFs allow us to easily tinker with our investments so we can find just that sweet spot.

Mixing and Matching Your Stock ETFs

Reaching for the elusive Efficient Frontier means having both stocks and bonds and having both domestic and international holdings in your portfolio. That part is fairly simple and not likely to stir much controversy. (Although, for sure, experts differ on what they consider optimal percentages.) But experts definitely don't agree on how to best diversify the domestic stock part of a portfolio. Two competing methods predominate:

- ✔ One method calls for the division of a stock portfolio into domestic and foreign, and then into different styles: large cap, small cap, mid cap, value, and growth.
- ✔ The other method calls for dividing the portfolio up by industry sector: healthcare, utilities, energy, financials, and so on.

My personal preference for the small to mid-sized investor, especially the ETF investor, is to go with the styles. But there's nothing wrong with dividing up a portfolio by industry sector. And for those of you with good-sized portfolios, a mixture of both, without going crazy, may be optimal.

Filling in your style box

Most savvy investors make certain to have some equity in each of the nine boxes of the grid in Figure 4-4, which is known as the *style box* or *grid* (sometimes called the *Morningstar grid*).

The reason for the style box is simple enough: History shows that companies of differing cap (capitalization) size (in other words, large companies and small companies) and value and growth companies tend to rise and fall in different economic conditions. I define *cap size, value,* and *growth* in Chapter 5, and I devote the next several chapters to showing the differences between styles, how to choose ETFs to match each one, and how to weight those ETFs for the highest potential return with the lowest possible risk.

Investing with style

The following chart shows how well various investment styles have fared in the past several years. Note that a number of ETFs are available to match each style.

	2000	2001	2002	2003	2004	2005
Small cap value	22.8%	14.0%	−11.4%	46.0%	22.2%	4.7%
Small cap growth	−22.5%	−9.2%	−30.3%	48.5%	14.3%	4.2%
Large cap value	6.1%	−11.7%	−20.8%	31.8%	15.7%	5.8%
Large cap growth	−22.1%	−12.7%	−23.6%	25.7%	6.13%	4.0%

Large cap value	Large cap blend	Large cap growth
Mid cap value	Mid cap blend	Mid cap growth
Small cap value	Small cap blend	Small cap growth

Figure 4-4: The style box or grid.

Buying by industry sector

A good number of investors of late, especially since the advent of ETFs, have started using sector investing as an alternative to the grid. Examining the two models toe-to-toe yields some interesting comparisons and much food for thought.

Investing by industry sector

This chart shows how well various industry sectors have fared in the past several years. Yes, there are ETFs that track each of these industry sectors — and many more.

	2000	2001	2002	2003	2004	2005
Energy	15.7%	−10.4%	−11.2%	25.6%	31.5%	31.4%
Healthcare	37.0%	−12.0%	−18.8%	15.1%	1.7%	6.5%
Materials	−15.7%	3.5%	−5.5%	38.2%	13.3%	4.4%
Information Technology	−40.9%	−25.9%	−37.4%	47.2%	2.6%	1.0%

One study on industry-sector investing, done by Chicago-based Ibbotson Associates in 2003, came to the very favorable conclusion that sector investing is potentially a superior diversifier than grid investing because times have changed since the 1960s when style investing first became popular. "Globalization has led to a rise in correlation between domestic and international stocks; large, mid and small cap stocks have high correlation to each other. A company's performance is tied more to its industry than to the country where it's based, or the size of its market cap," concluded Ibbotson.

The jury is still out, but I give an overview of the controversy in Chapter 9. For now, I invite you to do a little comparison of your own by comparing the charts in the sidebars "Investing with style" and "Investing by industry sector." Note that using either method of diversification, some of your investments should smell like roses in years when others stink.

Don't slice and dice your portfolio to death

One reason I tend to prefer the traditional style grid to industry sector investing, at least for the non-wealthy investor, is that there are simply fewer styles to contend with. You can build yourself, at least on the domestic side of your stock holdings, a pretty well diversified portfolio with but four ETFs: one small value, one small growth, one large value, and one large growth. With industry-sector investing, you would need a dozen or so ETFs to have a well-balanced portfolio. And that may be too many.

You don't want to chop up your portfolio into too many holdings, or the transaction costs (especially with ETFs that require trading costs) can start to bite into your returns.

What creates returns, and what kind of returns will the future bring?

In the world of stock markets, with their by-and-large juicy long-term returns, the juice comes from three sources:

- ✔ Dividends
- ✔ Earnings growth
- ✔ Price/earning multiples (the measure of market expectations), otherwise known as P/E

Dividends, it may surprise you to learn, account for the lion's share of stock market returns over the past two centuries. The stock market has given us roughly a 7 percent post-inflation rise during that period. Perhaps three-quarters of that 7 percent is attributable to dividends. That's history, of course. Today's dividend yield on the S&P 500, although it has grown in the past two years, is not much more than 1.5 percent and is very unlikely to exceed 5 percent ever again. Instead of paying dividends, companies today tend to funnel their profits into internal growth, repurchasing shares of their own stock and dishing out astronomical compensation for top executives.

In the future, we may be looking at a 2 percent dividend yield, tops, plus whatever good fortune brings us in the way of earnings growth. The price/earnings multiple — the factor by which investors are willing to invest in stocks in hopes of future earnings — soared wildly in the bull market of the 1990s but has since shrunk to pretty close to its historical norm (about 18). It may grow again, or it may shrink. Who knows? And whether earnings growth can take up where dividend yield left off and provide investors with 7 percent return after inflation — that is a big unknown.

When I look into my crystal ball (I really try not to do that very often), I can't see what returns will be, but I do know for sure that the stock market will continue to be volatile, perhaps even more so than it has been in the past. Many investors may be throwing up on the side of the ship long before they get to any port where they'll find the Holy Grail. Fortunately, with a well-balanced portfolio of ETFs, you may be chucking up fewer cookies than most passengers.

But don't assume you can avoid all risk, don't assume that the future will mirror the past, and don't put everything you have into stocks.

As a rule, if you have $10,000 to invest and you want ETFs, consider four or five that can give you some diversification. (Perhaps start with the four above and add in an international ETF. See my sample ETF portfolios for all sizes of nest eggs in Part IV.) If you have $50,000, consider something in the ballpark of a 10 to 15 ETF portfolio, and if you have $250,000 or more, perhaps look at a 20 to 30 ETF portfolio. If you invest in many more ETFs than this, the marginal benefits of added diversification will likely be outweighed by the additional trading costs every time you attempt to rebalance your holdings.

Chapter 5

Large Growth: Muscular Money Makers

*P*ick up a typical business magazine and look at the face adorning the cover. He's Mr. CEO. Tough and ambitious and looking for acquisitions under every rock, his pedigree is Harvard, his wife is the former Miss Missouri, his salary (not to mention other perks) exceeds the gross national product of Peru, and his house has 14 bathrooms. (Yeah, I know this seems like a stereotype, but U.S. CEOs do tend to be a rather homogenous lot.) The title of the cover story emblazoned across Mr. CEO's chest suggests that buying stock in his company will make you rich. Without knowing anything more, you can assume that Mr. CEO heads a large growth company.

In other words, Mr. CEO's company has *total market capitalization* (the value of all its outstanding stock) of at least $5 billion, earnings have been growing and growing fast, the company has a secure niche within its industry, and many people envision the Borg-like corporation eventually taking over the universe. Think Microsoft, Google, Yahoo, PepsiCo, Dell, Oracle, eBay, and Cisco Systems.

In this chapter, I explain what role such behemoths should play in your portfolio. But before getting into the meat of the matter, take a quick glance at Figures 5-1 and 5-2. Figure 5-1 shows where large growth stocks fit into a well-diversified stock portfolio. (I introduce this style box or grid, which divides a stock portfolio into large cap and small cap, value and growth, in Chapter 4.) Figure 5-2 shows their historical return.

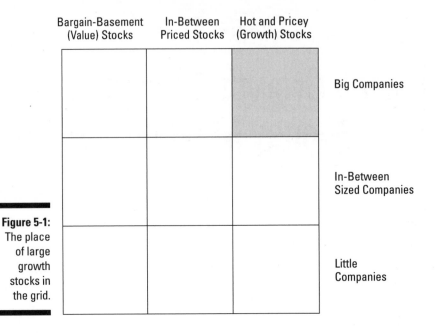

Bargain-Basement (Value) Stocks	In-Between Priced Stocks	Hot and Pricey (Growth) Stocks	
			Big Companies
			In-Between Sized Companies
			Little Companies

Figure 5-1:
The place of large growth stocks in the grid.

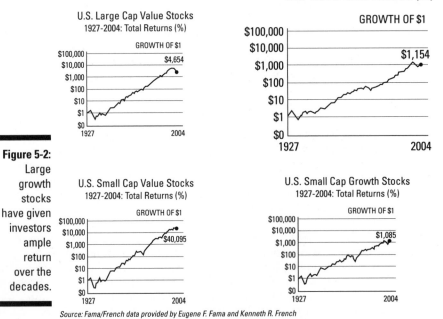

U.S. Large Cap Value Stocks
1927-2004: Total Returns (%)

GROWTH OF $1

$100,000
$10,000 — $4,654
$1,000
$100
$10
$1
$0
1927   2004

U.S. Large Cap Growth Stocks
1927-2004: Total Returns (%)

GROWTH OF $1

$100,000
$10,000
$1,000 — $1,154
$100
$10
$1
$0
1927   2004

U.S. Small Cap Value Stocks
1927-2004: Total Returns (%)

GROWTH OF $1

$100,000
$10,000
$1,000 — $40,095
$100
$10
$1
$0
1927   2004

U.S. Small Cap Growth Stocks
1927-2004: Total Returns (%)

GROWTH OF $1

$100,000
$10,000
$1,000 — $1,085
$100
$10
$1
$0
1927   2004

Figure 5-2:
Large growth stocks have given investors ample return over the decades.

Source: Fama/French data provided by Eugene F. Fama and Kenneth R. French

Style Review

In Chapter 4, I note that one approach to building a portfolio involves investing in different styles of stocks: large cap, mid cap, small cap, value, and growth. How did the whole business of style investing get started? Hard to say. Benjamin Graham, the "Dean of Wall Street," the "Father of Value Investing," who wrote several oft-quoted books in the 1930s and 1940s, didn't give us the popular style grid that you see in Figure 5-1. But Graham certainly helped provide the tools of fundamental analysis whereby more contemporary brains could help figure things out.

In the early 1980s, studies out of the University of Chicago began to quantify the concrete differences between large caps and small caps, and in 1992, two economists named Eugene Fama and Kenneth French delivered the seminal paper on the differences between value and growth stocks.

What makes large cap large?

Capitalization or *cap* refers to the combined value of all shares of a company's stock. The division lines between large cap, mid cap, and small cap are sometimes as blurry as the division lines between, say, *Rubenesque* and *fat*. The distinction is largely in the eye of the beholder. If you took a poll, however, I think you would find that the following divisions are generally accepted:

- ✔ **Large caps:** Companies with over $5 billion in capitalization

- ✔ **Mid caps:** Companies with $1 billion to $5 billion in capitalization

- ✔ **Small caps:** Companies with $250 million to $1 billion in capitalization

Anything from $50 million to $250 million would usually be deemed a *micro cap*. And your local pizza shop, if it were to go public, might be called a *nano cap (con aglio)*. There are no nano cap ETFs. For all the other categories, there are ETFs to your heart's content.

How does growth differ from value?

Many different criteria are used to determine whether a stock or basket of stocks (such as an ETF) qualifies as *growth* or *value*. (In Chapter 6, I list "Six Ways to Recognize Value.") But perhaps the most important measure is the ratio of price to earnings: the *P/E ratio,* sometimes referred to as the *multiple.*

The P/E ratio divides the price of the stock by the earnings per share. For example, suppose the McDummy Corporation stock is currently selling for $40 a share. And suppose that the company earned $2 last year for every share of stock outstanding. McDummy's P/E ratio would be 20. (The S&P 500 currently has a P/E of about 16.)

The higher the P/E, the more investors are willing to pay for the company earnings. Or to put it in terms of growth and value,

- ✔ The higher the P/E, the more *growthy* the company: Either the company is growing fast, or investors have high hopes (realistic or foolish) that it will.

- ✔ The lower the P/E, the more *valuey* the company. The business world doesn't see this company as a mover and shaker.

Each ETF carries a P/E reflecting the collective P/E of its holdings and giving you an indication of just how growthy or valuey that ETF is. A growth ETF is filled with companies that look like they are taking over the planet. A value ETF is filled with companies that seem to be meandering along but whose stock may be purchased for a bargain price.

Putting these terms to use

Today, all competent investment pros develop their portfolios with at least some consideration given to the cap size and growth or value orientation of their stock holdings. Why? Because study after study shows that, in fact, a portfolio's performance is inexorably linked to where that portfolio falls in the style grid. A mutual fund that holds all large growth stocks, for example, will generally (but certainly not always) rise or fall with the rise or fall of that asset class.

Some research shows that perhaps 90 to 95 percent of a mutual fund's or ETF's performance may be attributable to its asset class. I believe it. That's why the financial press's weekly wrap-ups of top performing funds will typically list a bunch of funds that mirror each other very closely. (That being the case, why not enjoy the low cost and tax efficiency of the ETF or index mutual fund?)

Big and Brawny

Large growth companies grab nearly all the headlines, for sure. The pundits are forever bestowing them with glory. The northeast corner of the style grid includes the most recognizable names in the corporate world. If you're seeking employment, I urge you strongly to latch on to such a growth company; your future will likely be bright. But do large growth stocks necessarily make the best investments?

Er, no.

Contrary to all appearances . . .

According to Fama and French (who are still operating as a research duo), over the course of the last 77 years, large growth stocks have seen an annualized return rate (not accounting for inflation) of about 9.5 percent. Not too bad at all. But that compares to 11.5 percent for large value stocks. And what's the relative volatility? Would you believe they're about on a par. Theories abound as to why large growth stocks haven't done as well as value stocks. Value stocks pay greater dividends, say some. Value stocks really *are* riskier; they just don't look it, argue others.

The theory that makes the most sense, in my opinion, is that growth stocks are simply hampered by their own immense popularity. Because growth companies grab all the headlines, because investors *think* they must be the best investments, the large growth stocks tend to get overpriced before you buy them. Think of how Google's stock shot up like a rocket in a matter of weeks after it hit the market. Weeks after that — after thousands and thousands of investors jumped on board — the stock began to cool.

Let history serve as only a rough guide

So given that large value stocks historically have done better than large growth stocks, and given (as I discuss in Chapters 7 and 8) that small caps historically have knocked the socks off large, does it still make sense to sink some of your investment dollars into large growth? Oh yes, it does. The past is only an indication of what the future may bring. No one knows whether value stocks will continue to outshine. In the past few years especially, growth stocks have lagged value by a wide margin, so perhaps we're going to see a reversal.

(Don't accuse me of market timing! I'm not saying that just because growth stocks have been depressed they are due for a big comeback. I have no idea. But to a small and limited degree, a little timely tactical tilting, I feel, is an okay thing. That is, it does make some sense to tilt a portfolio *gently* toward whatever sectors seem to be sagging and away from sectors that have been blazing. If you do that subtly, and regularly, and don't let emotions sway you, and if you watch out carefully for tax ramifications and trading costs, history shows that you may eek out some modest added return.)

Stocks of large companies — value and growth combined — should make up between 50 and 80 percent of your total domestic stock portfolio. The higher your risk tolerance, the more you should lean toward small cap.

Whatever your allocation to domestic large cap stocks, I recommend that you invest anywhere from 40 to 50 percent of that amount in large growth. Take a tilt toward value, if you wish, but don't tilt so far that you risk tipping over.

ETF Options Galore

The roster of ETFs on the market now includes about 30 broad-based domestic large cap funds, of which about 10 are large growth. The remainder of the broad-based (as opposed to industry sector or other specialized) large cap funds are either *blend* (a growth and value cocktail) or strictly large value. As I emphasize throughout this book, each and every investment you make should be evaluated in the context of your entire portfolio.

In this chapter, I'm focusing on large growth ETFs. But before you start shopping for a large growth ETF, you need to ask yourself whether a large growth ETF belongs in your portfolio. In a nutshell, it does, but only if your portfolio is large enough to warrant division into various styles.

Strictly large cap or blend?

All things being equal, I'd like to see you invest in both large growth and value stocks — separately. That approach gives you the opportunity to rebalance once a year and, by so doing, juice out added return and keep risk to a minimum. (More on rebalancing in Chapter 18.) But the profit you reap from that tweak must exceed the transaction costs of making two trades (generally selling the outperforming ETF for the year and purchasing the underperformer).

If your portfolio isn't big enough for the profit of the tweaking to outweigh the cost of the trading, you're better off with a blend of value and growth. If your portfolio is so small that any tweaking is likely to be unprofitable, I would suggest not only a blend of large value and growth, but a blend of *everything*. Keep these parameters in mind as you read on.

"Everything" investment options

I don't know where you park your money, and I don't know exactly how much you spend per trade, but I would say that if you have a portfolio of $10,000 or less, you should probably be thinking mutual funds, not ETFs. Otherwise, the trading costs could eat you alive. If, however, you are unlikely to do any trading in the next several years, an ETF portfolio may make sense. In that case, consider a simple and all-encompassing "everything" (total ball of wax) ETF for your domestic stock holdings.

Good options in the "everything" stock category include the iShares Dow Jones U.S. Total Market (IYY), the Vanguard Total Stock Market ETF (VTI), and the streetTRACKS Total Market (TMW). Of the three, I have a slight preference for the Vanguard choice for its ultra-low cost (0.07 percent versus 0.20 percent for either the iShares or the streetTRACKS).

Large and small cap blends

If you have more than $10,000 but less than $20,000 or so, and you're willing to invest it and keep it put for a good while, consider splitting up your domestic stock portfolio into large and small cap. In this case, I'd recommend a diversified small cap blend and a diversified large cap blend. Good options among the large cap blends would include the Vanguard Large Cap ETF (VV), the iShares S&P 500 (IW), the iShares Russell 1000 (IWB), and possibly the unconventional and somewhat sassy Rydex S&P 500 Equal Weight (RSP) ETF. I discuss these options in detail in the upcoming section "Blended options for large cap exposure."

Large cap growth and value options

If you have a portfolio of more than $20,000, you should split up the large caps into growth and value. Good large growth options would include the Vanguard Growth ETF (VUG), iShares Morningstar Large Growth (JKE), iShares S&P 500 Growth (IVW), streetTRACKS Dow Jones U.S. Large Cap Growth (ELG), and *possibly* the Rydex S&P 500 Pure Growth (RPG). See the upcoming section "Strictly large growth" for details on these ETFs.

Blended options for large cap exposure

Among the *blended* (large cap value and growth) options for smaller portfolios ($10,000 to $20,000), I feel comfortable recommending any of the four ETFs I discuss below. Note that there are subtle differences between the first three, while the fourth option — the Rydex baby — differs from the others by a good margin.

Please keep in mind that all the expense ratios, average cap sizes, price/earnings ratios, and top five holdings for the ETFs I list here and elsewhere in the book are true as of a certain date and are subject to change. You should verify before making any purchase.

Vanguard Large Cap ETF (VV)

Indexed to: MSCI U.S. Prime Market 750 Index (750 corporate biggies from both the value and growth sides of the grid)

Expense ratio: 0.07 percent

Average cap size: $44.8 billion

P/E ratio: 17.6

Top five holdings: Exxon Mobil Corp., General Electric, Microsoft, Citigroup, Bank of America

Russell's review: The ultra-low cost, as with nearly all Vanguard offerings, makes me want to stand up and cheer. The MSCI U.S. Prime Market 750, as the name implies, encompasses a larger universe of stocks than the more popular S&P 500, which translates to holdings with a somewhat smaller average cap size than you'll find with the iShares options. The MSCI index is also more "indexy" than the S&P 500: The choice of companies is purely quantitative, whereas with the S&P, there is some human choice. Personally, I like the hands-off approach. This ETF is an excellent choice for people with smaller portfolios trying to limit the number of ETFs they have to manage.

iShares S&P 500 (IVV)

Indexed to: S&P 500 (500 of the biggest and most stable U.S. companies)

Expense ratio: 0.09 percent

Average cap size: $47.0 billion

P/E ratio: 16.0

Top five holdings: General Electric, Exxon Mobil Corp., Citigroup, Microsoft, Procter & Gamble

Russell's review: I'm not all too crazy about the S&P 500 as an index; it's just too darned popular. That popularity may cost you a few cents here and there thanks to speculators who dip and dive around the index. The cost of this fund, however, is so delightfully low that it could help offset the speculation factor. The average cap size is way big. The iShares S&P 500 fund is a more-than-okay option, but I give a very slight preference to the Vanguard Large Cap ETF.

iShares Russell 1000 (IWB)

Indexed to: Russell 1000 (the largest 1,000 publicly traded companies in the land)

Expense ratio: 0.15 percent

Average cap size: $35.0 billion

P/E ratio: 16.2

Top five holdings: General Electric, Exxon Mobil Corp., Citigroup, Microsoft, Procter & Gamble

Russell's review: The cost isn't high, but it is higher than the comparable Vanguard fund. On the other hand, this ETF offers somewhat larger diversification — only a potential plus, really, if this is going to be a major part of your portfolio. Given the exposure to smaller companies, this fund may prove over the long run to be slightly more volatile but slightly more rewarding than either the Vanguard or the other comparable iShares options.

Rydex S&P 500 Equal Weight (RSP)

Indexed to: S&P 500, but each of the 500 companies in the index is given equal weight rather than the traditional market weighting

Expense ratio: 0.40 percent

Average cap size: $11.5 billion

P/E ratio: 16.3

Top five holdings: 500 stocks share equal weights (each about 0.25 of the portfolio)

Russell's review: Equal weighting is a novel and controversial approaching to investing. On one hand, it seems to make a lot of sense, offering perhaps better diversification and a relative overweighting of "cheaper" companies. I'm not crazy about the 0.40 percent expense ratio, which is considerably higher than comparable funds. Still, I wouldn't want to rule this fund out. If you decide you want to own it, note the much smaller average cap size than the other large blends. Arrange your other holdings accordingly to avoid a portfolio too oriented toward smaller companies.

Strictly large growth

For large growth and large growth alone (complimented by large value, of course) — a position I much prefer for people with adequate assets ($20,000+) — the four options I list here all provide good exposure to the asset class at very reasonable cost. You may also want to consider an offering from Rydex.

Vanguard Growth ETF (VUG)

Indexed to: MSCI U.S. Prime Market Growth Index (400 of the nation's largest growth stocks)

Expense ratio: 0.11 percent

Average cap size: $41.8 billion

P/E ratio: 22.2

Top five holdings: Microsoft, Procter & Gamble, General Electric, Johnson & Johnson, International Business Machines

Russell's review: The price is right. The index makes sense. There's good diversification. The companies represented are certainly large. This ETF is certainly a very good option, although I'd like it a wee bit more if it were a tad more growthy. There's also "The Vanguard edge" (see Chapter 3), which gives this fund another advantage for those who may already own the Vanguard Growth Index mutual fund.

iShares Morningstar Large Growth (JKE)

Indexed to: Morningstar Large Growth Index (105 of the largest and most growthy U.S. companies)

Expense ratio: 0.25 percent

Average cap size: $30.75 billion

P/E ratio: 28.9

Top five holdings: Microsoft, Johnson & Johnson, Cisco Systems, Intel, PepsiCo

Russell's review: Nothing in life is perfect. This ETF offers the growthiness that the Vanguard ETF lacks. The flip side is that the diversification leaves something to be desired. Microsoft and Johnson & Johnson together make up a tad more than 13 percent of the index; that's a little more than I would like to see. And perhaps because Morningstar indexes aren't nearly as popular as S&P indexes, this ETF is thinly traded, which could result in a larger spread when you buy or sell. What tips the scales for me, however, and makes this one of my faves is that Morningstar indexes are crisp and distinct: Any company that appears in the growth index is not going to be popping up in the value index. Even though that crispness could lead to slightly higher turnover, I like it.

iShares S&P 500 Growth (IVW)

Indexed to: S&P 500/Citigroup Growth Index (300 of the largest growth companies in the land, chosen from the S&P 500 universe)

Expense ratio: 0.18 percent

Average cap size: $19.1 billion

P/E ratio: 18.3

Top five holdings: Microsoft, Exxon Mobil Corp., Procter & Gamble, Pfizer, Johnson & Johnson

Russell's review: The price is good, and the diversification is more than adequate. My only beef — a small one — is that the selection could be growthier. (A growthier approach, however, might entail more turnover.) One certain plus: This ETF is the most popular among the large growth options, and therefore the buy and sell spreads should be slightly less than with, say, the Morningstar iShare or the Vanguard Large Growth.

streetTRACKS Dow Jones U.S. Large Cap Growth (ELG)

Indexed to: Start with the Wilshire 5000 (just about the whole shebang), and select the 400 or so largest and growthiest companies

Expense ratio: 0.20 percent

Average cap size: $61.0 billion

P/E ratio: 19.2

Top five holdings: Microsoft, Procter & Gamble, Johnson & Johnson, Cisco Systems, International Business Machines

Russell's review: Nothing wrong here: reasonable ratios, rational index. I'm not sure this would be my first choice, however; although the price is reasonable, it is still almost twice what Vanguard charges.

Rydex S&P 500 Pure Growth (RPG)

Indexed to: Approximately 140 of the most growthy of the S&P 500 companies

Expense ratio: 0.35 percent

Average cap size: $23.4 billion

P/E ratio: 19.1

Top five holdings: International Game Technology, Nvidia, XTO Energy, Forest Laboratories, Express Scripts

Russell's review: The promise here is one of "purity." You wouldn't know it by looking at the cap size and P/E ratio, neither of which make this fund look especially more pure than any other large growth ETF. It is possible that Rydex's other selection criteria somehow add to purity. But is that purity of style worth paying 0.35 percent for? Granted, that isn't high by mutual fund standards, but compared to the other large growth ETF options, it is pricey. I'd like to see this fund prove itself. It can do that if it maintains extremely low correlation with its value counterpart. That proof will take years.

ETFs I wouldn't go out of my way to own

None of the ETFs listed below is horrible — far from it. But given the plethora of choices, barring very special circumstances, I would not recommend these:

- ✔ **DIAMONDS Trust Series 1 (DIA).** Based on the index on which this ETF is based, I basically don't like it. The Dow Jones Industrial Average is an antiquated and somewhat arbitrary index of 30 large companies that look good to the editors of *The Wall Street Journal.* That isn't enough to build a portfolio on.

- ✔ **SPDR 500 (SPY).** It's the oldest and largest and perhaps even the cheapest (0.06 percent), but it's not the best thing on the ETF market. The S&P 500, which the fund tracks, isn't the greatest of indexes. The legal structure of SPY — unlike the vast majority of ETFs — does not allow for the immediate reinvestment of dividends, which can create a cash drag.

- ✔ **PowerShares Dynamic Large Cap Growth (PWB).** This ETF doesn't make me recoil in horror; you could do a lot worse. But the high-by-ETF-standards expense ratio (0.60 percent) is something of a turn-off. And the "enhanced" index reminds me too much of active investing, which has a less than gleaming track record. I may change my mind if this new fund still shines after years on the market, but for right now, I'd shy away.

Chapter 6

Large Value: Counterintuitive Cash Cows

*W*hy do American suburbanites gingerly cultivate their daisies, yet go nuts swinging spades or spraying poison chemicals at their dandelions? Why is a second cup of coffee in a diner free, but they charge you for a second cup of tea? Some things in this world just don't make a lot of sense. Why, for example, would slower-growing companies (the dandelions of the corporate world) historically reward investors better than faster-growing (daisy) companies? Welcome to the shoulder-shrugging world of value investing.

I'm talking about companies you've probably heard of, yes, but they aren't nearly as glamorous as Google or as exciting as Cisco. I'm talking about companies that usually ply their trade in older, slow growing industries, like insurance, petroleum, and transportation. I'm talking about companies such as Chevron, ConocoPhillips, Freddie Mac, American International Group (life insurance, anyone?), and Excelon (providing electricity and gas to customers in Illinois and Pennsylvania).

I see you yawning! But before you fall asleep, consider this: In the past 77 years, large value stocks have enjoyed an annualized growth rate of 11.4 percent, versus but 9.5 percent for large growth stocks — with roughly the same standard deviation (volatility). And thanks to ETFs, investing in value was never easier.

In this chapter, I explain not only the role that large value stocks play in a portfolio but why you may want them to be the largest single asset class in your portfolio. Take a gander at Figures 6-1 and 6-2. They show where large value stocks fit into the investment style grid (which I introduce in Chapter 4) and the impressive return of large value stocks over the past eight decades.

Pass the dandelion fertilizer, will ya?

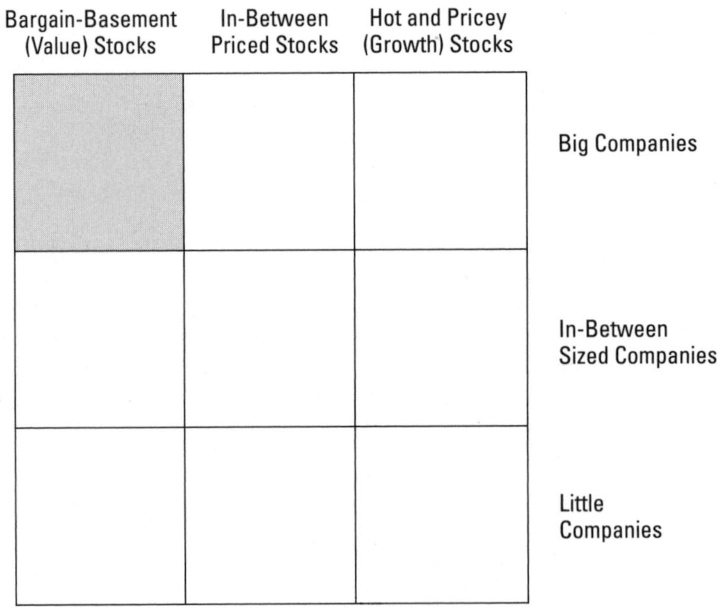

Figure 6-1:
Large value stocks occupy the northwest corner of the grid.

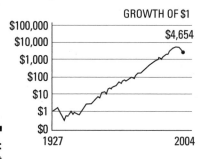

U.S. Large Cap Value Stocks
1927-2004: Total Returns (%)

GROWTH OF $1

$4,654

U.S. Large Cap Growth Stocks
1927-2004: Total Returns (%)

GROWTH OF $1

$1,154

U.S. Small Cap Value Stocks
1927-2004: Total Returns (%)

GROWTH OF $1

$40,095

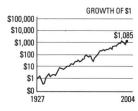

U.S. Small Cap Growth Stocks
1927-2004: Total Returns (%)

GROWTH OF $1

$1,085

Figure 6-2:
This chart shows the growth of $1 invested in a basket of large value stocks from 1927 to the present.

Source: Fama/French data provided by Eugene F. Fama and Kenneth R. French

Six Ways to Recognize Value

Warren Buffett knows a value stock when he sees one. Do you? Different investment pros and different indexes (upon which ETFs are fashioned) may use different criteria for making their selections of value stocks. But here are some of the most common criteria:

- ✓ **P/E ratio.** As early as 1934, Benjamin Graham and David Dodd (in their book with the gangbuster title *Security Analysis*) suggested that investors should pay heavy consideration to the ratio of a stock's market price (P) to its earnings per share (E). Sometimes called the *multiple,* this venerable ratio sheds light on how much the market is willing to cough up for a company's earning power. The lower the ratio, the more "valuey" the stock.

- ✓ **P/B ratio.** Graham and Dodd also advised that the ratio of market price to book value (B) be given at least "a fleeting glance." Many of today's investment gurus have awarded the P/B ratio the chief role in defining value versus growth. A ratio well below sea level is what floats a value investor's boat. *Book value* refers to the guesstimated value of a corporation's total assets, both tangible (factories, inventory, and so on) and intangible (goodwill, patents, and so on), minus any liabilities.

✔ **Dividend distributions.** You like dividends? Value stocks are the ones that pay them.

✔ **The cover of *Forbes.*** Magazine covers are rarely adorned with photos of the CEOs of value companies. Growth companies are followed more by everyone, and that includes Wall Street as well as the talking heads on CNBC. Value companies can be obscure.

✔ **Earnings growth.** Growth companies' earnings tend to impress. Value companies tend to have less than awe-inspiring growth in earnings.

✔ **The industry sector.** Growth stocks are typically found in adolescent industries, such as computers, biotech, wireless, and biotechnology. Value stocks are more often found in older-than-the-hills sectors, such as energy, banking, transportation, and toiletries.

Best Buys

Many academic types have looked at the so-called *value premium* and have tried to explain it. No one can agree on why value stocks have historically outperformed growth stocks. (A joke I remember from my college days: Put any three economists in a room, and you'll get at least five opinions.)

Some people say there is hidden risk in value investing that warrants greater returns. They explain that although the standard deviation for the two asset classes is about the same, value stocks tend to plummet at the worst economic times. Others say that value stocks outperform growth stocks because of the greater dividends paid by value companies. Growth companies tend to plow their cash into acquisitions and new product development rather than issuing dividends to those pesky shareholders.

Here's the best explanation for the value premium, if you ask this humble author: Value stocks simply tend to be ignored by the market — or have been in the past — and therefore come relatively cheap.

Doing it right

Famous value investors, like Warren Buffett, make their money finding stocks that come at an especially low price. They recognize that companies making lackluster profits, and even sometimes companies bleeding money, can turn around (especially when Mr. Buffett sends in his team of whip-cracking consultants). When a lackluster company turns around, the stock that was formerly seen as a financial turd (that's a technical term) can suddenly turn to 14-karat gold. It's a formula that has worked well for the Oracle of Omaha.

Good luck making it work for you.

For every Warren Buffett, there are a dozen stock pickers, maybe five dozen, who repeatedly take gambles on failing companies that continue to fail. I say the best way to invest in large value is to buy the index. There is no better way of doing that than through ETFs.

Making your selection

Of the 30 or so diversified large cap ETFs on the market, five are worth particular attention. The following offer good large value indexes at reasonable prices: the Vanguard Value ETF (VTV), iShares Morningstar Large Value (JKF), iShares S&P 500 Value (IVE), streetTRACKS Dow Jones U.S. Large Cap Value (ELV), and Rydex S&P 500 Pure Value (RPV).

I suggest that you read through my descriptions in the following section and make the choice that you think is best for you. Whatever your allocation to domestic large cap stocks (see Chapter 16 if you aren't sure), your allocation to value should be somewhere in the ballpark of 50 to 60 percent of that amount. In other words, I suggest that you tilt toward value, but don't go overboard.

The Large Cap Value Winners

The criteria you use in picking the best large cap value ETF should include expense ratios, appropriateness of the index, and tax efficiency. Here's how some of the top contenders compare. Note that the expense ratios, average cap sizes, price/earning ratios, and top five holdings are all subject to change; you should definitely check for updated figures before buying.

Vanguard Value ETF (VTV)

Indexed to: MSCI U.S. Prime Market Value Index (400 or so of the nation's largest value stocks)

Expense ratio: 0.11 percent

Average cap size: $45.1 billion

P/E ratio: 14.6

Top five holdings: Exxon Mobil Corp., Citigroup, Bank of America, Pfizer, General Electric

Russell's review: The price is right. The index makes sense. There's good diversification. The companies represented are certainly large. This ETF is a very good option, although I'd like it a wee bit more if it were a tad more valuey. (However, making it more valuey could increase turnover, which might increase costs.) All told, I like the Vanguard Value ETF. I like it a lot. If you already own the Vanguard Value Index mutual fund, and you're considering moving to ETFs, this fund would clearly be your choice (see "The Vanguard edge" sidebar in Chapter 3).

iShares Morningstar Large Value (JKF)

Indexed to: Morningstar Large Value Index (94 of the largest U.S. value stocks)

Expense ratio: 0.25 percent

Average cap size: $37.6 billion

P/E ratio: 12.7

Top five holdings: Exxon Mobil Corp., Citigroup, Bank of America, Pfizer, Altria Group

Russell's review: Nothing in life is perfect. This ETF offers a greater lean toward value than does the Vanguard option. The flip side is that the diversification leaves something to be desired: Exxon Mobil Corp. alone makes up over 10 percent of this ETF, and that, in my mind, is less than ideal. To boot, Morningstar indexes aren't nearly as popular as S&P indexes, so this ETF is thinly traded, which could result in a larger spread when you buy or sell. On the positive side, however, Morningstar indexes are neat boxes: Any company that appears in the value index is not going to pop up in the growth index. I think that's worth something, for sure.

iShares S&P 500 Value (IVE)

Indexed to: S&P 500/Citigroup Value Index (355 large value candidates plucked from the companies that make up the S&P 500)

Expense ratio: 0.18 percent

Average cap size: $15.7 billion

P/E ratio: 15.6

Top five holdings: Citigroup, General Electric, Bank of America, JPMorgan Chase & Co., Exxon Mobil Corp.

Russell's review: The price is good, and the diversification is more than adequate. My only beef — a small one — is that the selection could be more tilted toward value. On the other hand, this ETF is the most popular among the large value options, and therefore the buy and sell spreads (a penny here and a penny there, but it could add up) should be slightly less than with, say, the Morningstar iShare or the Vanguard Large Value. All in all, the iShares S&P 500 Value is a winner.

streetTRACKS Dow Jones U.S. Large Cap Value (ELV)

Indexed to: Start with the Wilshire 5000 (just about the whole shebang), and select out the 347 largest and most valuey companies

Expense ratio: 0.20 percent

Average cap size: $102.0 billion

P/E ratio: 13.4

Top five holdings: Exxon Mobil Corp., General Electric, Citigroup, Bank of America, Pfizer

Russell's review: Nothing wrong here: reasonable price, reasonable ratios, good company producing the index, and an index that makes sense. I'm not sure this would be my first choice, if only because the price could still be lower, but it wouldn't be a bad option for most.

Rydex S&P 500 Pure Value (RPV)

Indexed to: Approximately 150 of the most valuey of the S&P 500 companies

Expense ratio: 0.35 percent

Average cap size: $17.7 billion

P/E ratio: 30.9

Top five holdings: Ryder Systems, Dillard's, United States Steel, Ford Motor Company, Albertsons

Russell's review: The promise here is one of "purity." You wouldn't know it by looking at the cap size and P/E ratio, neither of which make this fund look especially more pure than any other large value ETF. It is possible that Rydex's other selection criteria somehow add to purity. But is that purity of style worth paying 0.35 percent for? Granted, that isn't high by mutual fund standards, but compared to the other large value options, it is pricey. I'd like to see this fund prove itself. It can do that if it maintains extremely low correlation to its growth counterpart. That proof will take time.

Chapter 7

Small Growth: Sweet Sounding Start-ups

*O*nce upon a time in the kingdom of Redmond, there was a young company called Microsoft. It was a very small company with very big ideas, and it grew and grew and grew. Its founder and its original investors became very, very rich and lived happily ever after.

Oh, you've heard that story? Then you understand the appeal of small growth companies. These are companies that typically have *market capitalization* (the market value of total outstanding stock) of under $1 billion. They frequently boast a hot product or patent, often fall into the high tech arena, and seem to be on their way to stardom. Some of them make it, and along with them, their investors take a joy ride all the way to early retirement.

Unfortunately, for every Microsoft, there are a dozen small companies that go belly up long before their prime. For every investor who gambles on a small company stock and takes early retirement, 100 others still take their cars to work every Monday morning.

Beep beep.

In this chapter, I ask you to take a ride with me through the world of small cap growth stocks. I explain what role, if any, they should play in your ETF portfolio. First stop along the ride: Figure 7-1, where you see how small growth fits into the investment style grid I introduce in Chapter 4. Second stop: Figure 7-2, which shows that small growth stocks, at least over the past eight decades, haven't exactly lit the world on fire.

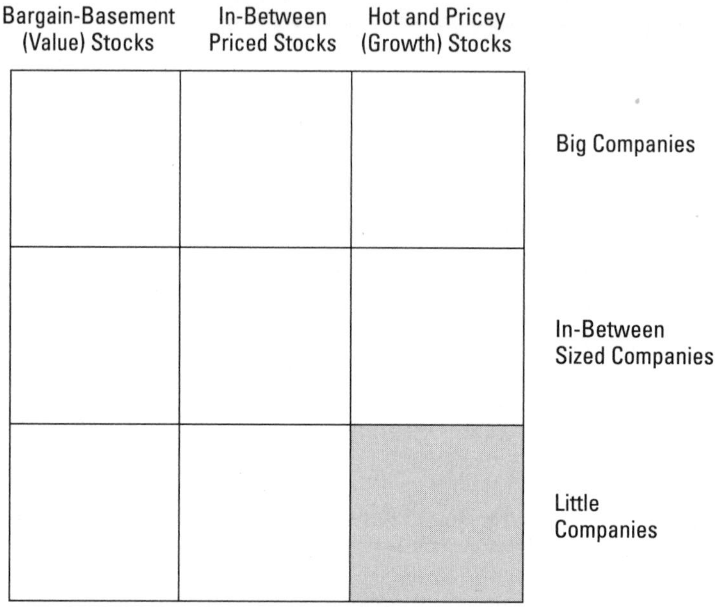

Bargain-Basement (Value) Stocks	In-Between Priced Stocks	Hot and Pricey (Growth) Stocks	
			Big Companies
			In-Between Sized Companies
			Little Companies

Figure 7-1: The shaded area represents the portion of the investment grid represented by small growth stocks.

Let's Get Real

In the past century, small cap stocks have outperformed large cap stocks just as assuredly as Honduras produces more Hondurans than the United States. The volatility of small cap stocks has also been greater, just as assuredly as the United States has more roller coasters than Honduras. In terms of return per unit of risk (risk-adjusted rate of return), however, small caps are clearly winners. And so it would seem that investing in small caps is a pretty smart thing to do. But please know that not all small caps are created equal.

As it happens, the true stars of the small cap world have been small cap *value* stocks rather than small cap *growth* stocks. (Take a look at Chapters 5 and 6 if you aren't sure what I mean by those terms.) How slow-growing, often ailing companies have beat out their hot-to-trot cousins remains one of the great unresolved mysteries of the investing world. But the numbers don't lie.

U.S. Large Cap Value Stocks
1927-2004: Total Returns (%)

U.S. Large Cap Growth Stocks
1927-2004: Total Returns (%)

Figure 7-2:
Historically, the growth of a basket of small growth stocks isn't anything to write home about.

U.S. Small Cap Value Stocks
1927-2004: Total Returns (%)

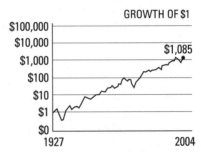

U.S. Small Cap Growth Stocks
1927-2004: Total Returns (%)

Source: Fama/French data provided by Eugene F. Fama and Kenneth R. French

In fact, if you look at the numbers, such as those in Figure 7-2, you may be inclined to treat small growth stocks as a pariah. Please don't. They belong in a well-diversified portfolio. Some years are clearly small growth years. The best example is rather recent: 2003. In that year, small growth was the undisputed King of Return, clocking in at an astounding 50.37 percent. And who is to say that the past wasn't a fluke and that small growth may actually go on to outperform all other asset classes in the next 20 years?

Your Choices for Small Growth

If you have a portfolio of under $20,000 or so, I recommend that you consider a small cap *blend* fund, which combines small value and small growth stocks. Small cap domestic stocks shouldn't occupy more than 20 percent or so of your portfolio (more on that in Chapter 16), and if you divide up 20 percent of less than $20,000, the trading costs could seriously impact your returns. So keep it simple until your portfolio grows to the point that you can start slicing and dicing a bit more economically.

If you have a portfolio of over $20,000 and you are a buy-and-hold kind of guy or gal, I suggest you break up your small cap holdings into growth and value. Given the dramatic outperformance of value in the past, I suggest that you tilt in that direction — more so than you do with large caps. A reasonable tilt may call for somewhere between 60 and 75 of your small cap exposure going to value, and 25 to 40 percent going to growth.

Small cap blend funds

A bit of growth, a bit of value, your choice in small cap blend funds should take into consideration such things as expense ratios, average cap size, and P/E ratio (which I explain in Chapter 5). Keep in mind that these numbers are subject to change, so I recommend checking them before you make any purchases.

Some pretty good ETF options for people with limited sized portfolios include the Vanguard Small Cap ETF (VB), iShares Morningstar Small Core (JKJ), iShares S&P Small Cap 600 (IJR), and streetTRACKS Dow Jones Wilshire Small Cap (DSC).

Vanguard Small Cap ETF (VB)

Indexed to: MSCI U.S. Small Cap 1750 Index (1,750 broadly diversified smaller U.S. companies)

Expense ratio: 0.10 percent

Average cap size: $1.6 billion

P/E ratio: 23.8

Top five holdings: Western Digital Corp., Martin Marietta Materials, AMR Corporation, Vertex Pharmaceuticals, Oshkosh Truck Corp.

Russell's review: The expense ratio is half that of any other offering in the small cap ETF arena. The diversification is lovely. And Vanguard's ETFs — largely because they are pegged to indexes with little turnover — are arguably the most tax-efficient of all ETFs. Those are the three positives. On the down side, the P/E ratio is higher than that of the competitors (an indication of a greater orientation toward growth and away from value), and so too is the cap size. On balance, this is a very good selection, but, as with all blend funds, I'd scrap it for something more refined — a growth and value split — as soon as your portfolio is large enough to allow for such refinement.

iShares Morningstar Small Core (JKJ)

Indexed to: 383 companies from the Morningstar Small Core Index that fall somewhere between growth and value

Expense ratio: 0.25 percent

Average cap size: $865 million

P/E ratio: 19.8

Top five holdings: Integrated Device Technology, Walter Industries, Manitowoc Co., Jones Lang Lasalle, Sierra Pacific Resources

Russell's review: The diversification isn't quite what you get with Vanguard, but it's adequate. The somewhat lower P/E could translate into slightly higher returns over the long haul, but that may be offset by the higher expense ratio. These Morningstar iShares aren't heavily traded, so you could get zonked with a larger spread when you buy and sell.

iShares S&P Small Cap 600 (IJR)

Indexed to: Roughly 600 companies that make up the S&P Small Cap 600 Index

Expense ratio: 0.20

Average cap size: $883 million

P/E ratio: 17.5

Top five holdings: Oshkosh Truck Corp., NVR, Cimarex Energy Co., Frontier Oil Corp., Resmed

Russell's review: This is a perfectly acceptable ETF for small cap exposure at a fair price. Vanguard's price, however, is even more fair. If you already own this ETF, that's not reason enough to switch unless you're holding a rather large position to minimize the trading cost. But if you're starting from scratch, I don't know if paying double the fee of Vanguard's would be warranted.

streetTRACKS Dow Jones Wilshire Small Cap (DSC)

Indexed to: Start with the Wilshire 5000 (just about the whole shebang), and select out the 1,744 smallest companies

Expense ratio: 0.25 percent

Average cap size: $1.8 billion

P/E ratio: 17.9

Top five holdings: Akamai Technologies, Glamis Gold Ltd., SL Green Realty Corp., Terex Corp., Intuitive Surgical

Russell's review: Great diversification — perhaps a little too good, as the selection of companies seems to edge into the mid cap area a bit. The expense ratio is higher — not ridiculously higher, but higher — than some others in this category. Still, you could do much worse.

Strictly small cap growth funds

If you have enough assets to warrant splitting up small value and small growth, go for it, by all means. Following are some very good small growth options from iShares, Vanguard, and streetTRACKS. In the next chapter, I present small value options to serve as compliments to the funds presented here.

Vanguard Small Cap Growth ETF (VBK)

Indexed to: MSCI U.S. Small Cap Growth Index (approximately 970 small growth capitalization companies in the United States)

Expense ratio: 0.12 percent

Average cap size: $1.6 billion

P/E ratio: 28.8

Top five holdings: Western Digital Corp., AMR Corp., Vertex Pharmaceuticals, Oshkosh Truck Corp., The Corporate Executive Board

Russell's review: I'm not entirely sure why Vanguard charges 0.02 percent more for this fund than it does for its small cap blend ETF, but, hey, that's only $2 a year for every $10,000 invested, and it's still the best deal in town. Add to that the wide diversification, tax efficiency beyond compare, and a very definite growth bias, and I really have no complaints. The Vanguard Small Cap Growth ETF offers an excellent way to tap into this asset class.

iShares Morningstar Small Growth Index (JKK)

Indexed to: Approximately 370 companies from the Morningstar Small Growth Index

Expense ratio: 0.30 percent

Average cap size: $850 million

P/E ratio: 28.3

Top five holdings: Rambus, Silicon Laboratories, PMC-Sierra, Hologic, Trimble Navigation Ltd.

Russell's review: My only beef with the Morningstar indexes is that they tend to be a bit too concentrated in the large cap arena. In small caps, that isn't a problem. The largest holding here, Rambus, gets but a 1.1 percent allocation, which is perfectly acceptable. The expense ratio, too, is acceptable, although higher than some others in this category. I like that Morningstar promises no crossover between growth and value. If you own this ETF along with the iShares Morningstar Small Value Index, you should get pleasantly low correlation.

iShares S&P Small Cap 600 Growth (IJT)

Indexed to: Despite the "600" in the title, this ETF represents 354 holdings chosen from the S&P Small Cap 600/Citigroup Growth Index

Expense ratio: 0.25 percent

Average cap size: $734 million

P/E ratio: 16.7

Top five holdings: NVR, Cimarex Energy Co., Global Payments, Frontier Oil Corp., Resmed

Russell's review: S&P indexes are a bit too subjective for me to really love them. I'm also a slight bit baffled by the current P/E ratio of this fund, which is actually lower than the iShares S&P Small Cap Value 600 Index fund (IJS). It should be the other way around. (See what I mean about subjective?) Of course, P/E ratios can fluctuate greatly from week to week, especially with small cap funds. Nonetheless, this fund's price is reasonable, and there's no reason to snub this iShares offering. Still, it isn't my first pick.

streetTRACKS DJ Wilshire Small Cap Growth (DSG)

Indexed to: Start with the Wilshire 5000 (just about the whole shebang), and select out the 875 smallest and growthiest companies

Expense ratio: 0.25 percent

Average cap size: $1.8 billion

P/E ratio: 21.5

Top five holdings: Glamis Gold Ltd., Akamai Technologies, Fmc Technologies, Intuitive Surgical, Western Gas Resources

Russell's review: Sure, I could live with this ETF in my portfolio. I might even be happy. But is there any reason to pay 0.25 percent, when Vanguard is charging half that? Maybe, but it would take something more than I see to convince me.

Rydex S&P 600 Small Cap Pure Growth (RZG)

Indexed to: Approximately 140 of the smallest and most growthy of the S&P 600 companies

Expense ratio: 0.35

Average cap size: $1.2 billion

P/E ratio: 27.5

Top five holdings: Coinstar, Biolase Technology, Ceradyne, Christopher & Banks Corp., Odyssey HealthCare

Russell's review: The price is higher than others in this category, and the promise of "purity" is a big murky — especially if the quest for purity leads to high turnover, which could reduce tax efficiency. Rydex also seems to cater most to traders rather than buy-and-hold investors, and that gives me something of a feeling of discomfort. Traders usually trade themselves into losses.

Smaller than Small: Meet the Micro Caps

If you want to invest your money in companies that are smaller than small, you're going to be investing in micro caps. These are companies larger than the corner delicatessen, but not by much. In general, micro caps are publicly held companies with less than $250 million in outstanding stock. Micro caps, as you can imagine, are volatile little suckers, but as a group they offer impressive long-term performance figures. In terms of diversification, micro caps — in conservative quantity — are a nice addition to most portfolios.

Micros move at a modestly different pace than do other equity asset classes. It is generally theorized that because micro caps are heavy borrowers, their performance is more tied to interest rates than are larger cap stocks. (Lower interest rates would be good; higher interest rates would not.) Micro caps also tend to be more tied to the vicissitudes of the U.S. economy and less to the world economy than, say, the fortunes of General Electric or McDonald's.

Given the high risk of owning any individual micro cap, it makes eminent sense to work micro caps into your portfolio with ETFs. To date, but three micro cap ETFs have been introduced. They differ from one another to a much greater extent than do the larger cap ETFs, although all three are certainly acceptable options.

iShares Russell Microcap Index (IWC)

Indexed to: 1,240 of the smallest publicly traded companies, all culled from the Russell 3000 Index

Expense ratio: 0.60 percent

Average cap size: $425 million

P/E ratio: 21

Top five holdings: Trident Microsystems, Brightpoint, Nuance Communications, Cubist Pharmaceuticals, Stratasys

Russell's review: There aren't a lot of choices in this field, so I'm glad this is one of them. I'm not crazy about paying 0.60 percent, which is high for an ETF, but there seems to be price collusion in the micro cap area, so what are you going to do? (Personal note to ETF firms' attorneys: Hey, I'm only kidding about the price collusion, guys! It just *seems* that way.)

PowerShares Zacks Microcap Index (PZI)

Indexed to: The proprietary ZAX Index, which includes roughly 400 micro cap stocks chosen for "investment merit criteria, including fundamental growth, stock valuation, investment timeliness . . . ." In other words, someone behind the scenes is stock picking.

Expense ratio: 0.60 percent

Average cap size: $342 million

P/E ratio: 19.7

Top five holdings: Biogen IDEC, Applera Applied Biosystems, Gilead Sciences, Sigma-Aldrich, Amgen

Russell's review: I don't like stock picking, and I don't generally trust any manager to know what qualifies as "investment timeliness." Still, this ETF's selections yield an average cap size that makes it, in my mind, a serious contender, despite the active management.

First Trust Dow Jones Select Microcap Index (FDM)

Indexed to: Dow Jones Select MicroCap Index, which contains about 280 of the smallest stocks listed on the New York Stock Exchange, the American Stock Exchange, and the NASDAQ

Expense ratio: 0.60

Average cap size: $622 million

P/E ratio: 20

Top five holdings: General Cable Corp., Brightpoint, Mobile Mini, Giant Industries, Atlas America

Russell's review: The price is competitive, and everything else looks okay, but the cap size is considerably larger than the other two micros — and isn't smallness the whole reason to be in micro caps in the first place?

Chapter 8

Small Value: Diminutive Dazzlers

*L*ook at the list of some the top ten companies represented in the Vanguard Small Value ETF: Martin Marietta Materials, United Dominion Realty, Federal Realty Investment Trust, Beazer Homes USA. These are not household names. Nor are they especially fast-growing companies. Nor are they industry leaders. Nor are they in exciting new industries poised for potential huge growth. As you go further down the list of holdings, you'll likely find some companies in financial distress. Others may be facing serious lawsuits, expiration of patents, or labor unrest. If you wanted to pick one of these companies to sink a wad of cash into, I would tell you that you're crazy.

But if you wanted to sink that cash into the entire small value index, well, that's another matter altogether. Assuming you could handle some risk, I'd tell you to go for it. By all means. Your odds of making money are pretty darned good. At least if history is our guide.

Don't take my word for it; see Figure 8-2, which shows the enormous growth of value stocks over the past eight decades. On the way there, see Figure 8-1, which shows where small value fits into the investment style grid I introduce in Chapter 4. And then, follow me as I explain the importance of small value stocks in a poised-for-performance ETF portfolio.

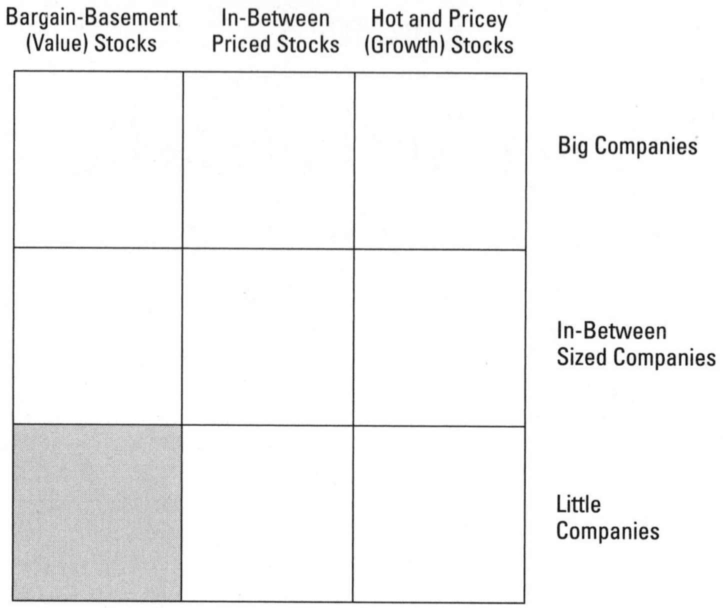

Bargain-Basement (Value) Stocks	In-Between Priced Stocks	Hot and Pricey (Growth) Stocks	
			Big Companies
			In-Between Sized Companies
			Little Companies

Figure 8-1: Small value stocks occupy the southwest corner of the investment style grid.

It's Been Quite a Ride

Small value stocks collectively have returned more to investors than have either large value stocks or any kind of growth stocks. In fact, the difference in returns has been somewhat staggering: I'm talking about an annualized return of about 14.5 percent over the past 77 years for small value, versus 11.5 percent for large value, 9.5 for large growth, and 9.4 for small growth. Compounded over time, the outperformance of small value stocks has been HUGE.

Latching on for fun and profit

To be sure, small value stocks are risky little suckers. Even the entire index (available to you in neat ETF form) is more volatile than any conservative investor would feel comfortable with. But as part — a very handsome part — of a diversified portfolio, a small value ETF can be a beautiful thing indeed.

U.S. Large Cap Value Stocks
1927-2004: Total Returns (%)

U.S. Large Cap Growth Stocks
1927-2004: Total Returns (%)

U.S. Small Cap Value Stocks
1927-2004: Total Returns (%)

Figure 8-2:
As you can
see, small
value has
truly shined
in the
past eight
decades.

U.S. Small Cap Growth Stocks
1927-2004: Total Returns (%)

Source: Fama/French data provided by Eugene F. Fama and Kenneth R. French

If we knew the past was going to repeat, such as it did in the movie *Ground-hog Day,* there'd be no reason to have anything but small value in your port-folio. But, of course, we don't know that the past will repeat. Bill Murray's radio alarm clock may not go off at sunrise. And the small value premium, like Bill Murray's hairline, may start to seriously recede. Still, the outperformance of small value has historically been so much greater than that of small growth that I favor a good tilt in the direction of value.

But keeping your balance

Whatever your total allocation to domestic small cap stocks (see Chapter 16 for advice), I recommend that anywhere from 60 to 75 percent of that amount be allocated to small value. But no more than that, please. If the value premium disappears or becomes a value discount, I don't want you left holding the bag. And even if small value continues to outperform, having both small value and small growth (along with their bigger cousins, all of which tend to rise and fall in different cycles) will help smooth out some of the inevitable volatility of holding stocks.

Good choices among small value ETFs include offerings from Vanguard, iShares, and streetTRACKS.

Vanguard Small Cap Value ETF (VBR)

Indexed to: MSCI U.S. Small Cap Value Index (about 950 small value domestic companies)

Expense ratio: 0.12 percent

Average cap size: $1.6 billion

P/E ratio: 20.1

Top five holdings: Camden Property Trust REIT, Conseco, Federal Realty Investment Trust REIT, Harsco, Ryder System

Russell's review: Low cost, wide diversification, tax efficiency beyond compare, and a very definite value bias — what's not to like? The Vanguard Small Cap Value ETF offers an excellent way to tap into this asset class.

iShares Morningstar Small Value Index (JKL)

Indexed to: 338 of Morningstar's Small Value Index

Expense ratio: 0.30 percent

Average cap size: $910 million

P/E ratio: 15.5

Top five holdings: Foster Wheeler Ltd., Trinity Industries, Ciena Corp., Brandywine Realty Trust, New Century Financial Corp.

Russell's review: My only complaint with the Morningstar indexes is that they tend to be a bit too concentrated in the large cap arena. In small caps, that isn't a problem. The largest holding here, Foster Wheeler Ltd., gets slightly less than a 1 percent allocation, which is perfectly good. The expense ratio, too, is acceptable, although higher than some others in this category. I like that Morningstar promises no crossover between growth and value. If you own this ETF along with the iShares Morningstar Small Growth Index, you should get pleasantly low correlation.

iShares S&P Small Cap 600 Value Index (IJS)

Indexed to: 457 of the S&P Small Cap 600/Citigroup Value Index

Expense ratio: 0.25 percent

Average cap size: $592 million

P/E ratio: 19.1

Top five holdings: Commercial Metals Co., Shurgard Storage Centers, Reliance Steel & Aluminum Co., Energen Corp., Standard Pacific Corp.

Russell's review: S&P indexes are a bit too subjective for me to want to marry them. I'm also a slight bit baffled by the current P/E ratio of this fund, which is actually higher than the iShares S&P Small Cap Growth fund (IJT). It shouldn't be that way. (That's what I mean about subjective.) Of course, P/E ratios can change from week to week, especially with small cap funds. Nonetheless, this fund's price is reasonable, and there's no reason to snub this iShares offering. But you may do better elsewhere.

streetTRACKS DJ Wilshire Small Cap Value (DSV)

Indexed to: Start with the Wilshire 5000 (just about the whole shebang), and select out the 876 smallest and most valuey companies

Expense ratio: 0.25 percent

Average cap size: $1.9 billion

P/E ratio: 15.9

Top five holdings: Allegheny Technologies, AMR Corp., LSI Logic Corp., Terex Corp, SL Green Realty Corp.

Russell's review: Sure, I could live with this ETF in my portfolio. I might even be happy. But is there any reason to pay 0.25 percent when Vanguard is charging half that for its small value offering? Maybe, but it would take something more than I see to convince me.

Rydex S&P 600 Small Cap Pure Value (RZV)

Indexed to: Approximately 180 of the most valuey and small of the S&P 600 companies

Expense ratio: 0.35

Average cap size: $590 million

P/E ratio: 43.2

Top five holdings: Alliance One International, Startek, Central Vermont Public Service Corp., Planar Systems, Schulman A

Russell's review: The price is higher than others in this category, and the promise of "purity" is a bit murky, especially if that quest for purity leads to high turnover and that blows the tax efficiency. Rydex also seems to cater most to traders rather than buy-and-hold investors, which gives me something of a feeling of discomfort. Traders usually trade themselves into misery.

What About the Mid Caps?

In a word, my take on mid cap ETFs is . . . *why*? Yes, even as I'm writing these words, mid cap stocks — investments in companies with roughly $5 to $20 billion in outstanding stock — have decidedly outperformed both large and small cap stocks for the past 12 months. But such outperformance of mid cap stocks is a fluke. So, too, is any underperformance.

If you look at the risk/return profile of mid caps over many years, you find that it generally falls right where you would expect it to fall: smack in between large and small cap. Owning both a large cap and small cap ETF, therefore, will give you an average return very similar to mid caps but with considerably less volatility because large and small cap stocks tend to move up and down at different times.

Other investment pros may disagree, but I really don't see the point of shopping for mid cap ETFs, even though there are many mid cap offerings. Keep in mind, too, that most large cap and small cap funds are rather fluid: You will get some mid cap exposure from both. Many sector funds — including real estate, technology, and utilities — are also chock full of mid caps (see Chapter 9).

Chapter 9

Sector Investing: ETFs According to Industry

*A*ny *Star Trek* fan (yeah, beam me up) knows that matter and antimatter, should they ever meet, would result in an explosion so violent as to possibly destroy the entire universe or, at the very least, mess Donald Trump's hair. Despite the firm convictions of zealots on both sides, style investing (large-small-growth-value) and sector investing (technology-utilities-healthcare-energy) are not matter and antimatter. They can, and sometimes do, exist very peacefully side-by-side.

In this chapter, I present the nuts and bolts of sector investing: how it can function alone, or in conjunction with style investing, to build a well-diversified portfolio. Either way you decide to slice the pie — style or sector — using ETFs as building blocks makes for an excellent strategy. (Hmm, am I starting to sound like a zealot myself?)

Yes, there are now 70 industry sector ETFs. You can find one to mirror every one of the major industry sectors in the U.S. economy, including energy, basic materials, financial services, consumer goods, and so on. See the industry sector map in Figure 9-1 for a bird's eye view of the U.S. economy split into industry sectors, each accorded its proper allotment.

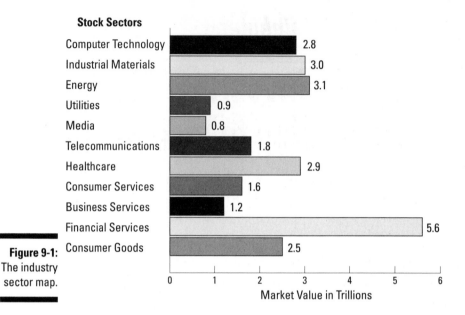

Figure 9-1:
The industry
sector map.

Based on Morningstar data, this map reveals the size of 11 major industry sectors of the U.S. economy. What you're seeing is the total capitalization of all public companies within each industry group.

Some of the newer ETFs mirror subsections of the economy, such as semiconductors (a subset of computer technology) and biotechnology (a subset of healthcare). In some cases, sectors of the economy you may not even know exist — such as nanotech and water resources — are represented with ETFs! A handful of the Barclays iShares, such as Global Healthcare and Global Telecommunications, even allow you to invest in industry sectors abroad (which are not represented in Figure 9-1).

Speculating on the Next Hot Industry

Is there a God? Does he have a long, white beard, and does he wear sandals? Why do sector investors tend to be speculators, while style investors tend to be buy-and-hold kinds of people? These are questions that sometimes keep me awake at night. I won't attempt to address the first two here. As for the third . . . heck, I have no idea. But there's little question that people who divide their portfolios into large-small-value-growth are much more likely to be long-term investors with long-term strategies than are people who buy into sectors (often through ETFs). That's just the way it is.

Sizzling and sinking

Sector funds are often purchased by investors who think they know which sectors are going to shine, and goshdarnit, they're going to profit by it. Unfortunately, they are often wrong.

I'm old enough to recall a day when environmental service companies, by dint of the realization that pollution was becoming a serious problem, were going to be a sure bet. But then, lo and behold, environmental service companies seriously lagged the overall market for years. Then it was computer and Web technology that couldn't possibly fail to outperform, yet for three brutal years (2000–2002), the technology sector fell like hail. At the time of this writing, energy is the sector that people are pouring money into. Utilities are also hot (just as they were prior to the stock market crash of 1929). By the time this book comes out, well . . .

Momentum riders and bottom feeders

Interestingly, while most investors are *momentum investors* — they tend to buy what's lately been hot — other investors look for what's been down, on the theory that everything reverts to the mean. The two camps are forever trading sector funds. Right now, the momentum investors are buying energy, utilities, real estate, and precious metals; the bottom feeders (I'm not sure what they call themselves) are buying technology and consumer goods. Fortunately (or unfortunately), there is no dearth of ETFs to please both crowds.

You can tell from my tone, no doubt, that I'm no big fan of sector speculation — or speculation of any sort. But what about using sector ETFs as buy-and-hold instruments? Even though few people do it, can a buy-and-hold portfolio be just as easily and effectively divided up by industry sector as it can by investment style?

Choosing Sector Investing Instead of the Grid?

An in-depth study on industry-sector investing, done several years ago by Chicago-based Ibbotson Associates (now part of Morningstar), came to the very favorable conclusion that sector investing — because times have allegedly changed — is potentially a superior diversifier than grid (style) investing. (I discuss the style grid in Chapters 4 and 5.) Globalization has led to a rise in correlation between domestic and international stocks; large, mid, and small cap stocks have high correlation to each other. A company's performance is tied more to its industry than to the country where it's based or the size of its market cap, concluded Ibbotson.

The Ibbotson report didn't end there. It also ballyhooed sector investing as a superior instrument for fine-tuning a portfolio to match an individual investor's risk tolerance. A conservative investor might overweight utilities and finances (two less volatile sectors); a more aggressive investor might tilt toward technology (whooeee).

That sounds like a good plan, although the lead author of that study once confided to me that he has the bulk of his personal portfolio still broken up into value, growth, large, and small — as do I. However, we both have some industry sector ETFs (for fine-tuning), as well.

Doing sector investing right

If you are going to go the sector route and build your entire stock portfolio, or a good part of it, out of industry sector ETFs, I suggest that before you do anything, take a look at Figure 9-1. Make sure you have allocations to all 11 major sectors of the economy.

Some advisors would tell you to keep your allocations roughly in accordance with each sector's overall size. I dunno. Had you done that in 1999, your portfolio would have been three-quarters technology, given the gross overpricing of the sector at that point. And you would have taken a bath the next year. I'd rather see a more even allocation.

Start perhaps with a roughly equal allocation as your home base, and then start tweaking — not based on crystal ball predictions of the future, but rather on the unique characteristics of each sector. What do I mean? Read on.

Seeking risk adjustment with high and low volatility sectors

Some industry sectors have historically evidenced greater return and greater risk. (Return and risk tend to go hand-in-hand, as I discuss in Chapter 4.) The same rules that apply to style investing apply to sector investing. Know how much volatility you can stomach, and then, and only then, build your portfolio in tune with your risk tolerance.

As far as historical risk and return, Figure 9-2 shows an approximation of how the major sectors rank. Keep in mind that *any* single sector — even utilities, the least volatile of all — will tend to be more volatile than the entire market because there is little diversification. Don't overindulge!

Also, keep in mind that your allocation between bonds and stocks will almost certainly have much more bearing on your overall level of risk and return than will your mix of stocks. In Part III of this book, I introduce bonds and discuss how an ETF investor should hold them.

The Most Volatile Sector ETFs (with highest return potential)

Technology

Financial (includes REITs)

Healthcare

Consumer Discretionary

Industrial

Materials

Energy

Consumer Staples

Utilities

Figure 9-2: Industry sectors, from most to least volatile.

The Least Volatile Sector ETFs (with lowest return potential)

Knowing where the grid comes through

There is nothing wrong per se with dividing up a stock portfolio into industry sectors, but please, don't be hasty in scraping style investing. I really believe that if you're going to pick one strategy over the other, the edge goes to style investing. For one thing, we know that it works. Style investing helps to diffuse (but certainly not eliminate) risk. Scads of data show that.

In addition, style investing allows you to take advantage of years of other data that indicate you can goose returns without raising your risk by leaning your portfolio toward value and small cap (see Chapters 6, 7, and 8). When you invest in industry sectors through ETFs, you are investing the vast majority of your funds in large caps, and you're splitting growth and value evenly. That may limit your investment success.

Another reason ETF investors shouldn't scrap style investing: Style ETFs are the way cheaper choice. For whatever reason — yes, another one of those eternal mysteries that keep me awake at night — style ETFs tend to cost one-half to one-third as much as industry-sector ETFs do. That's true for the Vanguard ETFs, the Barclays iShares, *and* the State Street Global Advisors' SPDRs and streetTRACKS. Go figure.

And one final reason to prefer style to sector for the core of your portfolio: You will require fewer funds. With large growth, large value, small growth, and small value, you pretty much can capture the entire stock market. With sector funds, well, you would need nearly a dozen to achieve the same effect. Each sector fund, because the performance of all companies within an industry sector tend to be closely correlated, offers minimal diversification.

Combining strategies to optimize your portfolio

There's no point to having dozens of ETFs in your portfolio if they are only going to replicate each other's holdings. So if you already own the entire market through diversified ETFs in all corner quadrants of the style grid — large, small, value, and growth — why add any industry sectors that are obviously already represented?

Well, it would make sense to add, say, a peppering of semiconductor stocks or utility stocks if you knew that semiconductors or utilities were going to blast off. Of course, a rational investor would never say he or she knew anything about the future.

And yet, taking on an added dose of semiconductors or utilities may still make sense if that added dose of either industry sector somehow were to raise your performance potential without raising risk. That could happen only if you chose an industry sector that is loosely correlated to the majority of the market.

Newness is a red flag

At about 70 and counting, you can find an ETF to mirror just about any sector or subsector of the economy. The latest arrivals include a host of commodity ETFs, including silver and oil futures. And new ones are sure to arrive shortly. Proceed with caution. New sector offerings occur most often after recent run-ups in price. The sector is hot. The public is buying. The financial industry is accommodating. Everyone is happy, for the moment. But there may be a balloon about to burst.

Seeking low correlations for added diversification

Some sectors, even though they are part of the stock market, tend to move out of lockstep with the rest of the market. By way of example, consider REITs: real estate investment trusts. (If you look for REITs in Figure 9-1, you find them buried under "Financial Services.") I devote Chapter 13 entirely to REITs, and especially REIT ETFs.

Another sector that fits the bill, at least of late, is energy. Yes, Exxon Mobil Corp. and Chevron are part of the entire market, but they tend to zig when everything else zags (probably because when the price of oil rises, these companies profit more, while the rest of the economy, at least outside of Texas, suffers).

For example, consider that in 2002, when the total U.S. stock market tanked by almost 11 percent, REITs were up 31 percent. In 2001, when the total U.S. stock market tanked by nearly 11 percent, REITs were up more than 12 percent. The year 2005 was pretty lackluster for the total stock market, yet energy stocks were up 31 percent.

Of course, there are years when it works the other way, and these sectors may fall way short of the overall market. *This* year perhaps?!

In Chapter 16, where I draw up some sample portfolios, you'll see more of REITs and energy.

If you decide to build your portfolio around industry sector funds, I urge you to at the very least dip into the style funds to give yourself the value/small cap tilt that I discuss in the four chapters prior to this one. That's especially true if you use SPDRs or HOLDRS to build your sector portfolio. Those two fund groups are especially weighted toward large cap. Again, in Chapter 16, I offer a few sample portfolios to illustrate workable allocations.

Sector Choices by the Dozen

After you decide which industry sectors you wish to invest in, you need to pick and choose among ETFs. Barclays iShares offers 20 selections. PowerShares has 21. State Street offers a dozen SPDRs and a half dozen streetTRACKS options. Vanguard has a dozen sector funds. And 16 Merrill Lynch HOLDRS focus on industry groupings.

Begin your sector selection here:

- **Do you want representation in large industry sectors (healthcare, technology, utilities)?** Your options include Vanguard ETFs, Barclays iShares, and Select Sector SPDRs.

- **Do you want to zero in on very narrow industry niches (insurance, oil service, nanotech)?** Consider streetTRACKS, PowerShares, and Merrill Lynch HOLDRS.

- **Do you want to keep your expense ratios to a minimum?** Vanguard ETFs and Select Sector SPDRs cost about half as much as PowerShares and Barclays iShares.

In the following sections, I give you a more in-depth view of the sector offerings available to you.

Vanguard ETFs

The Vanguard industry sector offerings are as follows:

Name	Ticker
Vanguard Consumer Discretionary ETF	VCR
Vanguard Consumer Staples ETF	VDC
Vanguard Energy ETF	VDE
Vanguard Financials ETF	VFH
Vanguard Health Care ETF	VHT
Vanguard Industrials ETF	VIS

Name	Ticker
Vanguard Information Technology ETF	VGT
Vanguard Materials ETF	VAW
Vanguard REIT Index ETF	VNQ
Vanguard Telecommunications Services ETF	VOX
Vanguard Utilities ETF	VPU

Fill your domestic stock portfolio with Vanguard's 11 industry sector ETFs, and presto! You've captured just about the entire universe of stocks. Granted, that universe will be weighted in such a manner that you'll have only token representation of mid and small caps (although you'll have more small cap exposure than you would with either SPDRs or HOLDRS).

The one exception is the Vanguard REIT Index ETF (VNQ). Principally a mid cap fund, VNQ is a prince among ETFs. With an expense ratio of 0.12 percent, it is the least expensive of all industry sector ETFs. It is also well diversified within its own real estate universe. If you're going to own a REIT ETF, Vanguard's selection is an excellent choice. (See Chapter 13 for more on REITs.) All other Vanguard ETFs carry an expense ratio of 0.25 percent — the same as most of the SPDRs.

In general, Vanguard ETFs, based on MSCI indexes, and the Select Sector SPDRs, based on S&P indexes, are your best building blocks for a portfolio sliced and diced by industry sectors. They are also excellent options for peppering a grid-based portfolio with sector funds.

Select Sector SPDRs

SPDR industry sector offerings are as follows:

Name	Ticker
Biotech Select Sector SPDR	XBI
Consumer Discretionary Select Sector SPDR	XLY
Consumer Staples Select Sector SPDR	XLP
Energy Select Sector SPDR	XLE
Financial Select Sector SPDR	XLF
Health Care Select Sector SPDR	XLV
Homebuilders Select Sector SPDR	XHB

Name	*Ticker*
Industrial Select Sector SPDR	XLI
Materials Select Sector SPDR	XLB
Semiconductor Select Sector SPDR	XSD
Technology Select Sector SPDR	XLK
Utilities Select Sector SPDR	XLU

Overall, I put the Select Sector SPDRs on a par with the Vanguard sector ETFs. The biotech, homebuilders, and semiconductor SPDRs will cost you 0.35 percent. The others — representing larger industry groupings — will cost you the same as the Vanguard ETFs, either 0.24 or 0.25 percent. Those nine others, however, are the ones that you most want if you wish to build a domestic stock portfolio around industry sectors.

As the S&P indexes upon which the Select Sector SPDRs are built tend to represent mostly large cap companies, I urge anyone building a SPDR portfolio to tap into small caps through some other means, such as buying into one of the small cap ETFs discussed in Chapters 7 and 8.

If you're going to invest in sector funds, know that the SPDRs Web site — www.spdrindex.com — is full of fabulous tools. Check out especially the Correlation Tracker, SPDR Map of the Market, and the Sector Tracker. (No, you don't have to be a SPDRs investor to use the tools.)

streetTRACKS

steetTRACKS industry sector offerings are as follows:

Name	*Ticker*
streetTRACKS KBW Bank	KBE
streetTRACKS KBW Capital Markets	KCE
streetTRACKS KBW Insurance	KIE
streetTRACKS Morgan Stanley Technology	MTK
streetTRACKS Dow Jones Wilshire REIT	RWR

The three KBW Capital Markets Index offerings are simply too narrow industry sectors to float my boat. The streetTRACKS Morgan Stanley Technology Index is too expensive: 0.50 percent. And the streetTRACKS REIT index — at 0.25 percent — is, although perfectly acceptable an investment, twice as expensive as the Vanguard alternative with no real advantage. Sorry, but streetTRACKS ETFs, although far, far from horrible investments, rate second-choice in Russell's world.

Barclays iShares

Barclays industry sector offerings are as follows:

Name	Ticker
iShares Dow Jones U.S. Basic Materials Index	IYM
iShares Dow Jones U.S. Consumer Goods Index	IYK
iShares Dow Jones U.S. Consumer Services Index	IYC
iShares Dow Jones U.S. Energy Index	IYE
iShares Dow Jones U.S. Financial Sector Index	IYF
iShares Dow Jones U.S. Financial Services Index	IYG
iShares Dow Jones U.S. Healthcare Index	IYH
iShares Dow Jones U.S. Industrial Index	IYJ
iShares Dow Jones U.S. Real Estate Index	IYR
iShares Dow Jones U.S. Technology Index	IYW
iShares Dow Jones U.S. Telecommunications Index	IYZ
iShares Dow Jones U.S. Transportation Index	IYT
iShares Dow Jones U.S. Utilities Index	IDU
iShares Cohen & Steers Realty Majors Index	ICF
iShares NASDAQ Biotechnology Index	IBB
iShares Goldman Sachs Networking Index	IGN
iShares Goldman Sachs Semiconductor Index	IGW
iShares Goldman Sachs Software Index	IGV
iShares Goldman Sachs Technology Index	IGM

As you may be aware by now, I like Barclays. I like their style funds. As I discuss in the next chapter, I like many of their international funds. As far as bond ETFs, they are the only game in town, and they don't abuse it. As for industry sector funds, however, Barclays simply charges too much. With the exception of the iShares Cohen & Steers Realty Majors Index (REIT) ETF, which carries an expense ratio of 0.35 percent, all the other iShares sector options are 0.50 or (in most cases) 0.60 percent. That's more than double the cost of either the Vanguard ETFs or Select Sector SPDRs.

PowerShares

PowerShares industry sector offerings are as follows:

Name	*Ticker*
PowerShares Dynamic Biotechnology & Genome	PBE
PowerShares Dynamic Building & Construction	PKB
PowerShares Dynamic Energy & Exploration	PXE
PowerShares Dynamic Food & Beverage	PBJ
PowerShares Dynamic Hardware & Consumer Electronics	PHW
PowerShares Dynamic Insurance	PIC
PowerShares Dynamic Leisure & Entertainment	PEJ
PowerShares Dynamic Media	PBS
PowerShares Dynamic Networking	PXQ
PowerShares Dynamic Oil & Gas Services	PXJ
PowerShares Dynamic Pharmaceuticals	PJP
PowerShares Dynamic Retail	PMR
PowerShares Dynamic Semiconductors	PSI
PowerShares Dynamic Software	PSJ
PowerShares Dynamic Telecommunications & Wireless	PTE
PowerShares Dynamic Utilities	PUI
PowerShares Lux Nanotech	PXN
PowerShares Aerospace & Defense	PPA
PowerShares WilderHill Clean Energy	PBW
PowerShares Water Resources	PHO

On the down side, PowerShares charges 0.60 percent: more than twice as much as Vanguard ETFs or Select Sector SPDRs. They are also "dynamic," which means that the indexes are actively managed (someone somewhere is picking stocks). Many investors would see that as a plus; I don't. It means added expense (both upfront and behind the scenes) and a possible loss of tax efficiency. On the up side, however, PowerShares's selection of industry groupings has been innovative, to say the least.

Whereas I wouldn't suggest building an entire portfolio of PowerShares sector ETFs, if you're looking to sprinkle some noncorrelating holdings into an otherwise well-diversified portfolio, PowerShares may have something to offer. I'm especially intrigued with the WilderHill Clean Energy ETF (PBW) and the Water Resources ETF (PHO). Investing in companies that provide alternative fuels and companies that provide filtration and delivery of drinking water, these two ETFs, so far, seem to have sweetly low correlations to the broad market. I'm keeping an eye on them.

Merrill Lynch HOLDRS

Merrill's industry sector offerings are as follows:

Name	*Ticker*
Biotech HOLDRS	BBH
Broadband HOLDRS	BDH
B2B Internet HOLDRS	BHH
Europe HOLDRS	EKH
Internet HOLDRS	HHH
Internet Architecture HOLDRS	IAH
Internet Infrastructure HOLDRS	IIH
Market 2000+ HOLDRS	MKH
Oil Services HOLDRS	OIH
Pharmaceutical HOLDRS	PPH
Regional Bank HOLDRS	RKH
Retail HOLDRS	RTH
Semiconductor HOLDRS	SMH
Software HOLDRS	SWH
Telecom HOLDRS	TTH
Utilities HOLDRS	UTH
Wireless HOLDRS	WMH

Unhealthy investments

Word on the street is that the Securities and Exchange Commission (SEC) is currently sitting on applications for a dozen new ETFs that would track companies involved in treating specific diseases. Soon, if the SEC allows it, you'll be able to invest in the Ferghana-Wellspring (FW) Derma and Wound Care Index Fund, or the FW Metabolic-Endocrine Disorders Index Fund, or the FW Respiratory/Pulmonary Index Fund. The firm has also applied to issue two Cancer Index funds: one for large caps, and another for small.

I can think of no good reason to take a gamble on such small market niches. Should a cure to cancer be found, the company that nails it will probably see its stock skyrocket, for sure. The other however-many companies? Their stocks may well plummet. If you're holding the entire basket, it's a flip of the coin to say which way your investment may head. If you like flipping coins, fine, but please don't bet your retirement money on such foolishness.

If it looks like a duck and it quacks like a duck, it probably is a duck, goes the old saying — which happens to be wrong. Holding Company Depositary Receipts (HOLDRS) look and quack just like ETFs, but technically, they're geese. They're close enough to the target, however, that I include a discussion of HOLDRS in the book. Ready? Here it comes.

You buy HOLDRS just like a stock or an ETF. But there's a difference. You get a basket of stocks — up to 20 — which you actually own. At any point, you can redeem your HOLDRS shares for the stocks themselves. (You can't do that with ETFs.) The price is dirt cheap, but the payment method is a bit complicated. Instead of a management fee, you pay $8 per HOLDR. Assuming you bought 100 shares of a HOLDR with a market price of $100, the annual fee on your $10,000 investment would be $8 (or 0.08 percent). That fee comes out of dividends and cash distributions, and if there are no dividends or cash distributions, you don't pay a thing.

I can't complain about any of the above, but what makes HOLDRS inappropriate investments for most laypeople is their concentration. Some of the HOLDRS have as few as a half dozen stocks. In some cases, such as with the Biotech HOLDRS, two company stocks — Genentech and Amgen — make up almost two-thirds of the value of the entire holdings. That isn't diversification.

Chapter 10

Going International: ETFs Without Borders

. . . .

. . . .

*I*f you were standing on a ship in the middle of the ocean (doesn't matter whether it's the Atlantic or Pacific), and you looked up and squinted real hard, you might see investment dollars sailing overhead. Of all the money that U.S. fund investors added to their portfolios in 2005, an astounding 70 percent went to funds that invest overseas.

The reason for the rush is clear: Simply look at the recent returns of U.S. stocks versus foreign stocks.

As of March 31, 2006, per Morningstar Principia, the three-year annualized return for the SPDR 500 (SPY), an ETF that tracks the S&P 500 Index, was an impressive 16.93 percent. The iShares Dow Jones U.S. Total Market (IYY) had even better gains: 18.53 percent. But those numbers pale in comparison to the 27.57 annualized return of the iShares S&P Europe 350 (IEV), or the 27.80 yearly return of the iShares MSCI Japan Index (EWJ). The average emerging markets fund, the undisputed leader of the pack, returned an astounding 44.50 percent per year.

Yes, investors just love to chase hot money. And usually, I would caution them not to. In this case, however, most Americans had been woefully under-invested abroad, so I see the recent turn as a decidedly good thing. I'm *glad* most investors have finally started to send their dollars abroad — even though they're doing it, by and large, for an entirely wrong reason.

In this chapter, I explain my love for international diversification and reveal how you can accomplish it painlessly with ETFs.

The Ups and Downs of Different Markets around the World

If you expect international stocks to continue to clock such phenomenal returns, you are sure to be disappointed. I do think you can expect that foreign stocks may do better than U.S. stocks in the coming decade or two. (If you want the nitty-gritty of my reasoning, see the section "Why ETFs are a great tool for international investing.") But I certainly wouldn't bet the farm on international stock outperforming. Or U.S. stock. The difference in returns in the future, as it has been in the past, is not likely to be all that extreme.

In all likelihood, international stocks will have their day. U.S. stocks will then come up from behind. Then international stocks will have their day again. And then U.S. stocks will get the jump. This type of horse race has been going on since, oh, long before *Mr. Ed* was on the air. Take a look at Figure 10-1. Note (as depicted by the hills and valleys in the chart) that over the past 30 years, outperformance by U.S. stocks versus non-U.S. stocks has been followed quite regularly by years of underperformance.

The reason to invest abroad isn't primarily to try to outperform the Joneses . . . or the LeBlancs, or the Yamashitas. Rather, the purpose is to diversify your portfolio so as to capture overall stock market gains while tempering risk. You reduce risk whenever you own two or more asset classes that move up and down at different times. Stocks of different nations tend to do exactly that.

Low correlation is the name of the game

Why, you may ask, do you need European and Japanese stocks when you already have all the lovely diversification discussed in past chapters: large, small, value, and growth stocks, and a good mix of industries? (See Chapter 5 if you need a reminder of what these terms mean.) The answer, *mon ami, mi amigo,* is quite simple: You get better diversification when you diversify across borders.

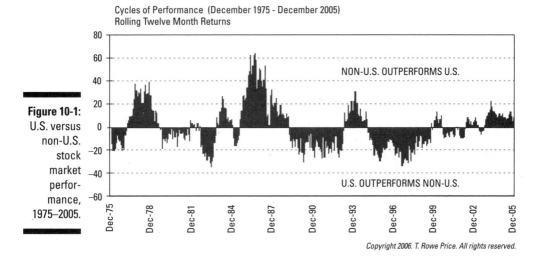

Cycles of Performance (December 1975 - December 2005)
Rolling Twelve Month Returns

Figure 10-1:
U.S. versus non-U.S. stock market performance, 1975–2005.

NON-U.S. OUTPERFORMS U.S.

U.S. OUTPERFORMS NON-U.S.

I'll use several of Barclays iShare ETFs to illustrate my point. Suppose you have a wad of money invested in the iShares S&P 500 Growth Index fund (IVW), and you want to diversify:

✔ If you combine your large growth ETF with the large value counterpart, the iShares S&P 500 Value Index fund (IVE), you find that your two investments have a five-year correlation of 0.92 percent. In other words, 92 percent of the time over the past five years, the funds moved in the same direction. Eight percent of the time, they moved in opposite directions.

✔ If you invest in the iShares S&P Small Cap 600 Growth Index fund (IJT), you find that your two investments have hugged the same performance line roughly 84 percent of the time in the past five years.

✔ If you invest in the iShares S&P Small Cap 600 Value Index fund (IJS), your investments tend to move in synch only 78 percent of time. Not bad. But not great.

But now consider adding some Japanese stock to your original portfolio of large growth stocks. The iShares MSCI Japan Index fund (EWJ) has tended to move in synch with large U.S. growth stocks only about 34 percent of the time. *That's* diversification. And that's what makes international investing a must for a well-balanced portfolio.

Remember what happened to Japan

To just "stay home" would be to exhibit the very same conceit seen among Japanese investors in 1990. If you recall, that's when the dynamic and seemingly all-powerful rising sun slipped and then sank. Japanese investors, holding domestic-stuffed portfolios, bid *sayonara* to two-thirds of their wealth, which, 16 years later, they have yet to fully recapture. It could happen here. Or worse.

Finding Your Best Mix of Domestic and International

About two-thirds of the entire world stock market is now outside of the United States. Should you invest two-thirds of your stock portfolio in foreign ETFs? No, I think that may be overdoing it. Many financial experts say 15 to 25 percent of your stock holdings should be international, which is woefully underdoing it. I say 40 to 50 percent of your stock portfolio should be international — and I feel rather strongly about that range.

Why putting two-thirds of your portfolio in foreign stocks is too much

First, when you invest abroad, you are usually investing in stocks that are denominated in other currencies. I *wish* someone would offer a series of dollar-hedged international ETFs, but such is not the case. And even in the mutual fund world, dollar-hedged international stock funds are hard to find. (The Tweedy, Browne International Value Fund was a good option, but the fund is now closed to new investors.)

Because your foreign ETFs are denominated in either Euros, Yen, or Pounds, they tend to be more volatile than the markets they represent. In other words, if European stock markets fall and the dollar rises (*vis a vis* the Euro) on the same day, your European ETF will fall doubly hard. If, however, the dollar falls on a day that the sun is shining on European stocks, your European ETF will soar.

A pure (and purely silly) currency play

If you would like to bet that the dollar is going to fall and the Euro is going to rise, you can purchase shares of the Rydex Euro Currency Shares ETF (FXE). You may turn out to be right, in which case, you'll make money. But I wouldn't call that successful investing. You made a lucky bet, not an investment. Currencies can move like a trash-can top in a hurricane, and you never know what direction they'll follow. This ETF (and about a dozen other currency ETFs recently to appear on the market) may indeed serve a purpose in the world of commerce (such as manufacturers hedging against currency losses), but for the average investor's portfolio, FXE deserves no allocation. If you follow my advice and invest in international stocks (and perhaps bonds, too, as I discuss in Chapter 12), you will get plenty of exposure to Euros (and Yen and Pounds) already — perhaps too much. You don't need any more.

Over the long-run, individual currencies tend to go up and down. It is unlikely that the dollar (or Euro) would permanently rise or fall to such a degree that it would seriously affect your nest egg. In the short-term, however, such currency fluctuations can be a bit nauseating. (See more on currency in the sidebar "A pure [and purely silly] currency play.")

Second, another risk with going whole hog for foreign stock ETFs is that to a certain extent, your fortunes are tied to those of your home economy. Stocks tend to do best in a heated economy. But in a heated economy, we also tend to see inflation. Because of that correlation between general price inflation and stock inflation, stock investors are generally able to stay ahead of the inflation game. If you were to invest all your money in Europe, and should the economy here take off while the economy there sits on the launch pad, you could potentially be rocketed into poverty.

Third, in the world of ETFs, the really, really good buys are to be had on the domestic side of the offerings. For whatever reason, global and international ETFs are about twice the price as broadly diversified U.S. ETFs. For example, while most Vanguard domestic ETFs carry management expenses of 0.11 or 0.12 percent, their foreign counterparts run anywhere between 0.18 and 0.30 percent. The iShares international ETFs run about 0.60 percent versus many of the domestic offerings that run 0.30 percent or less.

Fourth, part of the reason that international stocks now account for about two-thirds of the world stock market may simply be because they are over-heated. The timing to delve deeply abroad could be all wrong. As you see in the hills and valleys of Figure 10-1, periods in which foreign stocks beat the pants off U.S. stocks are regularly followed by periods in which those foreign-made pants fall to the ground. We may be on the verge of a big U.S. comeback.

Fifth, and finally, certain kinds of stock funds in the United States offer even lower correlation to the rest of the U.S. market than do international stock funds, and I suggest leaving room in your portfolio for some of those funds. I'm talking principally about so-called *market-neutral* funds, which I discuss in Chapter 15.

Why putting one-fifth of your portfolio in foreign stocks is insufficient

Scads of research indicates that an 80-percent-or-so domestic stock/20-percent-or-so foreign stock portfolio is optimal for maximizing return and minimizing risk. But almost all that research defines *domestic stock* as the S&P 500 and *foreign stock* as the MSCI EAFE. The MSCI EAFE is an index of mostly large companies in the developed world. This analysis takes little account of the fact that you are not limiting yourself to the S&P 500 or to the MSCI EAFE. You have the option of adding many asset classes to your portfolio of U.S. stocks. And among your international holdings, you can have developed-world stocks in Europe, Australia, and Japan; emerging market nation stocks; and large foreign stocks and small foreign stocks, maybe broken out into growth and value stocks.

Many investment pros know well — and several have even told me — that they favor a much larger international position than they publicly advocate. Some may be afraid of seeming unpatriotic. Much more prevalent is a lemming-over-the-cliff-cover-my-ass mentality. If I, as your financial advisor, suggest a portfolio that resembles the S&P 500, and your portfolio tanks, you'll feel a bit peeved but you won't hate me. That's because all your friends' and neighbors' portfolios will have sunk as well. Should I give you a portfolio that's 50 percent foreign, and should foreign stocks have a bad year, you'll compare your portfolio to your friends' and neighbors' portfolios, and you'll hate me. You may even sue me.

I wouldn't want that. Neither would most investment professionals. So most err on the side of caution and give you a portfolio that's more S&P 500 and less foreign — for their own protection, not your best interest.

Why ETFs are a great tool for international investing

By mixing and matching domestic and international — with 40 to 50 percent foreign — you will find your investment sweet spot. In Chapter 16, I pull together sample portfolios that use this methodology, using mostly ETFs and a few mutual funds. Time and time again, I've run the numbers through the most sophisticated (and perhaps most expensive) professional portfolio analysis software available, and time and time again, the 40 to 50 percent foreign is where I find the highest returns with minimal risk. Oh yes, this range has worked very well in the real world, too.

Although I try not to make forecasts because the markets are so incredibly unpredictable, I will say that if you were to err on either side of the U.S./foreign division question, I would err on the side of too much foreign. Even though foreign stocks have lately been hot, hot, hot, the world economic and political climate is telling me that the U.S. stock market is on relatively shakier ground. I could give you a long list of reasons (war in Iraq, raging federal deficit, trade deficit, aging population, healthcare crisis), but foremost, what really scares me about the United States is the extent to which it is becoming a nation of haves and have-nots. If history tells us anything, it is that great inequality leads to great dissension and upheaval.

Me, personally, I have fully half of my own stock portfolio in foreign stocks — the vast majority of it held in ETFs.

Not All Foreign Nations are Created Equal

At present, you have more than 60 global and international ETFs from which to choose. (*Global* ETFs may hold U.S. as well as international stocks; *international* ETFs are purely non-U.S.) I'd like you to consider the following half-dozen factors when deciding which ones to invest in:

✔ **What's the correlation?** Certain economies are more closely linked to the U.S. economy, and therefore the stock markets of those countries tend to be more closely linked to Wall Street. Canada, for example, offers limited diversification. Western Europe offers a bit more. For the least amount of correlation, you want Japan (the world's second-largest stock market, by far) or emerging market nations like Russia, Brazil, India, and China.

✔ **How large is the home market?** Although you can invest in individual countries, I wouldn't recommend it. You can't slice and dice your portfolio to include all 35 or so ETFs that represent individual countries (from Belgium to Austria and Singapore to Spain), so why try? Choose large regions in which to invest. (The only exception is Japan, which has such a large stock market that it qualifies, in my mind, as a region.)

✔ **Think style.** If you have a large enough portfolio, consider dividing your international holdings into value and growth, large and small, just as you do with your domestic holdings. Barclays iShares make the value/growth part possible by offering value and growth international options. The large and small part may have to be done outside the ETF universe (using mutual funds) until more small cap international ETFs hit the streets.

✔ **Consider your risk tolerance.** Developed countries (United Kingdom, France, Japan) tend to have less volatile stock markets than do emerging market nations (such as those of Latin America or the Middle East).

✔ **What's the bounce factor?** As with any other kind of investment, you can pretty safely assume that risk and return will have a close relationship over the years. Emerging market ETFs will likely be more volatile but, over the long-run, more rewarding than ETFs that track the stock markets of developed nations. One caveat: Don't assume that countries with fast-growing economies are necessarily those that make for the most profitable investments; see the sidebar "A boom economy doesn't necessarily mean a robust stock market."

✔ **Look to P/E ratios.** How expensive is the stock compared to the earnings you're buying? You may ask yourself this question when buying a company stock, and it's just as valid a question when buying a nation's stocks. In general, a lower P/E ratio is more indicative of promising returns than is a high P/E ratio.

Using ETFs as our proxies for world markets, we find that the Vanguard Total Stock Market ETF (VTI) currently has a P/E of about 18; the Vanguard European ETF (VGK) has a P/E of about 16; the Vanguard Pacific ETF (VPL) has a P/E of approximately 20; and the Vanguard Emerging Market ETF (VWO) has a P/E of roughly 13.5. The Emerging Market ETF is therefore the "value stock" of the world, with European stocks second on the value list.

A boom economy doesn't necessarily mean a robust stock market

You would think that a fast-growing economy would be the place of places to invest. And yet there is more to stock returns than the growth of a national economy. (Just ask those investors who poured money into China several years ago.) In fact, the mind-blowing conclusion of a handful of recent studies is that the reverse is true: If you look at the stock returns of various national markets over the past 100 years, you actually find an *inverse* relationship. *Slow-growing* economies (such as India's, whose stock market has lately left China's in the dust) generally make for better stock investments!

Several possible explanations exist. Some people say that rapid economic growth is attributable more to small, entrepreneurial businesses rather than to larger, publicly held corporations. Another explanation is that the fruits of economic growth may or may not go to shareholders — and often don't. Those fruits may also go to labor, or consumers, or (the United States is a prime example) top executives and option-holders. Another possible explanation is that the prices of stocks in fast-growing economies (just like domestic growth stocks) often start off overpriced due to higher-than-reasonable expectations. Stocks of slow-growing economies (just like value stocks) may tend to be underpriced.

The moral of the story is to spread your investment dollars around the world. Don't think you can pick countries that will outperform by using projected growth rates as your crystal ball.

Choosing the Best International ETFs for Your Portfolio

Although I'm (obviously) a huge fan of international investing, and I believe that ETFs are the best way to achieve that end, there are only a dozen or so foreign ETFs that I think really fit the bill for most portfolios. Following are my favorites, along with explanations of why I like them.

Note that I've split them up into three major regions: European, Pacific region, and emerging markets. For most people's portfolios, a reasonable split of your foreign stock holdings would be something in the ballpark of 40/40/20, with 40 percent going to Europe (England, France, Germany, Switzerland), 40 percent to the developed Pacific region (mostly Japan, with a smattering of Australia and Singapore), and 20 percent to the emerging market nations (Brazil, Russia, Turkey, South Africa, Mexico).

A special word on BLDRS

The BLDRS indexes, restricted to American Depository Receipts that trade on the NASDAQ, have attracted some criticism for their apparent randomness. In a way, the criticisms are right. Building a European ETF out of only ADRs that trade on the NASDAQ is a little like putting together a football team of men whose first names start with "R." But my feeling is that all indexes are somewhat random. Some are weighted according to cap size; others are equally weighted; yet others are weighted by number of shares outstanding. In point of fact, a team of football players named Robert, Rick, and Raul are not necessarily going to be any better or worse than a team with Clay, Dave, and Sam. And so it is with BLDRS: Their performance has been pretty much on a par with the other ETF options of the same regions.

Three brands to choose from

All the ETFs I discuss here belong to three ETF families: Vanguard ETFs; Barclays iShares; and BLDRS (pronounced "builders"), a small product line issued by NASDAQ and the Bank of New York.

BLDRS stands for "Baskets of Listed Depositary Receipts," which is a very fancy way of saying "foreign stocks that trade on American stock exchanges." Vanguard and Barclays iShares foreign ETFs are also made up mostly of Depositary Receipts (often referred to as ADRs — the A is for "American") but may hold other foreign stocks as well. For you, the investor, these nuances don't matter much, if at all.

For more information on any of the international ETFs I discuss below, keep the following contact information handy:

- ✔ **Vanguard:** www.vanguard.com; 1-877-662-7447
- ✔ **Barclays iShares:** www.ishares.com; 1-800-474-2737
- ✔ **BLDRS:** www.bldrsfunds.com; 1-888-627-3837

European stock ETFs: From the Northern Sea to the shores of the Mediterranean

Europe boasts the oldest, most established stock markets in the world: Netherlands, 1611; Germany, 1685; and the United Kingdom, 1698. Relative to the United States and Japan, European stocks, as a whole, are seemingly low-priced (low P/E ratio). Europe's strengths include political stability, an educated workforce, and the recent confederation of national economies making for the world's largest single market. Europe's great weakness is a seemingly stagnant high rate of unemployment with a very rapidly aging population.

Vanguard European ETF (VGK)

Indexed to: Morgan Stanley Capital International (MSCI) Europe Index, which tracks approximately 600 large cap companies in 18 European nations

Expense ratio: 0.18 percent

Top five country holdings: United Kingdom, France, Germany, Switzerland, Italy

Russell's review: This ETF has everything going for it: low cost, good diversification, and tax efficiency. You can't go wrong (unless the European stock market falters, which, of course, could happen). The mix of both many nations and currencies (Euro, British Pound, Swiss Franc, Swedish Krona) gives this fund an especially good balance and an especially good way to help protect your portfolio from any single-country (or currency) collapse.

BLDRS Europe 100 ADR (ADRU)

Indexed to: The Bank of New York Europe 100 ADR Index, a market-weighted basket of 100 European market-based ADRs trading on the NASDAQ, representing a total of 15 countries

Expense ratio: 0.30 percent

Top five country holdings: United Kingdom, France, Germany, Switzerland, Netherlands

Russell's review: Not as diverse as the Vanguard European ETF, but with 100 stocks, plenty diverse enough. The yearly expense ratio is about midway between the Vanguard European offering and the iShares Europe offering. All told, the BLDRS Europe is a good choice, although it may not be the best (that would be Vanguard). By the way, don't assume that because this ETF contains only NASDAQ listings it is in any way a technology-laden fund. Far from it. Industry-wise, the top three components of this ETF are oil and gas companies, banks, and pharmaceutical firms.

Make wheat, not war

In the stock market Olympics of the past century (1900–2000), the overall winner in terms of real stock market return (return *after* inflation — the kind of return that really counts) was . . . drumroll . . . the socialist, Volvo-producing, snow-covered nation of Sweden. Sweden's overall rate of return from beginning to end of century was 7.6 percent. In second place was Australia with 7.5 percent. In third place was South Africa with 6.8 percent. The United States came in fourth with 6.7 percent, and Canada was fifth with 6.4 percent. At the bottom of the world barrel, the Belgian equity market returned only 2.5 percent, with Italy, Germany, Spain, and France dragging closely behind with respective 100-year annualized post-inflation returns of 2.7, 3.6, 3.6, and 3.8 percent.

Here's the conclusion of the authors who pulled these numbers together, a group of distinguished professors from the London Business School: "Generally speaking, the worst performing equity markets were associated with countries which either lost major wars, or were most ravaged by international or civil wars." The best performers, point out professors Dimson, Marsh, and Staunton, were "resource rich countries."

iShares S&P Europe 350 (IEV)

Indexed to: Standard & Poor's Europe 350 Index, a collection of 350 large cap companies in 16 European countries

Expense ratio: 0.60 percent

Top five country holdings: United Kingdom, France, Germany, Switzerland, Spain

Russell's review: I really like iShares domestic offerings, and their foreign ETFs aren't bad products. Not at all. The diversification is excellent. The indexes make sense. The tax efficiency is top notch. I only wish the darned things didn't cost so much. At roughly 3.3 times the cost of the Vanguard European offering, IEV just isn't, I'm afraid, anything to write home about.

Pacific region stock ETFs: From Mt. Fuji to that big island with the kangaroos

The nations of the Pacific, led by Japan, have evidenced an astonishing comeback in recent years. Japan's economic and political troubles of late seem to be healing. With the rapid growth of China as the world's apparent soon-to-be largest consumer, surrounding nations may bask in economic glory. On the other hand, the threat of North Korea, the danger of avian flu, and the tension between China and Taiwan loom like black clouds over the region.

Vanguard Pacific ETF (VPL)

Indexed to: Morgan Stanley Capital International (MSCI) Pacific Index, which follows roughly 550 companies in five Pacific region nations

Expense ratio: 0.18 percent

Top five country holdings: Japan, Australia, Hong Kong, Singapore, New Zealand

Russell's review: The cost can't be beat. And 550 companies certainly allows for good diversification. As with all Vanguard funds, tax efficiency is tops. Japan — the world's second-largest stock market — makes up 77 percent of this fund, a bit more than the BLDRS Asia 50. I have a slight preference for VPL over all other Pacific options.

BLDRS Asia 50 ADR (ADRA)

Indexed to: The Bank of New York Asia 50 ADR Index, a market-weighted basket of 50 Asian market-based ADRs trading on the NASDAQ, representing a total of 8 countries (although Japan accounts for nearly two-thirds of the money pot)

Expense ratio: 0.30 percent

Top five country holdings: Japan, Australia, Korea, Taiwan, China

Russell's review: The cost is higher than Vanguard's Pacific ETF, and you're tapping into fewer companies. Nonetheless, 50 companies isn't bad diversification. This fund also gives a bit more weight to non-Japan stock markets, which may be a good thing. All in all, ADRA is a good investment, although if you bent my arm to choose, I'd probably choose Vanguard.

iShares MSCI Japan (EWJ)

Indexed to: MSCI Japan Index, representing approximately 280 of Japan's largest companies

Expense ratio: 0.59 percent

Top five country holdings: Just Japan here

Russell's review: For the life of me, I can't understand why Barclays doesn't offer a Pacific region ETF. If you want the equivalent of either the BLDRS or Vanguard Pacific ETFs, you need to buy two iShares ETFs: the MSCI Japan and the MSCI Pacific ex-Japan (EPP). That's a doable option for larger portfolios, but with a cost ratio of several times that of Vanguard's, I'm not sure I see the point.

Emerging market stock ETFs: Well, we hope that they're emerging

When economists feel optimistic, they call them "emerging market" nations. But these same countries are also sometimes referred to as the Third World, or, even more to the point, "poor countries." The recent astonishing returns of emerging market stocks are due largely to sharp increases in the price of commodities, such as oil, which come largely from these nations. But commodity prices fluctuate greatly. And political unrest, corruption, and over-population, as well as serious environmental challenges, plague much of this part of the world.

On the other hand, emerging market stocks are perhaps still (despite their recent rise) underpriced. Many of the economies (such as China's) are growing rapidly. And — perhaps most importantly — these countries have many children, children who will grow up to be workers, consumers, and perhaps even investors.

Vanguard Emerging Market ETF (VWO)

Indexed to: The Select Emerging Markets Index, a custom index of roughly 750 large cap companies in 18 emerging market nations

Expense ratio: 0.30 percent

Top five country holdings: Korea, Taiwan, Brazil, South Africa, China

Russell's review: There's no better way that I know to capture the potential growth of emerging market stocks than through VWO. The cost is the lowest in the pack (equal to the BLDRS option), and the diversity of investments is more than adequate.

BLDRS Emerging Markets 50 ADR (ADRE)

Indexed to: The Bank of New York Emerging Markets 50 ADR Index, a market-weighted basket of 50 emerging market-based ADRs trading on the NASDAQ, representing a total of 11 countries

Expense ratio: 0.30 percent

Top five country holdings: Brazil, Korea, Mexico, China, Taiwan

Russell's review: Yeah, 50 companies falls way short of Vanguard's 750, but 50 companies is really enough to give you pretty good diversification. I have no problem whatsoever recommending this ETF as a way to tap into the emerging markets, although I do have a wee preference, once again, for Vanguard.

iShares MSCI Emerging Markets (EEM)

Indexed to: MSCI Emerging Markets Index, a basket of approximately 270 large companies in 20 emerging-market nations

Expense ratio: 0.75 percent

Top five country holdings: South Korea, South Africa, Brazil, Taiwan, China

Russell's review: Good fund. Good company. Good index. If it weren't more than twice the price of the other options in this area, I'd jump to recommend it.

iShares value and growth: Two special ETFs for style investing abroad

Studies show that the same *value premium* — the tendency for value stocks to outperform growth stocks — that seemingly exists here in the United States exists around the world. (See the full value premium discussion in Chapters 6 and 8.) Therefore, I suggest a mild tilt toward value in your international stock portfolio, as well as in your domestic.

You can accomplish this tilt easily by allotting a small percentage of your international holdings to the iShares MSCI EAFE Value Index (EFV). For smaller portfolios with limited room to slice and dice, an investor may want to invest part of her holdings in EFV and part in the iShares MSCI EAFE Growth Index (EFG). The division into regions can come as the portfolio

---

A word on foreign taxes

If you are buying both a foreign and a domestic ETF, and you have room enough for only one in your IRA, Roth IRA, or other tax-advantaged retirement plan, choose the domestic fund and plug the foreign fund into your non-retirement account. That's because many foreign countries will slap you with a withholding tax on your dividends. Typically, such a tax may be 15 percent. (If you invest, say, $30,000 in a foreign fund with a dividend yield of 3 percent, you'll be losing $135 a year to foreign taxes.) If the foreign ETF is in a non-retirement account, your brokerage house will likely supply you with a year-end statement noting the foreign tax paid. You can then write that amount off in full against your U.S. taxes. (See line 43 of your friendly 1040.) If the foreign fund is held in your retirement account, however, no year-end statement, no write-off. You eat the loss.

---

grows. EAFE, by the way, stands for "Europe, Australia, and Far East" — in other words, the developed nations outside of the United States and Canada.

iShares MSCI EAFE Value Index (EFV)

Indexed to: MSCI EAFE Value Index, which is made up of approximately 535 large value companies in 21 developed-world nations, with about half the companies in either Japan or the United Kingdom

Expense ratio: 0.40 percent

Top five country holdings: Japan, United Kingdom, France, Switzerland, Germany

Russell's review: It's the only fund of its kind, and I'm greatly appreciative that it exists. My only beef is that at present, about 42 percent of the companies are concentrated in one industry: financials.

iShares MSCI EAFE Growth Index (EFG)

Indexed to: MSCI EAFE Growth Index, which is made up of approximately 550 large value companies in 22 developed-world nations, with about half the companies in either Japan or the United Kingdom

Expense ratio: 0.40 percent

Top five country holdings: Japan, United Kingdom, France, Switzerland, Germany

Russell's review: Like EFV, this international growth fund is the only one of its kind. I'm grateful for its existence, and I'm grateful that Barclays hasn't taken advantage of its monopoly and has kept the expense ratio reasonable.

Small cap international: Yes, you want it

Small cap international stocks have even less correlation to the U.S. stock market than do larger foreign stocks. The reason is simple: If the U.S. economy takes a swan dive, it will seriously hurt conglomerates — Nestle, Toyota, and British Petroleum, for example — that serve the U.S. market, regardless of where their corporate headquarters are located. A fall in the U.S. economy and U.S. stock market is less likely to affect smaller foreign corporations that sell mostly within national borders.

In the absence of a small international ETF until recently, I have been using small and mid cap international mutual funds from Fidelity, T. Rowe Price, Vanguard, Third Avenue, and Tweedy Browne. I discuss some of these funds further in Chapter 15 where I talk about the role of non-ETFs in your investment mix, and again in Chapter 16 where I present model portfolios. Given the recent popularity of these funds, a good number are closed to new investors. Take heart: I'm sure we'll see the introduction of a good number of small cap international ETFs before long.

For the time being, the only ETF offering that qualifies as small cap international is from WisdomTree. The WisdomTree International SmallCap Dividend Fund (DLS) is certainly a viable candidate to fill this slot in a portfolio. Because it's brand new, carries a fairly high expense ratio for an ETF (0.58 percent), and emphasizes dividends, I'm less than crazy about this fund. But for now, it may be one of the best options.

Regardless of the investment vehicle you choose, I suggest that a good chunk of your international stock holdings — perhaps as much as 50 percent, if you can stomach a lot of volatility — go to small and mid cap holdings. Future editions of this book will review and discuss whatever small cap international stock ETFs exist at that point.

Chapter 11

Specialized Stock ETFs

· ·

In This Chapter

▶ Unearthing some facts about socially responsible investing

▶ Determining the potential payoff of dividend funds

▶ Watching out for the taxman when those dividends come rolling in

▶ Introducing an opportunity to invest in initial public offerings

▶ Assessing funds that thrive when the market falters

▶ Considering a leveraged fund

· ·

*I*n this chapter, I introduce a few stock ETFs that don't fit into any of the categories I discuss in previous chapters. They are neither growth nor value, large nor small. They are not industry sector funds, nor are they international. If ETFs were ice cream, the funds presented here would not represent chocolate and vanilla, but rather, the outliers on the Baskin Robbins' menu: Turtle Cheesecake, Tiramisu, No Sugar Added Chocolate Chip, Pink Bubblegum, and Wild 'N Reckless (a swirl of green apple, blue raspberry, and fruit punch sherbets).

Wild 'N Reckless? I wouldn't say any of these funds are necessarily wild or reckless, but nonetheless, they are stock funds, and anything related to stocks — trust me on this — carries risk. That being said, I present you with two ETFs that bill themselves as socially responsible, a slew of funds that focus on companies paying high dividends (they're especially hot at the moment), one that invests only in corporations that have relatively recently begun selling shares to the public, and a few funds that go up when everything else is going down (don't get too excited; it isn't as good as it sounds). I also describe one hypothetical specialized stock ETF (see the sidebar "The author's pipedream") that I wish someone would introduce.

Socially Responsible Investing for a Better World

An increasing number of people — both individuals and institutions — are investing using some kind of moral compass. The investments chosen are screened not only for potential profitability but for social factors as well. Some screens, for example, attempt to eliminate all companies that profit from tobacco or weapons of mass destruction. Other screens try to block out the worst polluting companies or companies that use child labor in countries that have no effective child labor laws.

The total amount of money invested in socially screened portfolios (which include more than 100 mutual funds, certain state and city pension funds, union and church monies, some university endowments, and — count 'em — *two* ETFs) has grown from about $1 trillion in 1997 to over $2 trillion today.

Many of the funds that call themselves socially responsible not only invest, but they also use their financial muscle to lobby companies to become better world citizens. The movement seems to have had some impact on corporate America, most notably by pushing certain auto, oil, and utility companies to research ways to reduce emissions of greenhouse gasses. Other, smaller victories include a nearly nationwide ban on mercury thermometers and a recent commitment from a major tech company to start a recycling program.

Investments to help you sleep well at night

Whereas investing in a socially responsible mutual fund or ETF may do the world some good, the question remains whether it will do your portfolio any good. Proponents believe that nice companies, like nice salespeople, will naturally be more successful over time. Skeptics of investing with a social screen not only scoff at the notion of good karma; they say that limiting a fund manager's investment choices could lead to *lower* performance.

So far, no solid evidence exists that either side is right — or wrong. Over the past decade or so, the performance of socially responsible mutual funds has been, as a group, very similar to that of all other mutual funds.

What about the specific performance of the two ETFs I list here? Well, neither has been around long enough for its performance record to count for much. And, of course, performance is only one factor I look at when deciding whether to recommend an ETF.

Your two ETF choices

The two ETFs to use social screens introduced on the market thus far are as different as night and day. The iShares Select Social Index Fund (KLD) is a broad-based large cap blend (both value and growth) fund. The PowerShares WilderHill Clean Energy Fund (PBW) is a narrow industry sector fund *and* a style fund (overwhelmingly small growth) and — whew — something of a global fund as well. (Approximately 16 percent of the holdings are non-U.S.)

Unlike my reviews of other kinds of ETFs (found in Chapters 5 through 10), I review these two together. That way, I avoid repeating myself, for my feelings about both are the same: I'm absolutely, positively, conclusively ambivalent. My double-shot review follows a brief synopsis of the two funds.

The iShares Select Social Index Fund (KLD)

Based on the KLD Select Social Index, the fund starts with the 300 or so largest U.S. corporations. Based on each company's record for social justice and environmental performance, it overweights purportedly ethical companies and underweights supposedly unethical ones while making sure that all industries other than tobacco are represented. (Tobacco is totally snuffed.)

The resulting ETF looks like this:

Expense ratio: 0.50 percent

Top five companies: Wells Fargo, Johnson & Johnson, Microsoft, General Mills, American Express

Top five industries: Financials, technology, healthcare, consumer goods, industrials

The PowerShares WilderHill Clean Energy Fund (PBW)

Based on WilderHill Clean Energy Index, the fund tracks three dozen companies that invest in solar energy, windmills, hydrogen fuel cells, rechargeable batteries, and other forms of environment-friendly power.

The resulting ETF looks like this:

Expense ratio: 0.60 percent

Top five companies (which you've probably never heard of): Active Power, IMPCO Technologies, Ultralife Batteries, Mechanical Technology, Distributed Energy Systems

Top five countries: United States, Canada, United Kingdom, Japan, China

Russell's double-shot review: If you decide that you want to be a socially responsible investor, you have many choices: There are now 110 mutual funds that invest with some social screen. Some, like the iShares Select Social Index Fund, cover a large swatch of the market. Others, like the PowerShares WilderHill Clean Energy Fund, are more narrowly focused. The two ETFs, although fairly pricey by ETF standards, cost less than half of what the average socially conscious mutual fund would cost. And that is certainly a good thing. On the other hand, neither Barclays nor PowerShares promises the same kind of shareholder activism that you get with some of the more aggressive mutual fund companies. And that may lessen these ETFs' desirability in your eyes. The iShares Select fund is also quite liberal in its definition of "socially responsible" and makes many compromises in its selection of stocks. Certain socially conscious mutual funds have much tougher screening criteria.

From a strictly economic/diversification point of view, I like to see large cap stocks split distinctly into value and growth. With the iShares Select Social Index Fund, you get a mushier exposure to large caps. The PowerShares option, again from a strictly economic/diversification point of view, offers up a small sliver of the economy and, as such, involves considerable risk. On the other hand, all energy stocks — both clean and dirty — have lately shown a delightful lack of correlation to the market as a whole. I would caution you, should you want to sink any money into energy right now, that the sector has been one of the hottest, and what goes up sharply in the world of investments often comes down just as sharply. Be careful!

For more information on socially responsible investing

If you want to invest for a better world and a better portfolio, I suggest you do additional research. One person's idea of socially responsible may be very different than another's. What works for one portfolio may not work for another. There's a ton of information on the Web site of the Social Investment Forum: www.socialinvest.org.

Dividend Funds: The Search for Steady Money

The check is in the mail. When you know it's true (it isn't always), there are perhaps no sweeter words in the English language. To many investors, the thought of regular payments is a definite turn-on. And so, willing to oblige, the financial industry of late has been churning out "high dividend" funds — both mutual funds and ETFs — like there's no tomorrow.

The idea behind these funds is simple enough: They attempt to cull together the stocks of companies that are either issuing high dividends, have high dividend growth rates, or hold forth the promise of future high dividends.

Your ETF options

On the ETF side, the oldest and largest of the dividend funds is the iShares Dow Jones Select Dividend Index Fund (DVY). But you can also go with the SPDR Dividend (SDY), the Vanguard Dividend Appreciation ETF (VIG), the First Trust Morningstar Dividend Leaders Index Fund (FDL), or any of a bevy of PowerShares selections. The PowerShares dividend ETFs include the PowerShares Dividend Achievers Portfolio (PFM), the PowerShares High Yield Equity Dividend Achievers Portfolio (PEY), and the PowerShares High Growth Rate Dividend Achievers Portfolio (PHJ).

Why *three* PowerShares domestic dividend ETFs? The first one (PFM) "seeks to identify a diversified group of dividend paying companies." The second one (PEY) "seeks to deliver high current dividend income and capital appreciation." And the third (PHJ) "seeks to identify companies with the highest ten-year annual dividend growth rate."

If that weren't a big enough choice, you could also go with the PowerShares International Dividend Achievers Portfolio (PID), which "seeks international companies that have increased their annual dividend for five or more consecutive fiscal years." And if *that* weren't enough choice, the newest kid on the ETF block, WisdomTree, offers 20 *other* high dividend funds . . . with every wrinkle imaginable.

In a way, seeking dividends makes sense. In another, larger way, the logic is loopy. Let me explain . . .

Promise of riches or smoke and mirrors?

Dividends! Dividends! On the face of it, they look like free money. But nothing in life is quite so simple. Here are the typical arguments for buying a high dividend fund, along with my retort to each:

- ✔ **Argument for dividends #1: Steady money is just like honey.** Huh? Are you crazy, Russell? Who in his right mind wouldn't want dividends? Why even ask? A stock that pays dividends is *obviously* more valuable than a stock that doesn't pay dividends. If I buy a high dividend ETF, every month, my account balance will grow.

  Retort: Suppose you own an individual share of stock in the McDummy Corporation (ticker MCDM), and MCDM issues a dividend of $1. The market price of your one share of MCDM, as a rule, will fall by $1 as soon as the McDummy Corporation sends out the dividend. That's because the dividend comes from the McDummy's cash reserves, and as those cash reserves diminish, the value of the McDummy Corporation diminishes (just as it would if it gave away, say, 100 plastic pink flamingoes from the front lawn of its corporate headquarters, or any other asset for that matter). As the value of the company diminishes, so too does the value of its shares. And the very same holds true for a basket of stocks held in an ETF.

- ✔ **Argument for dividends #2: They lower my tax hit.** But . . . but . . . Suppose I need a steady stream of income? Isn't it better that I rely on dividends, which are generally taxed at 15 percent, than rely on bond or CD interest, which is taxed at my higher income-tax rate?

  First retort: First, if you need a steady stream of income, nothing is stopping you from creating *artificial dividends* by selling off any security you like. You may pay capital gains tax, but that will be no higher than the tax on dividends. In the end, whether you pull $1,000 from your account in the form of recently issued dividends, or whether you pull $1,000 from the sale of security, you are withdrawing the same amount. And what if one month you find you don't need the income? With a high dividend ETF, you need to pay the tax regardless, but with a non high dividend yielding ETF, you may pay no tax whatsoever. Of course, with an ETF, you pay a commission to buy and sell, so if you're regularly dipping in for small amounts of money, you may not even want an ETF in the first place.

  Second retort: The special dividend tax break is set to expire at the end of 2008. Then dividends will be taxed at ordinary income rates unless Congress extends the break.

Third retort: If you're really concerned about taxes, maybe you should be investing in tax-free municipal bonds.

✔ **Argument for dividends #3: Taxes, what taxes?** Russell, what gives? If I invest in an ETF, I won't have to worry about taxes because, as you've told us all along, ETFs are incredibly tax efficient.

Retort: ETFs are heads and shoulders above most mutual funds when it comes to tax efficiency, but that tax efficiency is aimed at reducing capital gains, not tax on dividends. An ETF can't do a whole lot to lessen the tax hit from dividends. ETF or mutual fund, you'll pay.

✔ **Argument for dividends #4: It's a new world!** Russell, you sound like a stick in the mud. This is an exciting new development in the world of investments. These high dividend paying funds will kick ass, you'll see.

Retort: New development? Really? Equity-income funds have been around for years and years, and they haven't exactly set the world on fire. And consider the ages-old *Dogs of the Dow* strategy. Many people have believed that if every year you purchase the ten highest-paying dividend stocks in the Dow (the so-called *Dogs*), you can rack up serious returns. The strategy has been well-studied, and it clearly isn't as powerful as the hype. The Dogs do seem to have some bark, but no more so than any other similarly sized and similarly volatile stocks.

✔ **Argument for dividends #5: Don't you read history?** Over the course of history, Russell, much of the stock market's returns have come from dividends. You should know that.

First retort: Yeah, so? During the longest bull market in history — the 1990s — stock market returns were running double digits a year, and very little was being shelled out in dividends. A company that isn't paying dividends is either investing its cash in operations or buying back its own stock. Either way, shareholders stand to gain.

Second retort: If you look at high dividend paying sectors of the economy — utilities is a perfect example — you don't necessarily find that those sectors beat the broader market over long periods of time. The utilities sector certainly hasn't.

✔ **Argument for dividends #6: Dividends offer protection.** Stocks that pay high dividends are going to be less risky than stocks that don't. Those dividends create a floor, at least a psychological floor. High dividend paying stocks cannot become worthless.

Retort: You would think that high dividend paying stock ETFs would likely fall less precipitously should there be a major downturn in the stock market. On the face of it, your argument seems logical. In the real world, however, studies of high dividend paying stocks reveal that they actually tend to be somewhat *more* volatile than the broad market. Go figure. Besides, if your main goal is to temper risk, you have other, probably more effective, ways of doing that. (See Chapter 12 on bonds.)

✔ **Argument for dividends #7: But still, it can't hurt.** All right, I concede, maybe these funds aren't the greatest thing since white bread. Still, can it hurt to buy one?

✔ **Retort:** Look, I don't *hate* these funds. Far from it. If you want to buy one, buy one. Put it into your retirement account, if there's room in there, and you won't even have to worry about any tax on dividends. But don't assume that you're going to beat the broad market over the long-haul. And know that you are buying a fund that is mostly large value stocks, typically within just a handful of industries (notably financial services, pharmaceuticals, and utilities). Your risk may be greater than you think.

✔ **Final argument: I want my dividends!** I don't care what you say. I'm going to buy a high dividend ETF.

✔ **Final retort:** Fine. Consider the Vanguard option (VIG) or the SPDR (SDY). At 0.28 percent and 0.30 percent, they are considerably less expensive than the competition. The iShares option (DVY) isn't too bad, either, with expenses of 0.40 percent.

I'd steer clear of the PowerShares options. The expense ratios — 0.50 percent — are problematic enough. And quite frankly, having to choose between "high dividend paying companies," "high current dividend income and capital appreciation," and "companies with the highest ten-year annual dividend growth rate" is enough to give me a big, fat headache. WisdomTree's many, many dividend offerings, which tend to be even more pricey than PowerShares, make my head explode.

By the way, don't forget Real Estate Investment Trusts (REITs); several ETF REIT options exists, which tend to pay *twice* the amount of dividends as any of the high dividend ETFs. (Plenty more on REITs in Chapter 13.)

Last but not least, if you're not going to be using that dividend money right away, make sure you have your ETF with a brokerage house that will reinvest your dividends without charging you a commission. The vast majority will do so, but not all.

A Fund for Initial Public Offerings: Google It, and You'll Discover FPX

Want to take a real joyride? In April 2006, First Trust Advisors introduced the First Trust IPOX-100 Index Fund (FPX). You can now invest in an ETF that, according to the prospectus, tracks the 100 "largest, typically best perform-ing, and most liquid initial public offerings ["IPOs"] in the . . . U.S." Just prior to the introduction of the fund, the index on which it is based clocked a three-year annualized return of 33.74 percent. Needless to say, with that kind of return, this new ETF got the attention of a good number of investors. But I wonder what's in store for them in the future.

A brief recent history of IPOs

Yes, when times are good for small and mid cap stocks, as they were in the three years prior to the launch of FPX, times are typically very good for IPOs. But when times are bad . . . The index suffered terribly during the bear market of 2000, 2001, and 2002, with annual returns, respectively, of –24.55 percent, –22.77 percent, and –21.64 percent. (If you started with $10,000, you would have been left with a rather pathetic $4,566.04.)

A brief longer-term history of IPOs

But what about the long-term performance of IPOs? Jay Ritter, a professor of Finance at the University of Florida, keeps studious records on the returns of IPOs, and he asserts that collectively, they haven't done all that well *vis a vis* the larger market. But he hastens to add that the long-term performance is dragged down by the smaller IPOs, and that larger IPOs — the ones included in the IPOX ETF — as a group have modestly outperformed the market, albeit with greater volatility.

Indeed. As the IPOX Index now stands, tech stocks make up 25 percent of the roster, and the two top companies — Google and Viacom — together make up 20 percent of the index. Do you really want that kind of volatility in your portfolio, on top of an expense ratio of 0.60 percent?

You may, yes, especially if you buy the arguments of some IPO proponents who say that recent laws (particularly the Sarbanes-Oxley Act, otherwise known as the Public Company Accounting Reform and Investor Protection Act of 2002) are likely to boost overall IPO performance. But if you are inclined to take a gamble, please don't do it with any more money than you can afford to lose, and consider waiting a while. Buying into IPOX now, after three glorious years of returns, may not be the wisest timing.

Funds That Thrive When the Market Takes a Dive

In June 2006, an outfit called ProShares introduced eight new ETFs. Four of the eight are designed to *short* the market. That is, these ETFs are designed to go up when the market goes down. Your selection of ProShares includes the Short QQQ fund (PSQ), which is betting against the NASDAQ-100; the Short S&P500 (SH), the Short MidCap400 (MYY), and the Short Dow30 (DOG).

DOG indeed. If I were to devise a ticker for the entire lot, it would be HUH?

Entering an upside down world

In other parts of this book, I talk about correlation and how wonderful it is when you can find two asset classes that go up and down at different times. Heck, it would seem that the ProShares Short funds are the ideal addition to a portfolio. Talk about diversification! Ah, but there's one little hitch: When you diversify, you want to find various asset classes that move out of synch but that are all moving upward, making money for you. ProShares are destined to go downward.

Sure, sometimes stocks decline. But over the long-run, they rise. They must rise. If they didn't, we wouldn't have a stock market. Who would invest? So over the long-run, you would expect ProShares Short funds to lose money. The only way to make money with these funds is to time the market right: to jump in just as the market is about to dive and then pull out before the market goes up. Good luck! Market timing, I'm not the first to say, is a fool's game.

Boasting a track record like none other

Don't take my word for anything I said in the previous section. Just check the long-term performance records of ProFunds, the mutual funds produced by the very same people who produce ProShares. The company's so-called *Inverse* mutual funds and the company's Short ETFs are very similar.

Ready for some depressing numbers? See `www.profunds.com/prices/performance.asp`.

Here, for example, are the annualized return figures for the ProFunds UltraShort OTC mutual fund, which has been proudly torturing investors since June 2, 1998:

- ✔ One year: –1.08 percent
- ✔ Five years: –21.04 percent
- ✔ Ten years: –15.63 percent
- ✔ Since inception: –36.58 percent

Sure, over the next 10 or 20 years, the stock market could tumble, and you can make money with inverse or short funds such as you can get with ProFunds or ProShares. But the odds are heavily, heavily stacked against you. And to play the game will cost you: All the ProShares carry an expense ratio of 0.95 percent, making them just about the most expensive ETFs on the market.

Funds That Double the Thrill of Investing (for Better or Worse)

The other four ETFs introduced by ProFunds appeal not to market pessimists but to extreme optimists. These are leveraged funds that include the Ultra QQQ (QLD), which "seeks daily investment results, before fees and expenses, that correspond to twice (200%) the daily performance of the NASDAQ-100 Index," and the similarly designed Ultra S&P500 (SSO), Ultra MidCap400 (MVV), and Ultra Dow30 (DDM).

You think the market is going to soar? These funds, which use futures and other derivatives to magnify market returns, promise to make you twice the money you would make by simply investing in the NASDAQ-100, the S&P 500, the S&P MidCap 400, or the Dow. Of course, you'll have to accept twice the volatility. It seems like a fair bet. But it really isn't.

Suppose you invest in the Ultra S&P500 (SSO), as opposed to, say, the SPDR 500 (SPY). On a daily basis, if the underlying index goes up, your investment will go up twice as much. If the underlying index goes down, your investment will go down twice as much. Clearly the volatility is double. But let's look at the potential returns, as well.

The SPY is going to cost you 0.10 percent in operating expenses. The SSO is going to cost you 0.95 percent. That's a difference of 0.85 percent a year, or $425 on a $50,000 investment (which will be compounded yearly). You can expect about 1.8 percent in dividends on SPY. Since SSO invests largely in futures, you aren't going to get much in dividends — probably less than half. That's a difference, on a $50,000 investment, of about another $450 or more. Already you've lost ($425 + $450) $875, regardless of which way the market goes.

And again, let's look at the long-term track record. ProShares Ultra funds, like their Short funds, have mutual fund equivalents (issued by the very same company) that have been in existence for many years. The UltraBull Fund, for example, has been around since November 27, 1997. Just like SSO, it promises you twice the punch of the S&P 500 and operates in much the same way. Let's see how well it has done.

Annualized return figures for the UltraBull Fund are as follows:

- ✔ One year: 9.32 percent
- ✔ Five years: 17.53 percent
- ✔ Ten years: –4.11 percent
- ✔ Since inception: –0.62 percent

How does this compare to SPY (inception date February 8, 1993)? Annualized return figures for the SPDR 500 (SPY) are as follows:

- ✔ One year: 8.51 percent
- ✔ Five years: 1.87 percent
- ✔ Ten years: 8.16 percent
- ✔ Since inception: 10.33 percent

Twice the volatility. Considerably less than half the return potential. Doesn't seem like anything to write home about, does it?

The author's pipedream

Throughout this book, I mention a few ETFs I'd like to see offered. In the area of specialized stock ETFs, one that doesn't exist is a "Reasonably-Paid-Top-Executives ETF." I might buy into it if it did exist. It stands to reason that when corporations pay their suits astronomical amounts of money, shareholders may stand to lose. After all, those millions and millions (sometimes billions) have to come from *somewhere*.

According to compensation researchers Lucian Bebchuk of Harvard University and Jesse Fried of the University of California at Berkeley, the pay of top executives eats seriously into U.S. corporate profits. In the period 1993–1995, public companies collectively paid their top five executives the equivalent of 5 percent of profits. By 2000–2002, that amount had reached 12.8 percent of corporate profits. That percentage declined but was still almost 10 percent in 2001–2003, the latest period of time the two law professors examined.

Not too surprisingly (at least in my mind), one study done by the Institute for Policy Studies and United for a Fair Economy found that those reduced profits are indeed hurting shareholders. The study looked at stock market returns for major U.S. corporations between 1991 and the end of 2004. Sure enough, the "Greedy CEO Portfolio" — a portfolio of those corporations that pay their CEOs the most — severely underperformed the S&P 500. Hence, an ETF comprised of stocks in companies that curb executive pay might be expected to outperform the market.

Part III
Adding Bonds, REITs, and Other ETFs to Your Portfolio

The 5th Wave — By Rich Tennant

"I've brought in Tom, Denise, and Kyle, to talk about our REIT, Bond, and metal ETFs respectively."

In this part . . .

The majority of ETFs — all those I discuss in Part II — represent common stock holdings. In this part, I introduce you to the minority: those two dozen or so ETFs that represent bonds, real estate investment trusts (REITs), and commodities such as gold, silver, and oil. Such holdings have enormous diversification power — the power to protect you if the stock market takes a big roll.

For sure, you have various means of owning such holdings. You can buy individual bonds, investment properties in Arizona (be careful not to step on a cactus), gold coins, and silver bullion. Heck, you can fill your garage with barrels of oil. But no method is as easy, efficient, and frugal as holding them as ETFs.

Chapter 12

The (Limited in Number, But Still Very Important) World of Bond ETFs

I love inline skating. Sometimes, I admit it, I take to the Pennsylvania hills a bit too fast. There's just something about the trees racing by and the wind in my face that I can't resist. Whoosh!

On occasion, I hit a bump, or some tiny woman in an SUV who can barely see over the steering wheel (they're all over my neighborhood) pulls out too fast in front of me, and I crash to the pavement. But thanks to the heavy black plastic armor that covers my knees, elbows, wrists, and head (just call me the Black Knight of Wealth Management), I've never been seriously injured.

Bonds are your portfolio's knee and elbow pads. When the going gets rough, and you hit the big bump (remember April 2000?), you'll be very glad to have bonds in your portfolio.

Plain and simple, there is no time-honored diversification tool for your portfolio that even comes close to bonds. They are as good as gold . . . even better than gold when you look at the long-term returns. Bonds are what may have saved your grandparents from selling apples on the street following the stock market crash of 1929.

The one thing that grandpa and grandma never had — but you do — is the ability to invest in bond ETFs. Like stock ETFs, bond ETFs are inexpensive, transparent (you know exactly what you're investing in), and highly liquid (you can sell them in a flash). Like individual bonds or bond mutual funds, bond ETFs can also be used to produce a reliable flow of cash in the form of interest payments, making them especially popular among grandparent types of any generation.

Throughout this chapter, I discuss a few things about bond investing in general. Then, without knowing the intimate particulars of your individual economics, I try my best to help you decide if bond ETFs belong in your portfolio, and if so, which ones. I also address that all-important and highly controversial question of how to achieve an optimal mix of stocks and bonds.

The single most important investment decision you ever make may be in determining the split between stocks and bonds in your portfolio. No pressure.

Tracing the Track Record of Bonds

Bonds, more or less in their present form, have been used as financial instruments since the Middle Ages. Then, as now, bonds of varying risk existed. (See the sidebar "The three risks of bond investing.") Then, as now, risk and return were highly correlated.

For the most part, bonds are less volatile than stocks, and their returns over time tend to be less. Over the past 80 years, the average annualized return of the S&P 500 has been around 10.0, while the return of long-term U.S. government bonds has been approximately 5.5 percent.

Comparing the *real* returns of stocks versus bonds (the return *after* inflation, the return that really counts), stocks over the past 80 years clock in at about 7.0 percent and bonds at 2.4 percent — a huge difference. A dollar invested in the stock market in 1926 (ignoring all taxes, investment fees, and so on) would today be worth $227.00. That same dollar invested in bonds would be worth about $6.40

These numbers may lead you to look at bonds and say to yourself, "Why bother?" Well, in fact, there's good reason to bother. Please read on before you decide to forsake this all-important asset class.

The three risks of bond investing

When you play a stock, your risks are plenty: The company you're investing in may go belly up; the public may simply lose interest in the stock, sending the price tumbling; or the entire economy may falter, in which case, your stock, like most others, may start to freefall. In the world of bonds, the risks aren't quite so high, and they tend to differ. Here are the three major risks of investing in bonds or a bond ETF:

✔ **Risk of default**. A bond is a promissory note. The note is only as good as the government, agency, or company that makes the promise to repay. If you buy a bond from ABC Corporation, and ABC Corporation can't pay, you lose. Risk of default is mostly an issue with high-yield ("junk") bonds. Don't invest in high-yield bonds unless you're willing to shoulder some serious risk. Keep in mind when buying a high-yield mutual fund that if the economy tanks and shaky companies start to sink, you'll possibly lose both the income from the bonds and the principal. And that could hurt. High-yield bonds, for example, were little comfort to those who lost money in the stock market in 2000; high-yields collectively lost about 6 percent that year. No high-yield bond ETFs exist, and none of the existing bond ETFs carry any substantial risk of default.

✔ **Interest-rate risk**. Suppose you are holding a bond with a 5 percent coupon rate, bought at a time when interest rates in general were 5 percent. Now suppose that the prevailing interest rate jumps to 10 percent. Are you going to be happy that you're holding a bond that is paying 5 percent? Of course not. If you hold the bond to maturity, there's a great opportunity cost. If you try to sell the bond before maturity, no one will give you full price; you'll need to sell it at a deep discount and take a loss. The longer the maturity of the bond, the greater the interest-rate risk. For that reason, the iShares Lehman 20+ Year Treasury Bond Fund (TLT) carries substantial interest-rate risk, while the iShares Lehman 1–3 Year Treasury Bond Fund (SHY) carries very little. All the other funds are somewhere in between. (There's a flip side to interest-rate risk: If you are holding a bond with a 5 percent coupon rate, and the prevailing interest rate drops to 3 percent, your bond will suddenly become a very hot ticket, selling at a juicy premium.)

✔ **Inflation risk**. Plain and simple, if you are holding a bond that pays 5 percent, and the inflation rate is 8 percent, you are in trouble. This is perhaps the biggest risk with bonds, especially low-yielding bonds, such as short-term and intermediate-term Treasurys. (The iShares Lehman 1–3 Year Treasury Bond Fund could very easily fall behind the inflation rate.) The only bonds immune to this risk are the inflation-protected bonds, which is why part of your bond portfolio should be invested in the iShares Lehman TIPS Bond Fund (TIP). Inflation-protected bonds, however, do carry interest-rate risk. And they also carry a risk that no other bonds do: *deflation* risk. If prices start to drop, your inflation adjustment will be worth zero, and you'll be left holding the lowest yielding bond in the land.

Portfolio protection when you need it most

When determining the attractiveness of bonds, we need to look not only at historical return but also at volatility: Long-term U.S. government bonds (which tend to be rather volatile bonds) in their worst year *ever* — 1967 — returned –9.2 percent. In their second worst year ever — 1958 — they returned –6.1 percent. That's a walk in the park compared to the worst stock market years of 1931 (–43.3 percent), 1937 (–35 percent), and 1974 (–26.5 percent).

As I note in the introduction to the chapter, during the Great Depression years, bonds may have saved your grandma and grandpa from destitution. The annualized real return of the S&P 500 from 1930–1932 was –20 percent. The annualized real return of long-term U.S. government bonds during the same three years was 14.9 percent.

There are two reasons that U.S. government bonds (and other high-quality bonds) often do well in the roughest economic times: 1) People flock to them for safety, raising demand; and 2) Interest rates often (not always, but often) drop during tough economic times. Interest rates and the price of bonds have an inverse relationship. When interest rates fall, already-issued bonds (carrying older, relatively high coupon rates) shoot up in price.

Bonds may similarly spare your hide should the upcoming years prove disastrous for Wall Street. (You never know.) Whereas international stocks, and certain industry sectors, like energy and real estate, have limited correlation to the broad U.S. stock market, bonds (not U.S. junk bonds, but most others) actually have a slight *negative* correlation to stocks. In other words, when the bear market is at its growliest, the complicated labyrinth of economic factors that typically coincide with that situation — lower inflation (possible deflation), lower interest rates — can bode quite well for fixed income. They certainly have in the past.

The way in which bonds and stocks tend to zigzag is beautifully illustrated in Figure 12-1, provided by Vanguard Investments.

History may or may not repeat

Of course, as investment experts say again and again (although few people listen), historical returns are only mildly indicative of what will happen in the future; they are merely reference points. Despite all the crystal balls, tea leaves, and CNBC commentators in the world, we simply don't know what the future will bring.

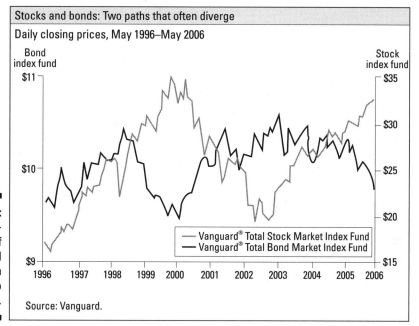

Figure 12-1:
The perfor-
mance of
stocks and
bonds from
May 1996 to
May 2006.

Although the vast majority of financial professionals use the past century as
pretty much their sole reference point, some point out that in the 19th century, stocks and bonds actually had more similar — nearly equal, in fact —
return rates. And perhaps that may be true for the 21st century as well. Time
will tell. In the meantime, having both stocks and bonds in a portfolio would
certainly seem to be the most prudent measure.

Tapping into Bonds in Various Ways

Like stocks, bonds can be bought individually, or you can invest in any of
hundreds of bond mutual funds or a handful of bond ETFs. The primary
reason for picking a bond fund over individual bonds is the same reason for
picking a stock fund over individual stocks: diversification.

Like stocks, bonds can (and should, if your portfolio is large enough) be
broken up into different categories. Instead of large, small, value, and growth
(the way stocks are often broken up), bond categories may include U.S.
Treasury, corporate, international, and municipal bonds — all of varying
maturity dates and credit ratings. Unless you're a billionaire, you simply can't

effectively own enough individual bonds to tap into each and every fixed income class.

Finding strength in numbers

To be honest, diversification in bonds isn't quite as crucial as it is with stocks. If you own high-quality U.S. government bonds or bonds from the most financially secure corporations, you are very unlikely to lose your principal, as you can with any stock. But there's more to diversification than protecting principal. There's also much to be said for smoothing out returns and mollifying risk.

Bond returns can vary greatly. In 2000, for example, U.S. Treasury bonds with maturities of more than one year returned over 13 percent. That same year, both high-yield bonds and international bonds lost money. Compare that to 2003 when high-yield bonds returned roughly 29 percent and international bonds almost 20 percent. U.S. Treasury bonds that year didn't even keep up with inflation.

By owning a handful of bond funds, you can effectively diversify across the map. You can have Treasurys of varying maturities, corporate bonds of varying credit worthiness, and international bonds of varying continents and currencies.

Of course, just as in the world of stocks funds, all bond funds are not created equal. Some Treasury funds are better than others. Some corporate bond funds are better than others.

Considering bond fund costs

As far as how to pick a bond fund, low costs are even more essential than they are in picking a stock fund. When (historically, at least over the past century) you're looking at maybe earning 2.4 percent above inflation, paying a manager even 1.2 percent a year is going to cut your profits in half. Do you really care to do that?

The most economical bond funds (like any kind of funds) are index funds, and you have a number of excellent index bond mutual funds to choose from. The bond ETFs, however, tend to be the cheapest of the cheap, which is a reason to like them.

Although I'm a big proponent of ETFs, I must tell you that the ETF edge in the fixed income arena isn't nearly as sharp as it is in stocks. The tax efficiency of a bond index mutual fund and a bond ETF are just about the same. The wonderful structure of ETFs that I discuss in Chapter 2 simply doesn't matter much when it comes to bonds. Bonds pay interest — that's how you make money with bonds — and they rarely see any substantial capital gains. To the extent that they do have capital gains, however, the ETF fund may have an edge over the mutual fund. But that's no big deal.

Casting a wide net

In the next section, I provide a menu of bond ETFs. These are, by and large, very good options for the fixed income side of your portfolio. If you have a modest portfolio, they may be sufficient to fill the entire fixed income side of your portfolio. If you have a larger portfolio, or you are in a very high tax bracket, you may need to look elsewhere. Only a handful of bond ETFs exist, and they do not yet include international bonds, high-yield bonds, or municipal bonds.

You may wish to consider various bond mutual funds to complement your bond ETF selections. I discuss a number of bond mutual funds in Chapter 15. I also use some of these non-ETF bond mutual funds to create sample portfolios in Chapter 16.

Sampling Your Basic Bond-ETF Menu

Of all the ETFs available to U.S. investors, only six are bond funds, and all are issued by Barclays iShares. The Securities and Exchange Commission, I happen to know, is sitting on applications for others. But for the time being, six is what we have to play with, so six is what I have to discuss in this chapter. So be it.

In this section, I present the six bond ETFs. A discussion of the risks and virtues of each leads us naturally to the ultimate question of whether you should invest in them, and if so, how much?

Please note that with the discussion of each bond ETF, I include the current yield — how much each share is paying as a percentage of your investment on the day I'm writing this chapter. I do this only to give you a flavor of how the yields differ between the funds. Current yield on a bond or bond fund, especially a long-term bond or bond fund, can change dramatically from week to week. So, too, can the difference in yields between the short- and long-term bonds (known as the yield *curve*). You can check the current yield of any bond fund, and the yield curve, on many Web sites, including www.etfconnect.com and www.morningstar.com.

Tapping the three Treasurys: Uncle Sam's IOUs

If the creator/issuer of a bond is a national government, the issue is called a *sovereign* bond. The vast majority of sovereign bonds sold in the United States are Uncle Sam's own Treasurys. (Yeah, that's how they're typically spelled. I don't know why.) Treasury bonds' claim to fame is the allegedly absolute assuredness that you'll get your principal back if you hold a bond to maturity. The United States government guarantees it. For that reason, Treasurys are sometimes called "risk-free."

Treasury-bond ETFs, thanks to Barclays iShares, come in a short-term, intermediate-term, and long-term variety, depending on the average maturity date of the bonds in the ETF's portfolio. The longer the term, generally the higher the interest rate, but the greater the volatility. Note that interest paid on Treasurys — including Barclays three Treasury ETFs — is federally taxable but not taxed by the states.

Following are detailed descriptions of the three Barclays iShare Treasury ETFs, along with my reviews.

iShares Lehman 1–3 Year Treasury Bond Fund (SHY)

Indexed to: The Lehman Brothers 1–3 Year U.S. Treasury Index, an index tracking the short-term sector of the United States Treasury market. The fund uses a representative sampling — typically around 30 individual bond issues.

Expense ratio: 0.15 percent

Current yield: 3.96 percent

Average weighted maturity: 1.8 years

Russell's review: This ETF is not a favorite of mine. Sure, it's an ultra-safe investment with little — almost no — volatility. And the yield is probably better than you can get in your local savings bank. But still, is this really where you want to stash your cash? Keep in mind that every time you make a deposit or withdrawal, you pay a commission. You may do better keeping your short-term money in a money market fund, a three- to six-month CD, or, better yet, an Internet bank like EmigrantDirect or ING Direct. The latter two options generally pay just as much as SHY, they are FDIC insured (making them just as safe), and you won't pay for each and every transaction.

iShares Lehman 7–10 Year Treasury Bond Fund (IEF)

Indexed to: The Lehman Brothers 7–10 Year U.S. Treasury Index, an index tracking the intermediate-term sector of the United States Treasury market. The fund uses a representative sampling — typically around 20 individual bond issues.

Expense ratio: 0.15 percent

Current yield: 4.40 percent

Average weighted maturity: 8.4 years

Russell's review: Expect modest returns and modest volatility. Of the three kinds of Treasurys, the intermediate-term bonds make most sense for most people's portfolios, and IEF is an excellent way to invest in them. Whatever your total allocation to fixed income, IEF deserves an allotment of perhaps one-fifth to one-third of that amount. See how I work it into several model portfolios in Chapter 16.

iShares Lehman 20+ Year Treasury Bond Fund (TLT)

Indexed to: The Lehman Brothers 20+ Year U.S. Treasury Index, an index tracking the long-term sector of the United States Treasury market. The fund uses a representative sampling — typically around 15 individual bond issues.

Expense ratio: 0.15 percent

Current yield: 4.73 percent

Average weighted maturity: 23.1 years

Russell's review: Hmmm. I believe that Treasurys are perhaps the safest investment in the land, but not *entirely* risk-free. I don't mean to sound unpatriotic. I don't mean to sound alarmist. But the steepness of this nation's deficit makes the hills of Pennsylvania look flat. It really scares me. The U.S. electorate seems to barely take notice. I may consider a short-term Treasury bill risk-free, but a 20+ year Treasury? Wag your flag all you like, but there is *some* risk of principal. And given the maturity of the bond, there is certainly going to be a heck of a lot of volatility. (If interest rates shoot up, the value of this fund will shoot down.) Long-term Treasurys may deserve a modest allocation in your portfolio, and this ETF is as good a way as any of getting it. But make sure that any money allocated to this fund is money that you aren't going to need to touch for a number of years, just in case the bond market takes a hit.

Gas at $4.00 a gallon? Getting inflation protection in a flash

Technically, U.S. Treasury Inflation-Protected Securities are Treasurys, but they are usually referred to as *TIPS*. I discuss them separately from the other Treasury obligations here because they play a distinctly different role in your portfolio.

The gig with TIPS is this: They pay you only a nominal amount of interest (currently about 2.5 percent), but they also kick in an adjustment for inflation. So, for example, if inflation is running at 4 percent, all things being equal, your TIPs will yield 6.5 percent. The iShares TIPS ETF is a fabulous way to tap into this almost essential ingredient in a well-balanced portfolio.

iShares Lehman TIPS Bond Fund (TIP)

Indexed to: The Lehman Brothers U.S. Treasury Inflation-protected sector of the United States Treasury market. The fund uses a representative sampling of roughly 15 bond issues.

Expense ratio: 0.20 percent

Current yield: 6.7 percent

Average weighted maturity: 10.5 years

Russell's review: TIPS belong in your portfolio, and this fund is the best way to hold them. You won't get rich off this fund, and the volatility may be more than you like. But if inflation goes on a tear, you are protected. Not so with other bonds. Of course, if inflation doesn't go on a tear, your money will get sub-market returns. But that is a risk worth paying. Note that TIPS are notoriously tax inefficient, even when held in an ETF. Preferably, you'll keep your shares of TIP in a tax-advantaged retirement account. In general, whatever your overall allocation is to fixed income (excluding short-term cash needs), one-quarter to one-third of that amount could be put into TIP.

Banking on business: A corporate bond ETF

Logically enough, corporations issue bonds called *corporate* bonds, and you can buy a dizzying array of them with varying maturities, yields, and ratings. Or you can buy a representative sampling through the Barclays iShare corporate bond ETF. Corporate bonds typically pay higher rates than government bonds, so you would expect the long-term payout from this ETF to be higher than any of the funds I discuss in previous sections.

Understanding bond ratings

United States Treasury bonds are considered the safest of all bonds because they are backed by the U.S. government. Bonds issued by federal government-agencies (such as Ginnie Mae) are typically one tiny step below Treasury bonds in terms of safety.

Bonds issued by corporations and municipalities (cities, counties, and their agencies) can vary in safety from quite high to very low, depending on the financial strength of the issuer. (Corporations tend to default more often than do municipalities.) The financial strength of the issuer is judged by credit rating agencies, such as Standard & Poors (S&P) and Moody's. Following are the ratings you most commonly find.

S&P Rating	*Moody's Rating*	*Quality*	*What it means*
AAA	Aaa	Highest grade	Your money is safe; there's no risk of default.
AA	Aa	High grade	Your money is safe; there's almost no risk of default.
A	A	Medium grade	Your money is likely safe.
BBB	Baa	A little shaky	Your money is probably safe.
BB	Ba	Somewhat speculative	You'll get your money back, with a little luck.
B	B	Very speculative	You'll get your money back, with considerable luck.
CCC	Caa	Possibly in default	Pray!
CC	Ca	Toilet paper	Pray! Pray harder!

In the area of corporate bonds, bond credit ratings are essential. Know that the average bond rating of the GS $ InvesTop Corporate Bond Fund is A, which means, more or less, that the bonds are issued by companies whose solvency is fairly solid (although certainly not on a par with the United States government). See the sidebar "Understanding bond ratings" if you wish to know more.

iShares GS $ InvesTop Corporate Bond Fund (LQD)

Indexed to: The GS $ InvesTop Index — an index of bond issues sponsored by a chorus line of companies rated "investment grade" (which means highly unlikely to go bankrupt any time soon) or above

Expense ratio: 0.15 percent

Current yield: 5.33 percent

Average credit quality: A

Average weighted maturity: 9.7 years

Russell's review: Investment-grade corporate bonds have done a pretty good job of holding their own in bad times. You get a bit more return than you do with Treasurys of equal maturity, although you pay state taxes on the dividends from corporate bonds. If your portfolio is large enough, you want LQD, as well as one of the Treasury ETFs and TIP. See how I include all three of these winners in the sample portfolios presented in Chapter 16.

The whole shebang: Investing in the entire U.S. bond market

The broadest fixed-income ETF is an all-around good bet.

iShares Lehman Aggregate Bond Fund (AGG)

Indexed to: The Lehman Aggregate Bond Index, which tracks the performance of the total U.S. investment grade bond market, including both government bonds and the highest quality corporate bonds. More than 6,000 bonds are in the index, but AGG uses a representative sampling of roughly 120 holdings. The average credit quality — AAA — indicates that there is very little chance any of the bonds in the index will default. (Even if one or two did, with 120 holdings, it wouldn't kill you.)

Expense ratio: 0.20 percent

The ultimate in simplicity

Want *real* simple investing? Combine The Lehman Brothers U.S. Aggregate (Bond) Index (AGG) with the Vanguard Total Stock Market ETF (VTI) and the iShares MSCI EAFE fund (EFA).

Presto! These three ETFs provide you with a fairly well-balanced portfolio at an incredibly low price.

Current yield: 4.6 percent

Average credit quality: AAA

Average weighted maturity: 6.9 years

Russell's review: Where can you go wrong with the world's largest ETF provider tracking the entire bond market for you and charging you only one-fifth of 1 percent? AGG makes an excellent building block in smaller portfolios or for any investor seeking the ultimate in simplicity. For larger portfolios, however, where you can afford to mix and match other bond funds of differing kinds, the need for AGG becomes less clear.

Determining the Optimal Fixed Income Allocation

Okay, now that I've talked about which bonds to buy, it's time to tackle the really tough question: How much of your portfolio should you allocate to bonds? The common thought on the subject — and I'm not above common thought, especially when it is right on the mark — is that the more conservative you want the portfolio to be, the higher the allocation to bonds.

But that answer begs the question, just how conservative do you want your portfolio to be? Different financial planners use different approaches to answer this monster question. And before I even start, let me say that I am about to oversimplify matters greatly for the sake of brevity.

Here's my take: I reckon that stocks are very likely to continue outperforming bonds into the foreseeable future. But as in the past, we will see up years and down years in both markets. The down years in the stock market are the far more dangerous. Bear stock markets, historically, don't last for more than a few years, although some have been particularly brutal and have lasted a decade or more. (Think 1930s and late 1960s to mid 1970s.)

For most investors over the past 100 years, stocks have paid off handsomely. So it's a balancing act. Too much in the way of stocks, and, should the markets go sour, you risk quick poverty. Too much in the way of bonds, and, should the general price level rise too much, you risk slow poverty as the interest just barely stays ahead of inflation, and you eat into your capital to pay the bills.

60/40? 50/50? Finding a split that makes sense

The balance point between stocks and bonds is usually expressed as the equation stocks/bonds, so a 60/40 portfolio means 40 percent bonds. The optimal balance point depends on many factors: age, size of portfolio, income stream, financial responsibilities, economic safety net, and emotional ability to deal with risk.

In general, I like to see investors hold three to six months' living expenses in cash (money markets or Internet savings accounts) or near-cash (very short-term bond funds, short-term CDs). Beyond that, the portfolio should be allocated to stocks and bonds, perhaps with a sliver to commodities.

In determining an optimal split, I would first ask you to pick a date when you think you may need to start withdrawing money from your nest egg. How much do you anticipate withdrawing? Maybe $30,000 a year? Or $40,000? Whatever the number, multiply it by 20. That amount, ideally, is what I'd like to see you have in your total portfolio, at a minimum, when you retire. Now multiply the same number by 10; that amount, ideally, is what I'd like to see you have in bonds, at minimum.

Meet Joe, age 64, with $600,000 in the bank

So let's consider Joe. He's a single guy with no kids who figures he's going to retire in one year. Joe has $600,000 in investments. He estimates that after Social Security and his very decent government pension, he needs to pull another $24,000 a year out of savings to pay all the bills. It seems to me that

Joe can do that and have a reasonable chance that his money will last as long as he lives. But how much should be in bonds and how much in stocks?

As a ballpark figure, without knowing much more about Joe, and ignoring for the moment such sticky things as present value and taxes and Joe's expected longevity, I'd start my portfolio construction with about $240,000 ($24,000 × 10) in mixed fixed income that would almost certainly include the Lehman 7–10 Treasury ETF (IEF) and the Lehman TIPS ETF (TIP).

The rest of Joe's money I would invest in a widely diversified portfolio made up mostly of stock ETFs. Thus, Joe might be looking at an allocation of $360,000 stocks/$240,000 bonds, or a 60/40 allocation. Joe also might be a good candidate for an immediate fixed annuity that would guarantee him the $24,000 a year. (Important note: Many annuities are financial dogs, and even the best annuities aren't for everyone. Please see my discussion in Chapter 15.)

A 60/40 allocation would generally be considered too risky for a 64-year-old. Most retirement models would allocate more to the tune of 40/60. So might I if Joe didn't have the secure government pension. Note, too, that I would use 60/40 only as my starting point. After taking all aspects of Joe's personal economics into consideration, I could wind up suggesting a 40/60 portfolio, or perhaps something in between the two, such as a 50/50 portfolio.

Meet Betsy and Mike, age 36, with $30,000 in the bank

Betsy and Mike are happily married. They both work and make decent incomes — enough so that if they needed to, they could live on one income. Betsy works in academia. Mike is a self-employed landscaper. They have no children. They have no debt. They would like to retire by age 62.

Betsy and Mike obviously need to accumulate a lot more than $30,000 if they want to retire by their early 60s. Their situation, I feel, warrants taking about as much risk as any investor should take. I might suggest an 85/15 portfolio or even (if Betsy and Mike were the type of people who could emotionally handle the volatility) a 90/10 portfolio. The 15 or 10 percent in bonds — $4,500 or $3,000 — I might allocate to The Lehman Brothers U.S. Aggregate Index (AGG).

In Chapter 16, I bring Joe, Betsy, and Mike back to look at how their portfolios might be broken up into various stock and bond ETFs. I also introduce you to some of their friends of various ages and means and suggest specific stock and bond ETFs for them, as well.

Chapter 13

Real Estate Investment Trusts (REITs): Becoming a Virtual Landlord

Why, land is the only thing in the world worth workin' for, worth fightin' for, worth dyin' for, because it's the only thing that lasts.

Spoken by the character Gerald O'Hara in *Gone with the Wind*

*W*hether you agree with Scarlett's father or not, you've undoubtedly noticed (gleefully) how the value of that little patch of land you call home has appreciated over the past several years. Oh, the price may have softened a bit lately, but still, you've done nicely. If you live in Boston, San Francisco, or the New Jersey Shore, you've won the lottery.

The value of commercial real estate — just about anywhere in the nation — has likewise been on the steep rise. And if you happen to own some, perhaps through a real estate investment trust, you likely have made out like a bandit.

In a nutshell, *real estate investment trusts,* popularly known as *REITs* (rhymes with "Pete's"), are companies that hold portfolios of properties, such as shopping malls, office buildings, hotels, amusement parks, or timberland. Or they may hold certain real estate related assets, such as commercial mortgages. About 200 REITs in the United States are publicly held, and their stock trades on the open market just like any other stock.

Via dozens of mutual funds, you can buy into a collection of REITs at one time. Via a handful of ETFs (currently four), you can similarly buy a bevy of REITs. And that may not be a bad idea. For the 20 years ended December 2005, the so-called NAREIT Composite Index has enjoyed an average annual return of 13.8 percent. That outshines the S&P 500's annual return of 12.7 percent for the same timeframe.

Some holders of REITs and REIT funds believe (and fervently hope) that such phenomenal performance will continue. Others argue that the glory of REITs may already be gone with the wind. I argue that REITs deserve a permanent allocation in most portfolios, and in this chapter, I provide you with several reasons (in addition to the reason given by Scarlett's dad).

Considering Five Distinguishing Characteristics of REITs

You may wonder why an entire chapter of this book is devoted to REIT ETFs. Why, you may ask, didn't I merely include them in Chapter 11 with the other specialized stock ETFs, like high dividend and socially responsible funds?

Good question!

I have *five* answers. Any one alone probably wouldn't justify giving REITs a chapter of their very own. All five together create a pretty good justification. The first three answers are solid explanations why REITs deserve special status in the world of investments. The final two answers are, well, a bit wishy-washy, but many people make these arguments, which means you're likely to hear them.

Limited correlation to the broad markets

According to investment analysts Callan Associates, the FTSE/NAREIT Equity Index, an index of U.S. REITs (similar to the NAREIT Composite Index I mention in the introduction to this chapter), has evidenced a correlation of 0.43 with the S&P 500 over the past 20 years. That means the prices of an S&P 500 index fund and the share prices of a REIT index fund have tended to move in the same direction less than half the time. The REIT index has practically no correlation to bonds.

Having had 20 percent REITs in your portfolio over the past 20 years — regardless of whether your portfolio was made up of mostly stocks or bonds — would have both raised your returns and lowered your volatility. It's the Efficient Frontier (as I discuss in Chapter 4) in action.

Will REITs continue to work their magic? No guarantees, but there's a pretty good chance, yes.

Unusually high dividends

REITs typically deliver annual dividend yields of between 5 and 7 percent — two to three times more than even the highest dividend paying non-REIT stocks, and easily three times more than the average stock. (Many stocks, of course, pay no dividends whatsoever.) The cash usually keeps flowing regardless of whether a particular REIT's share price rises or falls, just as long as the REIT is pulling in some money. That's because REITs, which get special tax status, are required by law to pay out 90 percent of their income as dividends to shareholders. Cool, huh?

Different taxation of dividends

Because REITs are blessed in that they don't have to pay income taxes, their dividends are usually fully taxable to shareholders as ordinary income. In other words, whatever dividends you get will be taxed at year-end according to your income tax bracket. Few, if any, REIT dividends you receive will qualify for the special 15 percent dividend tax rate. For that reason, your accountant will undoubtedly urge you to handle your REITs a bit carefully. I urge you to do so, as well.

Special status among financial professionals

The vast majority of wealth advisors — whether they primarily use style investing, sector investing, or astrology charts and tea leaves — recognize REITs as a separate asset class and tend to include it in most people's portfolios. Is that distinction logical and just? Yes, but . . . I've asked myself, if REITs deserve that distinction of honor, what about some other industry sectors, such as utilities and energy? After all, both utilities and energy have lately shown less correlation to the S&P 500 than have REITs. Don't they deserve their own slice of the portfolio pie?

I don't mean to slam REITs; I like REITs. But one possible reason they are seen as a separate asset class (in addition to the three reasons I explain in the previous sections) may be that the REIT marketers are more savvy than the marketers of utility stocks (which, in addition to having low correlation to the broad market, *also* pay exceptionally high dividends).

Connection to tangible property

Some people argue that REITs are different from other stocks because they represent tangible property. Well yeah, REITs do represent stores filled with useless junk and condos filled with single people desperately looking for dates, and I suppose that makes them different than, say, stock in Microsoft or Procter & Gamble. (Isn't toothpaste tangible?) But the reality is that REITs are stocks. And to a great degree, they behave like stocks. If REITs are different than other stocks, dividends and correlation are the likely culprits — not tangibility.

Picking the Best REIT ETF for Your Portfolio

If you want REITs in your portfolio, you won't get a whole lot of them unless you purchase a REIT fund. For all the room they take up, REITs simply don't make up that large a segment of the economy.

If, for example, you were to buy an S&P 500 index fund, only about 1 percent of that fund would be made up of stock from REITs. If you were to buy an S&P mid cap index fund (most REITs would probably qualify as mid caps), you would still be holding an investment with only about 4 percent REITs.

So if you want the diversification power of this special asset class, you need to go out of your way to get it. But thanks to ETFs, doing so shouldn't be much of a hassle, your expense ratio can be kept to a minimum, and you get many of the other benefits that you do with ETFs.

The tax efficiency of ETFs will help cap any capital gains you enjoy on your REIT fund, but it can't do anything to diminish the taxes you'll be paying on the dividends. For that reason, all REIT funds — ETFs or otherwise — are best kept in tax-advantaged retirement accounts, such as your IRA or Roth IRA.

Currently, four REIT ETFs are available to U.S. investors, and I outline them here. None are terrible investments — in fact, all are pretty darned good — but each is different, and I do have my preferences.

iShares Cohen & Steers Realty Majors Index Fund (ICF)

Indexed to: Cohen & Steers Realty Majors Index, which tracks 30 of the largest and most liquid REITs in the U.S. market. (Cohen & Steers is an investment firm that specializes in REITs.)

Expense ratio: 0.35 percent

Number of holdings: 31

Top five holdings: Simon Property Group, Vornado Realty Trust, ProLogis, Equity Residential, Boston Properties

Top sectors: Retail, office buildings, and residential (accounting for 72 percent of total assets)

Russell's review: Of the four REIT ETFs, the Cohen & Steers offering is the most selective in that it represents the largest REITs with the biggest volume of stocks. As such, you could expect the volatility of this fund to be a tad less than the others, which include smaller and less liquid REITs. You may also expect the long-term return of this fund to be a smidgen less. The cost — 0.35 percent — is reasonable by any investment standard but is still twice that of the cheapest REIT ETF. All in all, ICF isn't a bad investment choice, but it may not be optimal for all portfolios.

iShares Dow Jones U.S. Real Estate Index Fund (IYR)

Indexed to: Dow Jones U.S. Real Estate Index, a subset of the Dow Jones U.S. Financials Index that uses about 90 REIT stocks to track the U.S. commercial real estate market

Expense ratio: 0.60 percent

Number of holdings: 88

Top five holdings: Simon Property Group, Equity Office Properties Trust, Equity Residential, ProLogis, Vornado Realty Trust

Top sectors: Retail and office buildings (accounting for 43 percent of total assets)

Russell's review: The mix of investments is so close to the streetTRACKS Wilshire REIT Fund (RWR) that the two funds are almost indistinguishable. There's nothing wrong with this fund — nothing whatsoever — but why pay 0.60 percent when you can pay 0.25 percent for the streetTRACKS brand? Or, perhaps an even easier question to answer, why pay 0.60 percent when you can pay one-fifth that amount for the Vanguard REIT fund (VNQ), which uses a somewhat broader index?

streetTRACKS Wilshire REIT Index Fund (RWR)

Indexed to: Dow Jones Wilshire REIT Index, which employs roughly 90 stocks — mid caps, mostly — to track the U.S. REIT market

Expense ratio: 0.25 percent

Number of holdings: 88

Top five holdings: Simon Property Group, General Growth Properties, Equity Office Properties Trust, Archstone-Smith Trust, Equity Residential

Top sectors: Retail, office buildings, and apartments (accounting for 73 percent of total assets)

Russell's review: In essence, this is the same fund as the iShares Dow Jones U.S. Real Estate Index Fund (IYR), or very close to it, at less than half the price. If you wish to tap into the U.S. REIT market — which you should, for dividends, growth, or diversification — RWR is one of your best options, although I urge you to also consider the Vanguard REIT ETF (VNQ).

Vanguard REIT ETF (VNQ)

Indexed to: The Morgan Stanley U.S. REIT index, which tracks roughly 105 U.S. REITs — representing about half of all publicly traded REITS and roughly two-thirds the value of the total U.S. REIT market

Expense ratio: 0.12 percent

Number of holdings: 107

Top five holdings: Simon Property Group, Equity Office Properties Trust, Equity Residential, ProLogis, Vornado Realty Trust

Top sectors: Retail, apartments, and office buildings (accounting for roughly 62 percent of total assets)

Russell's review: Once again, Vanguard brings to market the most economical investment vehicle. You can't find a better way to invest in the U.S. REIT market than through VNQ. This is a broadly based ETF with an ultra low expense ratio. Be aware, however, that even with all the advantages of an ETF and the considerable tax-minimizing prowess of Vanguard, this ETF will represent something of a tax burden. For that reason, I recommend that you consider purchasing an ETF as a long-term investment and keeping it in a tax-advantaged retirement account.

Calculating a Proper REIT Allocation

You don't really need REITs for the income that dividends provide. Some people have this notion that withdrawing dividends from savings is somehow okay, but withdrawing principal is not. Don't confuse the issue, please. Do the math: If you withdraw $100 from your account, it is withdrawn, and it doesn't matter whether it comes from cash created by dividends or from elsewhere.

If you need cash, you can always create your own "artificial dividend" by selling any security you like (preferably one that has been appreciating). Not that I have anything against dividends — they're fine — but they shouldn't be your primary reason for purchasing REITs.

Your primary motivations for buying REITs should be diversification and potential growth. In the past, the diversification afforded by REITs has been significant, as has the growth.

Judging from the past

If we could go back in a time machine 20 years, I'd have you put, heck, *everything* in Microsoft. But REITs would not have been a bad option either. After all, they've done fabulously, kicking the pants off the S&P 500 and most other investments. Looking forward, of course, I don't know what will be. However, I think we can fairly safely assume that REITs will continue to move in somewhat different cycles from other stocks.

I think we can also fairly safely assume that REITs will *not* continue to outpace most other investments, for the simple reason that no investment does so indefinitely.

Putting all factors together, I suggest that most investors devote 10 to 20 percent of the equity side of their portfolios to REITs. If your portfolio is 50 percent stock and 50 percent bonds, I might suggest that 5 to 10 percent of your entire portfolio be devoted to REITs.

What if, like many people, your net worth is largely made up by the value of your home? You may want to play it a little light on the REITs, but don't let the value of your home affect your portfolio decisions to any great degree. (See the sidebar "Your residence, your portfolio.")

Splitting the baby

You can certainly put most of your REIT allotment into one of the REIT ETFs I discuss in this chapter. I suggest, however, that you also consider a position in international REITs. As yet, no ETFs allow you to tap into international REITs, so you'll have to go the mutual fund route. If you have a very handsome portfolio ($500,000+), you may also want to consider a highly specialized REIT fund, such as a lumber REIT, which can sometimes zig when other REITs zag.

Lumber on over to Chapter 15, where I discuss working non-ETFs into your portfolio, and you'll get all the specifics.

Your residence, your portfolio

If you bought your home for, say, $130,000 some 22 years ago, and that home is now worth $1,300,000, I say "Congratulations!" But don't let that bounty affect your portfolio decisions very much. After all, you'll always need a place to live. Sell the house today, and you'll presumably need to buy another (made of similarly over-priced bundle of tiles and plywood).

Of course, someday you may downsize, and you will be able to allot part of the value of your home to your portfolio. For that reason, and that reason alone, you may want to consider that the value of domestic real estate and the value of commercial real estate, while two different animals, are related. If your net worth is heavily into home, and especially if you are approaching a stage in life when you may consider downsizing, you may want to play it easier on REITs than would, say, an apartment dweller of similar means. Or you may forget about U.S. REITs and take a position in foreign REITs. (No foreign REIT ETFs are available yet, but several mutual funds exist, which I introduce in Chapter 15.)

Chapter 14

All That Glitters: Gold, Silver, and Other Commodities

*O*ne of my childhood passions was collecting coins from around the world. Sometime during the Johnson administration, on my meager allowance of $1 a week, I saved up for three months or so to buy myself a gold coin: an uncirculated 1923 50-kurush piece from Turkey. Maybe you can remember getting a shiny new bicycle for Christmas when you were 5 or 6. Maybe, like Citizen Kane, you remember getting your first sled. My most prized possession from childhood was that gold coin, smaller than a dime but absolutely gorgeous.

I still have it.

I never thought of my piece of gold as an investment. But for many people, gold is just that. Historically, the soft and shiny metal has been seen as the ultimate hedge against both inflation and market turmoil. Most people through the ages have bought gold just as I did: as coins, or sometimes in bricks. Alternatively, in more recent decades, they may have invested in shares of gold-mining companies.

Either way, investing in gold was always a pain in the neck. With shares of gold-mining companies, you had to factor in other things beside the price of pure gold. Political turbulence in South Africa, for example, or a fall in the value of the rand might send your stock down the mines. Buying gold coins involved (and still does) paying hefty commissions. Buying gold bricks also meant (and still does) sizeable commissions and possible assaying expenses. And both bricks and coins have to be stored and should be insured.

All that hassle changed with the introduction of the first gold ETF in November 2005. Suddenly, it became possible to buy gold at spot price — in an instant — with very little commission and no need to fret about storage or insurance. Thanks to ETFs, you can now also buy silver in the same way. Even crude oil, if that's your cup of Texas tea, can be purchased (sort of) with an ETF, as can coffee futures and contacts on wheat. In this chapter, I discuss commodities, and especially the commodity ETFs, and whether they belong in your portfolio.

Oh, by the way, I recently saw that a 50-kurush gold coin just like mine sold online for $127. *But I'm not selling mine!*

Gold, Gold, Gold!

Stocks and bonds may rise and fall. Currencies may ebb and flow. Economies go boom and then bust. Inflation tears nest eggs apart. And through it all, gold retains its value. Or so goes the old yarn.

The primary reason for buying gold, according to the World Gold Council (www.gold.org), is that

> *Market cycles come and go, but gold has maintained its long term value. Jastram [1977] demonstrated that in inflationary and deflationary times, in the very long term, gold kept its purchasing power. The value of gold, in terms of real goods and services that it can buy, has remained remarkably stable.*

Hmm. I'm not sure who Jastram was, and I don't know exactly what he means by "very long term," but I've done a bit of research on the subject. Although I don't claim that my research is exhaustive or in any way conclusive of the investment value of gold, it does shed *some* doubt on the veracity of the World Gold Council's claim.

If you look at Table 14-1, you'll see the price of gold for a sampling of years between 1920 and 2006, the average price of a basic Hershey chocolate bar in those years (which I found on a Web site called www.foodtimeline.org), and how many Hershey bars you could buy with an ounce of gold. Note that one ounce of gold in 1980 bought 2,460 Hershey bars, while 20 years later, in 2000, it bought a mere 558 bars. At today's prices — about $680 for an ounce of gold and about 75 cents for a Hershey bar — you'd get 906 chocolate bars for the same nugget.

Table 14-1	Trading Gold for Hershey Bars		
Year	Average price of a Hershey chocolate bar	Average price of an ounce of gold	Hershey bars per ounce of gold
1920	$0.03	$21	700
1965	$0.05	$35	700
1980	$0.25	$615	2,460
2000	$0.50	$279	558
2006	$0.75	$679	906

Midas touch or fool's gold?

Okay, let's give the World Gold Council the benefit of the doubt and assume that gold, in the very long term, does maintain its purchasing power. Maybe Hershey bars are an anomaly. Maybe the past couple decades are the anomaly. Still, you would hope that your investments would do better than merely keep up with inflation. If that is all gold can do, why hold it as an investment? (After all, it is a nonproductive lump of metal, so what should you really expect?)

Well, if you type "gold" into your favorite search engine, you'll find 10,000 vendors selling it and 10,000 reasons, according to those vendors, why *now* is the time to buy. (Um, excuse me, but if the price of gold "can only go up," why are you trying so hard to sell it?) Every day, I hear one explanation or another as to why gold "must" go up from here on (India's demand for gold . . . dentists' demand for gold . . . the mines are drying up . . . gold demand in the tech industry . . . and so on and so on). These are the very same arguments I've been hearing for years.

I really expect that the best you'll do over the very long run, as the World Gold Council puts it, is to maintain purchasing power. But, hey, even that isn't a bad thing when every other investment is tanking. Gold, as it happens, does show little long-term correlation to other assets. And when the going gets really rough, or seems rough, and people run from more active kinds of investment, they often turn to gold. Then, as a self-fulfilling prophecy, the price rises. That's possibly what's been happening in the past years since 9/11, the war in Iraq, the growing deficit, and what have you.

In the final analysis, if you want to hold gold, it probably wouldn't hurt. But please don't buy the nonsense that gold "must go up." It will go up. It will go down. It will go up again. Have a ball. But don't bank your retirement on it, okay? (Personally, I don't own shares in either gold ETF, but I'm not ruling it out.)

If you allot a small percentage of your portfolio to gold — no more than, say, 5 percent please (actually make that 5 percent *total* precious metals) — and keep that percentage constant, you'll likely eek out a few dollars over time. Every year, if the price of gold falls, you buy a bit; if the price rises, perhaps you sell. That strategy is called *rebalancing,* and I recommend it for all your portfolio allocations. (See my discussion of yearly portfolio rebalancing in Chapter 18.)

And if all goes to hell in a hand basket, your gold may offer you some protection.

A vastly improved way to buy the precious metal

When, in November 2005, State Street's streetTRACKS introduced the first gold ETF, it was a truly revolutionary moment. You buy a share just as you would buy a share of any other security, and each share gives you ownership of one-tenth of an ounce of gold held by the fund. Yes, the gold is actually held in various bank vaults. You can even see pictures of one such vault filled to near capacity (very cool!) on www.streettracksgoldshares.com.

If you are going to buy gold, this is far and away the easiest and most sensible way to do it.

You currently have two ETF options, the original from State Street — the **streetTRACKS Gold Trust (GLD)** — and a second introduced months later from Barclays — the **iShares COMEX Gold Trust (IAU)**. Both funds have expense ratios of 0.40 percent. Both funds are essentially the same. Flip a coin (gold or other).

The tax man cometh

Strange as it seems, the ownership of gold, according to the Internal Revenue Service, is considered ownership of a collectible. A share of either IAU or GLD is considered the same as, say, a gold Turkish coin from 1923 and, therefore, is treated as a collectible. (Don't ask.) So what? As it happens, the long-term capital gains tax rate on collectibles is 28 percent, and not the more favorable 15 percent afforded to capital gains on stocks.

Holding the ETF should be no problem as far as taxes (gold certainly won't pay dividends), but when you sell, you could get hit hard on any gains. Gold ETFs, therefore, are best kept in tax-advantaged accounts, such as your IRA.

Silver: The Second Metal

Talk about a silver bullet. After years of lackluster prices, in the early part of 2006, the price of silver suddenly, within three short months, shot up 67 percent. Why? Largely, it was a testimony to the growing power of ETFs!

The price jump was in anticipation of the introduction of Barclays **iShares Silver Trust (SLV)** ETF. The fund, introduced in April 2006, works much the same as the iShares COMEX Gold Trust (IAU). When you buy a share of SLV, you obtain virtual ownership of 10 ounces of silver.

To provide you with that ownership, Barclays had to buy many ounces of silver (initially 1.5 million), and that pending demand caused the silver market to bubble and fizz. Within several weeks after the introduction of the ETF, the price of silver continued to rise, reaching a 23-year high in May 2006 ($14.69 an ounce) before tumbling double digits in the following weeks.

Quick silver on the move

To say that silver is volatile is a gross understatement. In 1979, the price of silver was about $5 an ounce. In early 1980, the infamous Hunt brothers cornered the silver market (before they were caught), and the metal was briefly selling for $54 an ounce. Then it fell again. Hard.

If there is any reason to stomach such volatility, it is the fact that silver has a very low correlation to other investments. For the past five years, the price of silver has had very, very little correlation to stocks, no correlation to bonds, and a modest correlation (0.66) to the price of gold.

If you must . . .

If you're going to take a position in silver, the iShares ETF is the way to go. The expense ratio of 0.50 percent will eat into your profits or magnify your losses, but it will still likely be cheaper than paying a commission to buy silver bars or coins and then paying for a good-sized lockbox.

In the very long run, I don't think you're likely to do as well with silver as you would with either stocks or bonds. After all, you will be buying a lump of metal that will sit in a vault. It isn't a productive asset like you get when you buy ownership in a company. In the short run, who knows? Silver could be a good hedge. But I would urge you to invest very modestly; no more than 5 percent of your portfolio should be allocated to precious metals.

Keep in mind that the same strange tax law pertains to silver as to gold. Any capital gains will be taxed on the "collectibles" rate of 28 percent. You may want to keep your silver shares in a tax-advantaged account.

Oil: The Liquid Commodity

The **United States Oil Fund (USO)** opened on the American Stock Exchange on April 10, 2006. Even though the fund is technically not an ETF but a very close cousin called a *commodity pool,* in my mind, that date marks a sort of end to the Age of Innocence for ETFs. The United States Oil Fund, as official as that sounds, is run by a group called Victoria Bay Asset Management, which I will return to in just a moment.

Don't mistake this fund for something like the Vanguard Energy ETF (VDE) or the Energy Select Sector SPDR (XLE) funds, both of which invest in oil companies, like Exxon Mobil Corp. Don't mistake this fund for something like any of the precious metal commodity funds discussed in this chapter thus far. Victoria Bay, wherever that is, is not filled with oil. Whereas Barclays and State Street maintain vaults filled with gold and silver, Victoria Bay deals in paper: futures contracts, to be exact.

In other words, they use your money to speculate on tomorrow's price of oil. If the price of oil goes up 10 percent in the next several weeks, you should, theoretically, earn a 10 percent profit minus the fund's expense ratio of 0.85 percent. The price of oil and gas, as everyone knows, has been on a tear lately. And so this fund promises to give you a piece of that action, perhaps offering warm comfort every time you pull up to the pump and have to yank out your credit card.

Oily business

Yes, you may profit if you buy this ETF and the price of oil continues to escalate. Then again, is there reason to believe that the price of oil will continue to escalate? The famed economist John Maynard Keynes in 1930 theorized that commodity futures, over time, will offer compensation above and beyond any rise in the price of a commodity. He speculated that speculators will somehow be rewarded for taking the risk of future price uncertainly. Keynes's theory is unproven and very controversial.

But even if Keynes proves right, why pick one single commodity to invest in? Why not diversify your risks with a variety of commodities? Several ETFs already attempt to do that, and others are on the way. (I discuss these just as soon as I'm done with USO.) I equate the arrival of USO with the end of an Age of Innocence because it clearly, in my mind, is pandering to recent headlines about high oil prices and people's disgust at the pumps.

No experience necessary

In addition, the issuer of the USO fund is not a major investment bank but rather Victoria Bay Asset Management, LLC, "a wholly-owned subsidiary of Wainwright Holdings, Inc., a Delaware Corporation . . . that also owns an insurance company organized under Bermuda law." The fund's prospectus, especially the part about the management of Victoria Bay, makes for *very* interesting reading.

Two of the top people running the fund also manage a mutual fund called Ameristock, and a third, Malcolm R. Fobes III (no relation to Malcolm Forbes), is the founder of the Berkshire Focus Fund (no relation to the fabulously successful Berkshire Hathaway.) Both Ameristock and Berkshire Focus (both with Morningstar one-star ratings) have track records that would probably make you cringe.

But the part of the prospectus that really raises an eyebrow is where it explains that "the managing and directing of day-to-day activities and affairs [of the fund] relies heavily on . . . Mr. John Love," who, we later learn, is not only employed by Ameristock but also "holds a BFA in cinema-television from the University of Southern California. Mr. Love does not have any experience running a commodity pool." His experience: "from December 2000 to February 2001 [sic], Mr. Love was employed by Digital Boardwalk, Inc."

Even if John Maynard Keynes was right, no one running this fund seems nearly as smart as J.M. Keynes — or Jed Clampett. I would not invest in this fund; neither should you.

(Somewhat) Safer Commodity Plays

Just as diversification works to dampen the risk of stock investing, it can similarly smooth out — to a degree — the ups and downs of investing in commodities.

General commodity funds

Make no mistake, the **Deutsche Bank Commodity Index Tracking Fund (DBC)**, issued in February 2006, is one volatile investment. Rather than a true ETF, this fund (like the USO) is a *commodity pool* that deals in commodities futures.

Unlike the USO, or the gold and silver ETFs, the Deutsche Bank offering has a bit of diversity to protect you if one commodity suddenly goes way south. That diversity, alas, is limited. It entails six commodity classes: crude oil (35 percent), home heating oil (20 percent), aluminum (12.5 percent), corn (11.25 percent), wheat (11.25 percent), and gold (10 percent). The expense ratio — 0.68 percent — isn't outrageous but is still high by ETF standards.

I like the idea of a general commodity fund, although I'm not wild about DBC. As it happens, in June 2006, Barclays issued two ETFs that offer perhaps the best option yet for investing directly in commodities.

Just like the Deutsche Bank fund, the Barclays offerings aren't true ETFs; Barclays calls them ETNs for *exchange-traded notes.* They are the **iPath GSCI Total Return Index ETN (GSP)** and the **iPath Dow Jones-AIG Commodity Index Total Return ETN (DJP).** These are, in fact, *very* different from Barclays iShares ETFs. They are actually debt instruments, more like bonds than anything else. By buying them, you are lending Barclays your money, and you are counting on Barclays to give it back. (If Barclays were to go under, you lose.) That's not the case with iShares or any other ETF, where the ETF provider is acting more as a custodian of your funds than anything else.

If it were any other company but Barclays, I might worry. But Barclays is rated a very stable company, so I wouldn't worry too much about it going under. Your bigger worry is the future of commodity prices. Barclays promises to use "any tool necessary" to use your money to track commodity prices. Presumably, it works something like the Deutsche Bank fund in that it uses primarily futures contracts. But Barclays won't say. ETNs are not transparent like ETFs. You don't know exactly what you're holding.

So why do I like these funds more than the Deutsche Bank fund? It isn't the expense ratio. At 0.75 percent, the Barclay's funds are actually a tad more expensive. Here are the three reasons I prefer the Barclay's funds:

- ✓ I have a good amount of faith in the company; it's huge, it's well-managed, and it's profitable.

- ✓ The Barclays funds, by promising to curtail capital gains and dividends, will likely be much more tax efficient than the Deutsche Bank fund.

✔ The Barclays ETNs offer somewhat better diversification. Both ETNs invest in a number of commodities, from oil and natural gas to gold and silver to cocoa and coffee.

Of the two new funds, I prefer the iPath Dow Jones-AIG Commodity Index Total Return ETN (DJP) for its well-established index and the balanced weightings of its holdings: energy (30 percent), livestock (9 percent), precious metals (9 percent), industrial metals (21 percent), and agriculture (31 percent). Still, even when diversified, commodities are volatile, and their long-term returns are not as well established as the long-term return on stocks and bonds.

If you buy into a Barclays ETN, you should do so for the right reason: lack of correlation. Both the iPath funds have shown almost no correlation to either stocks or bonds. For more information on these funds, Barclays has a special Website: www.ipathetn.com.

As with precious metals funds, devoting 5 percent of your portfolio to either of the iPath funds would be plenty. No more than that, please. Oh, one little caveat: The IRS isn't entirely certain how it will be taxing these new funds yet. If you're not going to stash them into a tax-advantaged retirement account, you could be in for an unpleasant surprise.

Tapping into commodity companies

Another option for hitching your star, or part of your star, to commodities is to invest in commodity providing companies. There are perhaps a dozen ETFs that allow you to invest in oil and gas company stocks. Among them are

✔ Vanguard Energy ETF (VDE)

✔ Energy Select Sector SPDR (XLE)

✔ iShares Dow Jones U.S. Energy Index (IYE)

✔ PowerShares Dynamic Energy & Exploration (PXE)

✔ iShares Dow Jones U.S. Oil & Gas Exploration/Production Index Fund (IOE)

✔ iShares Dow Jones U.S. Oil Equipment & Services Index Fund (IEZ)

✔ iShares S&P Global Energy Index Fund (IXC)

They all sound different, but when you look at the roster of companies, they are all actually quite similar, and I feel equally lukewarm about all of them.

Keep in mind that the energy sector, unlike something like REITs (see Chapter 13), is a large sector of the U.S. economy. Energy companies make up about 10 percent of the capitalization of the U.S. stock market. So just being invested in the market, you have some decent exposure to energy already.

If you really want to grab any profits ensuing from rising demand for commodities and would rather not invest directly in commodities, a better fund may be the iShares Goldman Sachs Natural Resources Index Fund (IGE). Like all the other funds I list in this section, the fund invests in oil companies, but it invests in other commodity providers, too. Unfortunately, the fund is so heavy in energy (57 percent oil and 19.50 percent oil services) that its performance will match all the other energy funds rather closely. (Other than energy, the fund offers very limited exposure to metals and mining companies, and paper and forest firms.)

Tapping into commodity countries

As commodity prices go, so often go the stock markets of countries that provide the world with much of its commodities. By and large, those nations are the emerging market nations.

Although they can be just as volatile as commodities themselves, you can invest, through Barclays iShares, in the stock markets of nations such as gold-rich South Africa (the iShares MSCI South Africa fund [EZA]), timber giant Brazil (iShares MSCI Brazil [EWZ]), or mineral-laden Malaysia (iShares MSCI Malaysia [EWM]).

I would suggest, however, that your play in emerging markets be diversified through one of several ETFs that allow you to invest in a broad array of emerging market nations. Those include the iShares MSCI Emerging Market fund (EEM), the BLDRS Emerging Markets 50 ADR (ADRE), and the Vanguard Emerging Market ETF (VWO). I discuss these funds in some depth in Chapter 10.

Chapter 15

Working Non-ETFs into Your Investment Mix

In This Chapter

▶ Incorporating ETFs into an existing portfolio of mutual funds or individual securities

▶ Spotting holes in an ETF portfolio

▶ Choosing investments that best complement your stock ETFs

▶ Constructing the fixed income side of your portfolio

As new ETFs spring up, it has become easy to build a universe of investments using these low-cost vehicles. With 240 and counting, you can now invest in just about any area of the market. You've got your option of large company stock and small stock ETFs, various industry sectors, international stocks, Treasury bonds and corporate bonds, commodities, and more. And yet, for all their variety, ETFs also serve up a lot of repetition. Count 'em: There are no fewer than 30 broad-based large cap U.S. stock ETFs, for example.

Plus, for all the variety, the ETF universe still has some black holes. You can't, for example, buy an ETF that gives you exposure to either tax-free municipal or high-yield bonds. Or international bonds. Or international REITs. Well, at least as I sit down to write this chapter, these asset classes are not yet available in ETF form. That situation will surely change. Just as I was finishing up this book, WisdomTree issued the first ever small international stock ETFs.

For the time being, you have to look elsewhere to tap into several asset classes. This chapter serves as a quick guide to doing so.

This chapter also serves as a reference for those of you who already have non-ETF portfolios in place and want to keep them more or less intact. Perhaps you have huge unrealized tax gains and don't care to donate to the IRS just yet. Or your investment options may be limited by your employer's 401(k) plan options. Or you may be happy with your indexed mutual funds, which is fine.

For some of you — ah, yes, I know you're out there — no amount of cajoling will ever convince you to index your investments. You fervently believe that by picking stocks (or hiring someone to do so for you), you can clobber the market. So be it. I can still urge you to consider investing in an ETF here and there.

So, without further ado, I now give you my take on how ETFs and non-ETFs can get along in peace and harmony.

Tinkering with an Existing Stock or Mutual Fund Portfolio

Alright. Maybe you're intent on staying put with your existing portfolio. I understand that. But even you can benefit from an occasional ETF holding. (And I'm sure you know that, or else you wouldn't be reading this page right now.)

Improving your diversification

I'll start by assuming that you are invested in individual stocks and bonds, saving mutual funds for the next section.

Unless you are really rich, like Warren Buffett rich, you simply cannot have a truly well-diversified portfolio of individual securities — not nearly as well-diversified as even the simplest ETF or mutual fund portfolio. Where would you even start? You'd have to hold a bevy of large company stocks (both growth and value), small company stocks (again, both growth and value), foreign stocks (Asia and Europe and emerging markets, growth and value, large and small), REIT stocks, and, of course, fixed income investments.

Get real. Examine your portfolio. If you, like so many U.S. investors, have the large majority of your equity holdings in large company U.S. stocks, you can diversify in a flash by adding a small cap ETF or two (see Chapters 7 and 8) and a couple international ETFs (see Chapter 10). If you, like so many investors who lost their shirts in 2000, are heavily invested in exciting but somewhat perilous technology companies, you may balance that off by purchasing a few ETFs in boring but less jumpy sectors like utilities or consumer staples (see Chapter 9).

Minimizing your investment costs

Now, let's assume you're basically a mutual fund kind of guy or gal. You've been reading *Money* magazine and *Kiplinger's* for years. You believe that you have winnowed down the universe of mutual funds to a handful of winners, and goshdarnit, you're going to keep them in your portfolio.

You may have heard the term *core and satellite*. It refers to an investment strategy that has been very much in vogue lately. Core and satellite calls for a portfolio core of basically the entire market, or close to it. Then, you have your satellites: smaller investments designed to outdo the market. It isn't such a bad strategy.

Suppose you have four mutual funds that you love: one tech fund, one health-care fund, one energy fund, and one international growth fund. Each charges you a yearly fee of 1.67 percent (the mutual fund average). And suppose you have $250,000 invested in all four. You are paying ($250,000 × 1.67 percent) a total of $4,175 a year in management fees, and that's to say nothing of any taxes you're paying on dividends and capital gains.

Consider trimming those investments down and moving half the money into an ETF. Turn your present core into satellites, and create a new core with the Vanguard Total Stock Market ETF (VTI). It carries an expense ratio of 0.07 percent. Your total management fees are now ($125,000 × 1.67 percent) + ($125,000 × 0.07 percent), or $2087.50 + $87.50, which totals $2,175. You've just saved yourself a very nifty $2,000 a year, and you'll likely save considerable money on taxes, too.

Using ETFs to tax harvest

Regardless of whether you hold individual stocks or mutual funds, you should hope for nothing but good times ahead but be prepared for something less. Historically, the stock market takes something of a dip in one out of every three years. In those years, ETFs can help ease the pain.

Say it's a particularly bad year for tech stocks, and you happen to own a few of the most beaten down of the dogs. Come late December, you can sell your losing tech stocks or mutual funds. As long as you don't buy them back for 31 days, you can claim a tax loss for the year, and Uncle Sam, in a sense, helps foot the bill for your losses. Ah, but do you really want to be out of the market for the entire month of January (typically one of the best months for stocks)? You don't need to be.

Buy yourself a technology ETF, such as the Technology Select Sector SPDR (XLK), and you're covered should the market suddenly take a jump. Although I'd much rather you simply hold onto your ETF as a permanent investment, if you wish, at the end of 31 days, you can always sell your ETF and buy back your beloved individual stocks or mutual funds.

I believe that tax harvesting has its value, but it is by and large an overvalued and overdone strategy. After all, there are costs involved whenever making a trade. With ETFs and stocks, you pay a commission when you buy or sell. With any security, there is a spread. You can't just buy and sell without some middleman somewhere taking a small cut. Many investors cling to tax harvesting religiously. All I'm saying is please discuss the strategy with your tax adviser (or clergy) before proceeding next year, okay?

Building the Equity Side of Your New ETF Portfolio

In this section, I address those of you who are convinced that ETFs are the best thing since the abolition of pay toilets. You're ready to build a portfolio of ETFs but are concerned about those black holes I mention in the introduction to this chapter.

Unlike the bond side of your portfolio, where the ETF options are meager, you have many, many stock ETFs to choose from. It really doesn't take much outside of the ETF world to build a very well-diversified stock portfolio. A few minor asset classes are missing, which would be nice to have in larger portfolios but certainly aren't necessary. These include non-U.S. real estate and timber.

For those asset classes not yet represented by ETFs, you'll have to go the mutual fund route. I suggest that you read the latest edition of Eric Tyson's *Mutual Funds For Dummies* (Wiley) and investigate mutual fund options on www.morningstar.com or http://finance.yahoo.com. The options I give in the following sections are some of the mutual funds that I have used personally or in client portfolios. They are all *no load* (meaning you'll pay no commission), have reasonable management expenses, and are run by mutual fund companies with reputations for honesty. I include Web sites and telephone numbers in case you want to go directly to the fund provider. Please read the prospectus before purchasing any mutual fund.

International small cap

Once upon a time, the diversification afforded by investing in foreign companies like Toyota, Sony, Volkswagen, and British Petroleum was a beautiful complement to your domestic investments in Ford, General Electric, General Motors, and Texaco. Lately, however, the world has become a smaller place, and the fortunes of international conglomerates are arguably more bound to the world economy than to the economy of any nation.

As such, large international companies just don't offer the diversification power they once did. But small international companies — those that cater more to their own home markets than to an international audience — still do. I'm talking about businesses such as a bank in Tokyo that lends money to local firms, a company in the U.K. that delivers natural gas to British households, and a German construction and architectural firm. The correlation of small international stocks to the U.S. stock market has recently been, according to good a number of studies, perhaps half that of large international stocks.

If you can take some serious volatility, I suggest that of whatever you allocate to foreign stocks (preferably 40 to 50 percent of your total allocation to stock), one-third to one-half be allocated to foreign small and mid cap. In other words, if you have a $250,000 portfolio and you've decided to allocate $150,000 to stocks, consider allocating perhaps $20,000 to $37,500 to small and mid cap international funds.

WisdomTree came out with a handful of small international stock ETFs in June 2006. These include the WisdomTree International SmallCap Dividend Fund (DLS), the WisdomTree Europe SmallCap Dividend Fund (DFE), and the WisdomTree Japan SmallCap Dividend Fund (DFJ). All carry expense ratios of 0.58 percent.

Of the three, my favorite would be the broader International SmallCap Dividend Fund (DLS), which I may very well begin using in my portfolios soon. As you may have read in Chapter 11, I'm generally not too crazy about dividend funds, but for the moment, this is all that is available ETF-wise in the world of small cap international. For more information, see www.wisdom tree.com.

If DLS doesn't float your boat, I suggest looking into the following no load, well-managed, reasonably priced mutual funds. I've used all these for either my own portfolio or those of clients:

- **Fidelity International Small Cap Opportunities Fund (FSCOX):** 800-544-8888; www.fidelity.com

- **Third Avenue International Value (TAVIX):** 800-443-1021; www.thirdavenuefunds.com

- **T Rowe Price International Discovery (PRIDX):** 800-225-7720; www.troweprice.com

- **Tweedy, Browne Global Value (TBGVX):** 800-432-4789; www.tweedybrowne.com

- **Vanguard International Explorer (VINEX):** 800-662-7447; www.vanguard.com

The Tweedy, Browne fund (funny name, I know) is a mid and small cap international fund with a *value tilt,* meaning you get more value stocks than you do growth stocks. It is also the only international stock fund that is *dollar-hedged:* If the dollar goes up or down *vis a vis* other currencies, it won't affect your balance. The Tweedy, Browne fund reflects only the value of the foreign markets themselves. That little feature removes half the volatility of investing abroad and, in a way, almost creates a separate asset class. I use Tweedy, Browne for roughly half my allocation to foreign small and mid cap stocks and may continue to do so even after the introduction of more small cap international ETFs. Unfortunately, the Tweedy, Browne Global Value fund is currently closed to new investors, but it could possibly reopen.

International REITs

Real estate investment trusts, or *REITs* (see a full discussion in Chapter 13), offer sweet diversification to any portfolio. Foreign REITs offer even more diversification. After all, what could be more local than real estate?

The international REIT market is still in its adolescence. Australia and the Netherlands have had REITs or REIT-like structures since the early 1970s, Belgium and Canada since the early 1990s. In none of those countries, however, does the market cap for such securities even touch the market cap of U.S. REITs ($250 billion or more). The room for growth in such nations is enormous.

In other countries, including Japan, France, and Korea, REITs or REIT-like trusts are much more recent inventions. There, too, the market can seemingly only grow. And in the case of Germany, Italy, and the United Kingdom, nothing quite resembling REITs yet exists, but plans are on the drawing board. (Other kinds of real estate securities are presently available in those countries.)

With the growing availability of foreign REITs, as well as other publicly traded real estate securities, a handful of firms now offer global real estate funds to U.S. investors. And a number of others have such funds currently in development. Unfortunately, I know of no such ETF in development, so you'll have to go with a mutual fund to tap into this asset class.

Whatever your allocation to small and mid cap international stocks, I suggest that perhaps one-fifth to one-quarter of that amount be allocated to either of the following two funds:

- ✔ **Alpine International Real Estate Equity Fund (EGLRX):** 885-558-8875; `www.alpinefunds.com`

- ✔ **Fidelity International Real Estate Fund (FIREX):** 800-544-8888; `www.fidelity.com`

Be aware that foreign REITs, like other foreign stocks, tend to move up and down in accordance with currency flux, as well as with the value of the underlying securities. Therefore, you may see the value of your holding move considerably. If the past is any guide, however, you should do well. Both of these funds have thus far rewarded their investors richly.

Timber REITs

Real estate comes in many forms, from shopping malls to condos to office buildings. A handful of REITs own timberland — gazillions of acres of trees. The land under which the trees are grown tends to rise and fall in value along with the going price for timber. Therefore, these special REITs behave almost as a separate asset class. There are days and weeks when most REITs go one way and timber REITs go another. For that reason, if I have a client with a fairly large portfolio, I may take a percentage of the U.S. REIT allocation and move it into timber.

Alas, no timber REIT ETFs exist yet. No timber REIT mutual funds are available either. For that reason, I buy individual REIT stocks. Two of the largest timber REITs are the following:

- ✔ **Plum Creek Timber Company (PCL):** 800-254-4961; `www.plumcreek.com`

- ✔ **Rayonier Timber (RYN):** 904-357-9155; `www.rayonier.com`

Keep in mind that these are individual company stocks. Throughout this book I say that you really shouldn't invest in individual companies, but I'm making a small exception here for timber. Individual stocks can be volatile and sometimes awfully capricious. I suggest limiting your allocation to absolutely no more than 5 percent of the equity side of your portfolio. Perhaps take that 5 percent and split it between PCL and RYN.

Just like all REITs, timber REITs must distribute 90 percent of their income as dividends. And those dividends will be taxed. Keep your timber REITs, if possible, in a tax advantaged retirement account.

Where few investors have gone before: DFA funds

Perhaps you've never heard of the mutual fund company called Dimensional Fund Advisors, or DFA. For the ultimate in slicing and dicing a portfolio, no fund company compares. Only through DFA can you, for example, find a fund that allows you to invest in emerging markets small cap, emerging markets value, and U.K. small company. All of DFA's funds are expertly managed index funds with reasonable expense ratios.

The only problem with DFA is that you can invest in their funds only if you are an institution with huge bucks, or if you go through a *fee-only* wealth manager (meaning he takes no commissions). The problem with that, of course, is that you have to pay the fee-only wealth manager. Since you are reading this book, you are probably a hands-on, do-it-yourself kind of investor, and you may not want to pay someone to manage your money.

If, however, you have a handsome portfolio, and if you can find a fee-only wealth manager who charges you a reasonable amount (try The National Association of Personal Financial Advisors, www.napfa.org), by all means, consider DFA (www.dfaus.com). What I'd really love to see is DFA get into the ETF business!

Building the Fixed Income Side of Your New ETF Portfolio

A much as I enjoy in-line skating, I recognize that it does not make for an entire fitness program. So I accompany my in-line skating with other activities, like a kick boxing class and lots of walking. With that kind of cross training, I manage to stay in pretty good shape.

And to keep the fixed income side of my clients' portfolios in shape, I cannot rely entirely on bond ETFs. Not yet, at least. For right now, the only kinds of fixed income represented by ETFs are Treasurys, TIPS, and investment-grade corporate (see Chapter 12). These three categories do not provide the diversity within fixed income that I would like to see. So for the time being, I would ask you — especially if you have a portfolio of $50,000 or more — to complement your bond ETF holdings with one or more of the following other kinds of fixed income.

Tax-free glory: Municipal bonds

If the creator of the bond is a city or perhaps a municipal authority, the issue is called a *municipal bond* or *muni*. Interest income from munis is exempt from federal income tax and, in many cases (especially if you live in the state that issued the bond), state and local taxes as well. For that reason, the interest rate you get on munis is typically lower than you would get on a taxable bond of similar maturity.

A simple formula allows you to compare the return you'll get on a muni to the return you'll get on a taxable bond. Here's the formula: Subtract the federal marginal tax bracket percentage from the number one, and divide that number by the tax-free rate.

For example: Assume you are in the 25 percent tax bracket and are considering a 5.00 percent tax-free bond. You divide 5.00 by 0.75 (1 less 0.25) and find that the taxable-equivalent yield is 6.67 percent. In other words, you would need a taxable bond to pay 6.67 percent to match the return on the 5.00 percent tax-exempt.

Got that? Good! Now forget it! Unless you are in an exceptionally high tax bracket, I urge a position in munis for the diversification power, even if the simple formula tells you that you're going to get a lesser return. Munis tend to move in cycles somewhat different from most taxable bonds.

To date, no ETF allows you to invest in munis, but I have little doubt that one will appear before very long.

In the meantime, consider the following municipal bond funds. (Note: The following funds are federally tax-free but not state tax-free. If you live in a state with a high income tax, you may want to investigate munis that are exempt from both federal and state taxes. You'll find many offerings at both Vanguard and Fidelity.)

> ✔ **Fidelity Intermediate Municipal Income (FLTMX):** 800-544-8888; www.fidelity.com
>
> ✔ **Vanguard High-Yield Tax-Exempt (VWAHX):** 800-662-7447; www.vanguard.com

> This fund is somewhat more volatile than the Vanguard Intermediate-Term Tax-Exempt but should yield a higher return over time.
>
> ✔ **Vanguard Intermediate-Term Tax-Exempt (VWITX):** 800-662-7447; www.vanguard.com

Maes and Macs: Agency bonds with a break on tax

Bonds issued by U.S. government-sponsored organizations, such as the Government National Mortgage Association (Ginnie Mae), Student Loan Marketing Association (Sallie Mae), Federal National Mortgage Association (Fannie Mae), or Federal Home Loan Mortgage Corporation (Freddie Mac), are called *agency bonds.* They are usually exempt from state and local taxes. Unlike munis, however, they are not exempt from federal tax. Agency bonds usually fall somewhere between Treasurys and corporate bonds on the risk/return continuum.

Following are several more-than-acceptable agency bond funds:

- ✔ **American Century Ginnie Mae (BGNMX):** 800-345-2021; www.american century.com
- ✔ **Fidelity Ginnie Mae Fund (FGMNX):** 800-544-8888; www.fidelity.com
- ✔ **Vanguard GNMA Fund (VFIIX):** 800-662-7447; www.vanguard.com

I Bonds: An Uncle Sam bond with a twist

Like TIPS (see Chapter 12), I Bonds are inflation indexed. Unlike TIPS, they are available as individual bonds in very small denominations — as small as $25.

On the upside: The interest earned tends to be greater than TIPS. The correlation to inflation is also more closely matched, as I Bonds change their inflation adjustment every six months. And — a potentially very sweet bonus if you have young ones — if you use the I Bonds for higher education expenses, that interest, along with any inflation adjustments, may be yours to keep and spend tax-free.

On the downside: You must hold I Bonds for at least one year, and you forfeit three months' interest if you redeem them before they mature in five years.

You can buy I Bonds by calling 800-722-2678 or visiting www.treasury direct.gov.

Le bond du jour: International fixed income

Foreign bonds make up more than 75 percent of fixed-income opportunities worldwide, yet the asset class remains largely snubbed by U.S. investors.

That's a shame, because the world of international bonds offers many possibilities all the way up and down the risk/return ladder. They present another asset class to add to a portfolio, lending yet greater diversification. Just as in the world of stocks, some years are better for international bonds, some are better for U.S. If you have both, you'll enjoy a smoother ride on the road to accumulating wealth.

Morningstar currently lists 79 bond mutual funds categorized as either international or global. (No ETFs are available yet, but I'm certain they're coming.) I suggest that international bonds play a modest role in the portfolio of any investor with $50,000 or more in fixed income. For those with even larger fixed income positions, I may suggest both a dollar-hedged and unhedged position in foreign bonds. The dollar-hedged funds are less volatile. The unhedged funds offer greater growth potential. (*Hedged* means that the exchange rate between the dollar and other currencies is corrected for. *Unhedged* means that the return you get on your investment will depend in part on which way the dollar blows.)

Following are several international bond funds to consider:

- ✔ **American Century International Bond (BEGBX):** 800-345-2021; www.americancentury.com
- ✔ **PIMCO Foreign Bond, Unhedged (PFBDX):** 800-426-0107; www.allianzinvestors.com
- ✔ **PIMCO Foreign Bond, Dollar-Hedged (PFODX):** 800-426-0107; www.allianzinvestors.com
- ✔ **T. Rowe Price International Bond (RPIBX):** 800-225-7720; www.troweprice.com

Hold on tight: Junk city

You're undoubtedly familiar with the term *high-yield* bond, otherwise known (when we're being honest) as a *junk* bond. A high-yield bond — one that yields high dividends to compensate for the shaky nature of the bond — can be sovereign (think Latin American countries), corporate (think General Motors), or muni (think California). No high-yield bond ETFs exist . . . yet.

Of all the different kinds of high-yield bonds, my favorite are emerging market bonds issued by governments of countries like Brazil, Venezuela, Korea, and Russia. If you're going to have only one kind of junk bond, this is probably the one to have. Reason: Emerging market bonds have no correlation to U.S. stocks or bonds. On the other hand, U.S. junk bonds, especially corporate junk, tend to correlate with the stock market. When things get rough, they may not offer much protection the way, say, Treasurys would.

Consider a position in junk, especially emerging market bonds, but don't allocate it to the fixed income side of your portfolio. Allocate it to the stock side. Even though junk bonds aren't stocks, the potential return and volatility are closer to stocks than to most other bonds. Take, for example, the ten years ended December 31, 2005. Emerging market bonds during that period saw an average annual return of 13 percent, with a standard deviation of 14.18 percent.

As for U.S. junk, I generally suggest buying into the asset class — believe it or not — in more conservative portfolios, where I may substitute U.S. stock for high-yield bonds. It's my way of shooting for a fairly good return with limited risk. In a sense, I see U.S. junk as a hybrid of sorts. Not quite stock; not quite bond; somewhere in between on both risk and return.

Following are several U.S. high-yield bond funds to consider:

- ✓ **Fidelity High Income Fund (SPHIX):** 800-544-8888; www.fidelity.com
- ✓ **Payden High Income Fund (PYHRX):** 213-625-1900; www.payden-rygel.com
- ✓ **Vanguard High-Yield Corporate Bond Fund (VWEHX):** 800-662-7447; www.vanguard.com

And here are some emerging market bond funds to consider:

- ✓ **Fidelity New Markets Income Fund (FNMIX):** 800-544-8888; www.fidelity.com
- ✓ **Payden Emerging Markets Bond Fund (PYEMX):** 213-625-1900; www.payden-rygel.com
- ✓ **T. Rowe Price Emerging Markets Bond (PREMX):** 800-683-5660; www.troweprice.com

Market-neutral mutual funds

By no means are so-called *market-neutral* funds bond funds of any sort, but permit me the literary license to discuss them here. The reason: Unlike junk bonds, which *are* bonds but should be allocated to the equity side of your portfolio, market-neutral funds are actually stock funds that I'd like you to allocate to the fixed income side of your portfolio. That's simply because they tend to behave more like bonds than stocks: The return is somewhat predictable like bonds, and the volatility is limited.

Market-neutral funds use vastly different strategies to meet their ends. The goal of most is to produce long-term returns that are more similar to bonds than stocks (perhaps a tad higher than bonds) while having no correlation to either the bond or stock market.

Some market-neutral funds use a *long–short* strategy. That is, they buy stocks to enjoy the potential appreciation. They also *short* stocks (often stock ETFs) to make money when the market is going down. It's a tricky business, and you want to find an experienced manager who has been doing it for a while. Another strategy involves investing in companies very short-term just on the cusp of their merging with other companies.

Here are a few market-neutral funds worthy of investigation:

- **Gabelli ABC (GABCX):** 800-422-3554; www.gabelli.com
- **Hussman Strategic Growth (HSGFX):** 800-487-7626; www.hussmanfunds.com
- **Merger Fund (MERFX):** 800-343-8959; no Web site

Fixed immediate annuities

For older people especially, and almost definitely for those with no heirs, an annuity — either a fixed annuity or a variable — can make enormous sense. With an annuity, you abandon your principal, and in return you enjoy a fully insured yield typically far greater than you would likely get with any other fixed-income option.

There are many horrible annuities out there. I can't tell you how often a new client walks into my office, throws his annuity papers on the table, and says, "*Why* did I ever buy this stupid thing."

If you are interested in an annuity, start with Charles Schwab, Raymond James Financial, or Vanguard. In general, brokerage houses offer much, much better deals than insurance companies. Their annuity products tend to be cheaper, less complicated, and easier to back out of should you change your mind:

- **Charles Schwab:** 866-232-9890; www.schwab.com
- **Raymond James Financial:** 800-248-8863; www.raymondjames.com
- **Vanguard:** 800-522-5555; www.vanguard.com

A few odd ducks

I talk in this chapter about mutual funds, individual securities (stocks or bonds), and annuities as possible alternatives to, or complements to, ETFs. But the investment world offers other options as well. Here are a few of the less common kinds of investments, some of which may be worth consideration for your portfolio:

✔ **Closed-end mutual funds:** Just as the word *burger* without any qualifiers is usually understood to mean *ham*burger — not veggie burger or turkey burger — so are the words *mutual fund* usually understood to mean *open-end* mutual fund. The vast majority of mutual funds are open-ended. That means that the fund has no set limit of shares. As more investors buy into the fund, the fund grows, acquiring more securities and issuing more shares.

Closed-end funds, on the other hand, are created with a certain amount of shares, and they forever retain that same amount of shares. If any new investors want to buy in, they must buy shares from existing investors. For that reason, closed-end mutual funds, unlike open-end mutual funds, may sell shares at a premium or a discount. (ETFs may also trade at a premium or discount, but it tends to be negligible. Closed-end funds may sometimes be bought or sold for 50 percent more or less than the value of the underlying securities.) Closed-end mutual funds tend to be more volatile than open-end mutual funds, and the management fees tend to be higher.

✔ **Unit investment trusts:** Some ETFs, especially the older ones such as the QQQQ (Qubes) and SPDR 500 and SPDR 400, actually are unit investment trusts (UITs). However, not all UITs are ETFs.

A *UIT* is a fixed portfolio of stocks or bonds generally sold to investors by brokers. The UIT is usually sold through a one-time public offering. It has a termination date, which could be anywhere from several months to 50 years down the road. Upon termination, the UIT dissolves.

In the case of ETF/UITs, however, it's a slightly different story. When the first ETFs were created, there was an original termination date of 25 years hence. But as the ETFs grew in popularity, ETF providers petitioned the Securities and Exchange Commission (SEC) to make an exception, which the SEC did.

✔ **Hedge funds/Limited partnerships:** *Hedge funds* — funds that promise insurance against bad markets — come in many different flavors and use any number of strategies to achieve (or try to achieve) their objective. Of late, a number of mutual funds have been billing themselves as hedge funds. No ETFs have done so to date, but the time is coming, I'm sure. Traditionally, however, most hedge funds are neither mutual funds nor ETFs; rather, they are organized as limited partnerships. Limited partnerships are largely unregulated, fees tend to be high, and *liquidity* (the ability to get your money out if you need it) can be very limited. Proceed with great caution.

Part IV
Putting It All Together

The 5th Wave · By Rich Tennant

"You may want to talk to Phil — he's one of our more aggressive financial planners."

In this part . . .

Pick up your hammer and grab some nails. It's time now to get your hands dirty actually building an ETF portfolio. In the next four chapters, I walk you through the entire construction process. I then share some important maintenance tips, such as when to tweak your portfolio and when to leave hands off. And finally, I take you into the world of retirement, to see how your ETF portfolio may someday provide you with a steady and secure income.

Chapter 16

Sample ETF Portfolio Menus

*I*f there is such a thing as a personal hell, and if, for whatever reason, I piss off the Big Guy before I die, I'm fairly certain that I will spend eternity in either a Home Depot or a Lowe's. The only real question I have is whether His wrath will place me in plumbing supply, home décor, or flooring.

I'm not the handyman type. Even the words "home renovation" are enough to send shivers up my spine. The last thing I built out of metal or wood — a car-shaped napkin holder — was in shop class at Lincoln Orens Junior High School. I brought the thing home to my mother, and she said, "Oh, Russell, um, what a lovely birdhouse."

And yet, despite my failed relationship with power tools, there is one kind of construction that I absolutely love: portfolio construction.

I enjoy crafting portfolios not only because it involves multicolored pie charts (I've always had a soft spot for multicolored pie charts) but because the process involves so much more than running a piece of wood through a jigsaw and hoping not to lose any fingers. Portfolio construction is — or should be — a highly individualized, creative exercise that takes into consideration many factors: economics, history, statistics, and psychology among them.

The ideal portfolio (if such a thing exists) for a 30-year-old who makes $70,000 a year is very different from the portfolio of a 75-year-old who makes $30,000 a year. The optimal portfolio for a 40-year-old worrywart differs from the optimal portfolio for a 40-year-old devil-may-care type. The portfolio-of-dreams following a three-year bear market may look a wee bit different than a prime portfolio following a ten-year bull run.

Every financial professional I know goes about portfolio construction in a somewhat different way. In this chapter, I walk you through the steps that I take and that have worked well for me. I don't mean to present my way as the only way, so I also mention an alternative strategy (see the sidebar "Dividing up the pie either conservatively or aggressively by industry sector").

Needless to say (since this is, after all, a book about exchange-traded funds), my primary construction materials are ETFs, as I believe they should be for most, but not all, investors. My building tools involve some sophisticated Morningstar software, my HP 12C financial calculator, a premise called *Modern Portfolio Theory,* a statistical phenomenon called *reversion to the mean,* and various measures of risk and return. But rest assured that this isn't brain surgery, or even elbow surgery. You can be a pretty good portfolio builder yourself by the time you finish this chapter.

So please follow along. I promise you that nothing you are about to see will resemble either a napkin holder or a birdhouse!

So, How Much Risk Can You Handle and Still Sleep at Night?

The first question I ask myself — and the first question anyone building a portfolio should ask — is this: *How much volatility can the portfolio-holder stomach?* So few things in the world of investments are sure bets. One thing is a sure bet: The amount of risk you take or don't take will have a great bearing on your long-term return. You simply are not going to get rich investing in bank CDs. On the other hand, you aren't going to lose your nest egg in a single week, either. The same cannot be said of a tech stock — or even a bevy of tech stocks wrapped up in an ETF.

A well-built ETF portfolio can help to mitigate risks, not eliminate them.

Please forget the dumb old rules about portfolio building and risk. How much risk you can or should handle depends on your wealth, your age, your income, your health, your financial responsibilities, your potential inheritances, and whether you're the kind of person who tosses and turns over life's upsets. If anyone gives you a pat formula — "Take your age, subtract it from 100, and that, dear friend, is how much you should have in stocks" — run away! It isn't nearly that simple.

A few things that just don't matter

Before I lay out what matters most in determining appropriate risk and appropriate allocations to stocks, bonds, and cash (or stock ETFs and bond ETFs), I want to throw out just a few things that really *shouldn't* play into your decision, even though they play into many people's portfolio decisions:

- ✔ The portfolio of your best friend, which has done great guns.

- ✔ Your personal feelings on the state of the economy, the current administration, where the Fed stands on the prime interest rate, and exchanges rates between the dollar, the Euro, and the yen.

- ✔ The article you clipped out of *Lotsa Dough* magazine that tells you that you can earn 50 percent a year by investing in . . . whatever.

Listen: Your best friend may be in a completely different economic place than you are. His well-polished ETF portfolio, laid out by a first-rate financial planner, may be just perfect for him and all wrong for you.

As far as the state of the nation and where the Dow is headed, you simply don't know. Neither do I. The talking heads on TV pretend to know, but they don't know squat. Nor does the author of that article in the glossy magazine (filled with ads from mutual fund companies) that tells you how you can get rich quickly in the markets. The secrets to financial success cannot be had by forking over $3.50 for a magazine.

(Whenever I read some prognosticator suggesting a handful of stocks or mutual funds for the coming year, I Google his name to see what projections he made a year prior. Then I check to see how his picks have done. You should do the same! Inevitably, my dog Norman, the killer poodle, could do a better job picking stocks.)

The stock market over the course of the past century has returned about 10 percent nominally (7 percent or so after inflation). Bonds have returned about half as much. A well-diversified portfolio, by historical standards, has returned something in between stocks and bonds — maybe 7 to 8 percent (4 to 5 percent after inflation). With some of the advice in this book, you should be able to do that, and maybe even a wee bit better. But don't take inordinate risk with any sizeable chunk of your portfolio in the hope that you are going to earn 50 percent a year after inflation — or even before inflation. It won't happen.

On the other hand, don't pooh-pooh a 7 to 8 percent return. Compound interest is a truly miraculous thing. Invest $20,000 today, add $2,000 each year, and within 20 years, with "only" a 7.5 percent return, you'll have $171,566. (If inflation is running in the 3 percent ballpark, that $171,566 will be worth about $110,000 in today's dollars.)

The irony of risk and return

In a few pages, I provide you with some sample portfolios appropriate for someone who should be taking minimal risk as opposed to someone who should be taking more risk. At this point, I want to digress for a moment to say that in a perfect world, those who need to take the most risk would be the most able to take it. In the real world, sometimes sadly ironic, those who need to take the most risk really can't afford to.

Specifically, a poor person needs whatever financial cushion he has. He can't afford to risk the farm on emerging market or high tech ETFs. A rich person has plenty of financial cushion and can take out a chunk of discretionary money to invest in emerging market stocks and high tech ETFs, but he really doesn't need to because he's living comfortably and can do without the potential high return. It just isn't fair. Yet no one is to blame, and nothing can be done about it. It is what it is.

Let's move on.

The 20x rule

Whatever your age, whatever your station in life, you probably wouldn't object if your investments could support you. How much do you need to have your investments support you? That's actually not very complicated and has been very well studied: You need about 20 times your annual expenses to live off your investments and not have the principal start to disappear.

That is, if you need $30,000 a year to live — in addition to Social Security and any other income — you should ideally have $600,000 in your portfolio when you retire. You can have less, but you'll have to eat into principal. Eating into principal may be perfectly appropriate, especially after a certain age, but to play it safe, I'd like for you to at least aim to retire with 20 times your annual expenses in your portfolio.

(Factor in the value or partial value of your home only if it is paid up and if you foresee a day when you can downsize.)

If you are still far away from that 20x landmark, and you are not in debt, and your income is secure, and you have enough cash to live on for six months, then with the rest of your loot, you should probably err toward the riskier ETF portfolio (mostly stock ETFs). You need the return.

If you have your 20 times annual expenses already locked up or are close to it, you should probably err toward a less risky ETF portfolio (more bond ETFs). After all, you have more to lose than you have to gain. (See the sidebar

"Russell's 'today and tomorrow' portfolio modeling technique" for my suggestion on how you should have not one, but two portfolio models: one for right now, and one for the future.) You do need to be careful, however, that your investments keep up with inflation. Savings accounts are unlikely to do that.

If you have way more than 20 times annual expenses, congratulations! You have many options, and how much risk you take will be a decision external to any material needs. You may, for example, want to leave behind a grand legacy, in which case you may want to shoot for higher returns. Or you may not care what you leave behind, in which case leaving your money in a tired savings account wouldn't make much difference.

Other risk/return considerations

I doubt I can list everything you should consider when determining the proper amount of risk to take with your investments, but here are a few additional things to keep in mind:

- ✔ **What is your safety net?** If worse came to worst, do you have family or friends who would help you if you got in a real financial bind? If the answer is yes, you can add a tablespoon of risk.

- ✔ **What is your family health history? Do you lead a healthy lifestyle?** These are the two greatest predictors of your longevity. If Mom and Dad lived to 100, and you don't smoke and you do eat your vegetables, you may be looking at a long retirement. Add a dollop of risk — you'll need the return.

- ✔ **How secure is your job?** The less secure your employment, the more you should keep in nonvolatile investments (like short-term bonds or bond funds); you may need to pull from them if you get the pink slip next Friday afternoon.

- ✔ **Can you downsize?** Say you are close to retirement, and you live in a McMansion. If you think that sooner or later (sooner, if necessary) you can sell the McMansion and buy a smaller place, you have some financial cushion. You can afford to take a bit more risk.

Why not just fill out an online risk questionnaire?

Yes, I give my clients a risk questionnaire. And then I go through it with them to help them interpret their answers. Lots of Web sites offer investment risk questionnaires, but instead of having anyone interpret the answers, a computer just spits out a few numbers: You should invest x in stock and y in bonds. Yikes!

Please, please, don't allow a computer-generated questionnaire to determine your financial future! I've tried dozens of them, and the answers are consistently wacky!

For example: One of the questions that appears on nearly *all* the Web questionnaires is this: *Please rate your previous investment experience and level of satisfaction with the following six asset classes.* And then they list money market funds, bonds, stocks, and so on.

I had a client named Jason who was a 30-year-old with a solid job and no kids. After taking an online questionnaire, he was told he should be nearly all in money market accounts and bonds based on his previous "very low" satisfaction with stocks and stock mutual funds. This young man definitely should not invest in any foreign stocks or bonds, the computer-generated program told him, because of his "very low" satisfaction with foreign funds he had invested in previously.

Oh, jeesh. The reason Jason had "very low" satisfaction with stocks and foreign funds is because in 2004, he got snookered by some stock broker (posing as a "financial planner") into buying a handful of full load, high expense ratio, actively managed mutual funds that (predictably) lost him money. That experience should have *no* bearing on the development of this young man's portfolio, which should have the lion's share in stock ETFs or mutual funds.

What I'm saying is that after reading this book, if you aren't too certain where you belong on the risk/return continuum, perhaps you should hire an experienced and impartial financial advisor — if only for a couple of hours — to review your portfolio with you. I write more about seeking professional help in Chapter 20.

Keys to Optimal Investing

When you have a rough idea of where you should be riskwise, your attention should turn next to fun matters such as Modern Portfolio Theory, reversion to the mean, cost minimization, and tax efficiency. Please allow me to explain.

Incorporating Modern Portfolio Theory into your investment decisions

The subject I'm about to discuss is a theory much in the same way evolution is a theory: The people who don't believe it are those who decide to disregard all the science. Modern Portfolio Theory (MPT) says that if you diversify your portfolio — putting all kinds of eggs into all kinds of baskets — you reduce risk and optimize return.

You get the most bang for your buck, according to MPT, when you mix and match investments that have little *correlation.* In other words, if you build your portfolio with different ETFs that tend to do well (and not so well) in different kinds of markets, you'll have a lean and mean portfolio.

Lately, MPT has been the source of a lot of controversy. It hasn't been working as well as it did in the past. At times in the past few years, there have been stretches of days, even weeks and months, when different asset classes — U.S. stocks, foreign stocks, bonds, commodities, and real estate — have all moved up and down nearly in lockstep.

While correlations can change over history — and lately the major asset classes have shown alarmingly high rates of correlation — you shouldn't simply scrap the idea that diversification and the quest for noncorrelation are crucial. However, you may want to be cautious of too much reliance on diversification. Yes, you can diversify away much risk. But you should also have certain low-risk investments in your portfolio, investments that hold their own in any kind of market. Low-risk investments include money market funds, short- and intermediate-term high quality bonds (especially Treasury bonds), and bank CDs.

Maximizing the importance of cost minimization

ETFs are cheap, which is one of the things I love about them. The difference between a typical mutual fund that charges 1.6 percent and a typical ETF that charges 0.2 percent adds up to a *lot* of money over time. One of my favorite financial Web sites, www.moneychimp.com, offers a fund-cost calculator. Invest $100,000 for 20 years at 8 percent and deduct 0.2 for expenses; you're left with $449,133. Deduct 1.6 percent, and you're left with $345,806. That's a difference of over $100,000.

Because the vast majority of ETFs fall into the super-cheap to cheap range (generally 0.1 to 0.6 percent), the differences won't be quite so huge. Still, in picking and choosing ETFs, cost should always be a factor.

Of course, with ETFs, you pay a small trading fee every time you buy and sell. That too should be examined and minimized. Do all your trades online, and choose a brokerage house that gives you the best deal. If you're going to make frequent buys and sells, perhaps ETFs aren't for you; rather, you should build your portfolio with mostly low cost, no-load index funds.

Striving for tax efficiency

Keeping your investment dollars in your pocket and not lining Uncle Sam's is one big reason to choose ETFs over mutual funds. ETFs are, by and large, much more tax efficient than mutual funds. But some ETFs are going to be more tax efficient than others. I cover this issue in-depth in Chapter 19 where I talk about tax-advantaged retirement accounts, such as Roth IRAs.

For now, let me say that you must choose wisely which ETFs get put into which baskets. In general, high dividend and interest paying ETFs (REIT ETFs, bond ETFs) belong in tax-advantaged accounts.

Timing your investments (modestly and conservatively)

If you've read much of this book already, by now you realize that I'm largely an *efficient market* kind of guy. I believe that the ups and downs of the stock and bond market — and of any individual security — are, in absence of true inside information, unpredictable. (And trading on true inside information is illegal.) For that reason, I prefer indexed ETFs and mutual funds over actively managed funds.

That being said, however . . .

I also believe in something called *reversion to the mean*. This is a statistical phenomenon that colloquially translates to the following: What goes up must come down; what goes waaaay up, you need to be careful about investing too much money in.

At the time I'm writing this, for example, energy stocks, commodities, and small international stocks have been flying high for years. As far as all three of these kinds of stocks are concerned, I like them. I think they can be wonderful diversifiers. But I'm holding back, keeping my exposure to these asset classes a bit in check.

I'm *not* suggesting that you go out and buy any ETF that has underperformed the market for years, or sell any ETF that has outperformed. But to a small degree, you should factor in reversion to the mean when constructing a portfolio.

For example, say you decide that your $100,000 portfolio should include $15,000 of the iShares S&P 500 Growth ETF (IVW), and large growth stocks have for years seriously underperformed large value, small stocks, and just about every other asset class. You may want to allocate, say, $16,000 or perhaps as much as $17,000 to IVW. If you would normally invest $10,000 in the Energy Select Sector SPDR (XLE), and that ETF has outperformed the broad market by leaps and bounds for the past several years, you may wish to allocate, say, only $9,000.

Please don't go overboard. I'm suggesting that you use reversion to the mean to very gently tweak your portfolio percentages — not ignore them!

Finding the Perfect Portfolio Fit

Time now to peek into my private world, as I reveal some of the ETF-based portfolios I've worked out for clients over the years. You should look for the client that you most resemble, and that example will give you some *rough* idea of the kind of advice I would give you if you were a client. All names, of course, have been changed to protect privacy. For the sake of brevity, I provide you with only a thumbnail sketch of each of my client's financial situations.

Considering the simplest of the simple

Before I get into anything complicated or present any real client portfolios, I want to introduce an easier-than-easy ETF portfolio. What I've constructed is a perfectly fine, workable investment model with decent (although not great) diversification. It may be enough for anyone with limited funds (say $30,000 to $50,000), but funds they are willing to plunk down and leave put. (For less than $30,000, or for a portfolio that is likely to see a good amount of buying or selling, an entire ETF portfolio probably isn't going to make sense because the trading costs will gobble up too much.)

I've thrown in (in order of appearance) large cap stocks, small cap stocks, international stocks (EAFA stands for *Europe, Australia, and Far East index*), and bonds.

This portfolio can be tailored to suit the aggressive investor who can deal with some serious ups and downs in the hopes of high long-term returns, the conservative investor who can't stand to lose too much money, or the middle-of-the-road investor. Keep in mind that you should always have three to six months living expenses in cash or near-cash (money market, short-term CD, Internet banking account, or very short-term high-quality bond fund). You should also have all your credit card and other high-interest debt paid up. The rest of your money is what you may invest.

	Aggressive	Middle-of-the-road	Conservative
PowerShares FTSE RAFI U.S. 1000 (PRF)	30 percent	30 percent	20 percent
Vanguard Small Cap ETF (VB)	15 percent	10 percent	5 percent
iShares MSCI EAFE Index Fund (EFA)	30 percent	25 percent	15 percent
Vanguard Emerging Markets ETF (VWO)	10 percent	5 percent	0 percent
iShares Lehman Aggregate Bond Fund (AGG)	15 percent	30 percent	60 percent

Racing toward riches: A portfolio that may require a crash helmet

High-risk/high-return ETF portfolios are made up mostly of stock ETFs. After all, stocks have a very long history of clobbering most other investments — *if* you give them enough time. A high risk/high return portfolio should have a good percentage of small cap stocks and a good chunk of international, including emerging markets. If the portfolio is diversified into industry sectors (an acceptable strategy, as I discuss in Chapter 9), a high risk/high return strategy would emphasize fast-growing sectors, such as technology and healthcare.

Let's consider the case of Jason, a single, 30-year-old pharmaceutical sales-man. Jason came to me after getting burned badly by several high cost, load mutual funds that performed miserably over the years. Still, given his steady income of $90,000 and his minimal living expenses (he rents a one-bedroom apartment in Allentown, PA), Jason has managed to sock away $165,000. His job is secure. He has good disability insurance. He anticipates saving $20,000 to $30,000 a year over the next several years. He enjoys his work and intends to work till normal retirement age. He plans to buy a new car (ballpark $30,000) in the next few months but otherwise has no major expenditures earmarked.

Jason can clearly take some risk. Following is the ETF-based portfolio that I designed for him, which is represented in Figure 16-1. Note that I had Jason put four to six months emergency money, plus the $30,000 for the car, into a money market account, and that amount is not factored into this portfolio.

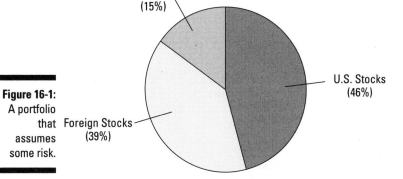

Figure 16-1:
A portfolio that assumes some risk.

Also note that although this portfolio is mostly made up of ETFs, I do include a few no-load mutual funds to gain access to asset classes not yet represented by ETFs. These are the Fidelity International Small Cap Opportunities Fund (FSCOX) and the Vanguard High-Yield Tax-Exempt bond fund (VWAHX), which makes particular sense for Jason because he is currently earning a high income and has no appreciable write-offs.

U.S. stocks: 46 percent

iShares Morningstar Large Value (JKF)	13 percent
iShares Morningstar Large Growth (JKE)	12 percent
iShares Morningstar Small Value (JKL)	9 percent
iShares Morningstar Small Growth (JKK)	6 percent
Vanguard REIT ETF (VNQ)	6 percent

Foreign stocks: 39 percent

iShares MSCI EAFE Value Index (EFV)	13 percent
iShares MSCI EAFE Growth Index (EFG)	12 percent
WisdomTree International SmallCap Dividend Fund (DLS)	7 percent
Vanguard Emerging Markets ETF (VWO)	7 percent

Bonds: 15 percent

iShares Lehman TIPS Bond Fund (TIP)	5 percent
iShares Lehman Aggregate Bond Fund (AGG)	5 percent
Vanguard High-Yield Tax-Exempt (VWAHX)	5 percent

Sticking to the middle of the road

Next, I present Jay and Racquel, who are ages 58 and 54, married, and have successful careers. Even though they are old enough to be Jason's parents, their economic situation actually warrants a quite similar high-risk/high-return portfolio. Both husband and wife, however, are risk-averse kind of people.

Jay is an independent businessman with several retail properties (valued at roughly $1.6 million); Racquel is a vice president at a major publishing house. Their portfolio: $800,000 and growing. Within several years, the couple will qualify for combined Social Security benefits of roughly $42,000. Racquel also will receive a fixed pension annuity of about $30,000. The couple's goal is to retire within five to seven years, and they have no dreams of living too lavishly; they should have more than enough money. The fruits of their investments, by and large, should pass to their three grown children and any charities named in their wills.

Being risk-averse, Jay and Racquel keep 30 percent of their portfolio in high-quality municipal bonds. They handed me the other 70 percent ($560,000) and told me to invest it as I saw fit. My feeling was that 30 percent high-quality bonds was probably overkill in terms of safety, so I saw no need to add to their bond position. I therefore constructed a portfolio of largely domestic and foreign stock ETFs. The size of their portfolio, versus Jason's, warranted the addition of a few more asset classes, such as international Real Estate Investment Trusts (REITs), an alternative energy fund (PowerShares WilderHill Clean Energy), a couple of market-neutral mutual funds (Hussman, Merger), and holdings in two large timber REITs. At the couple's request, I also invested a small amount in two commodity ETFs.

I did not include any U.S. REITs other than the timber REITs, given that so much of the couple's wealth is already tied up in commercial real estate. Figure 16-2 represents the portfolio breakdown, which I detail here.

Russell's "today and tomorrow" portfolio modeling technique

Career coaches constantly tout the importance of having a career plan; I'm going to tout the importance of having a portfolio plan. Times change; circumstances change. Your portfolio needs to keep up with the times. Suppose you are 45 years old and saving for retirement. Using the 20x rule I discuss in this chapter, you decide that your goal is to someday have a portfolio of $1.2 million. Your current portfolio has $600,000, so you have a ways to go. To get where you want, you realize you need to take some risk, but when you start to approach your goal, you want to lower your risk. After all, at that point, you'll have more to lose than gain with any market swings. You should model your portfolio today but also have a picture of what your portfolio may look like when you reach, say, $1.0 million . . . whenever that is.

Your picture may look something like this:

Today's $600,000 portfolio

Vanguard Large Cap ETF (VV)	30 percent
Vanguard Small Cap ETF (VB)	20 percent
iShares MSCI EAFE (EFA)	30 percent
iShares Lehman 7–10 Year Treasury Bond Fund (IEF)	10 percent
iShares Lehman TIPS Bond Fund (TIP)	10 percent

Tomorrow's $1.0 million portfolio

Vanguard Large Cap ETF (VV)	30 percent
Vanguard Small Cap ETF (VB)	15 percent
iShares MSCI EAFE (EFA)	25 percent
iShares Lehman 7–10 Year Treasury Bond Fund (IEF)	15 percent
iShares Lehman TIPS Bond (TIP)	15 percent

By having your portfolio model for today, and your picture of what it may look like tomorrow, you'll always know where you're heading. Trust me, it makes sense. Or trust Yogi Berra, who said, "If you don't know where you're going, you may wind up someplace else."

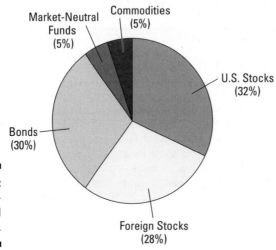

Market-Neutral Funds (5%)

Commodities (5%)

U.S. Stocks (32%)

Bonds (30%)

Foreign Stocks (28%)

Figure 16-2:
A middle-of-the-road portfolio.

U.S. stocks: 32 percent

iShares Morningstar Large Value (JKF)	9 percent
iShares Morningstar Large Growth (JKE)	8 percent
iShares Morningstar Small Value (JKL)	4 percent
iShares Morningstar Small Growth (JKK)	3 percent
iShares Russell Microcap Index (IWC)	2 percent
PowerShares WilderHill Clean Energy Fund (PBW)	2 percent
Plum Creek Timber Company (PCL)	2 percent
Rayonier Timber (RYN)	2 percent

Foreign stocks: 28 percent

iShares MSCI EAFE Value Index (EFV)	6 percent
iShares MSCI EAFE Growth Index (EFG)	5 percent
Tweedy, Browne Global Value (TBGVX)	5 percent

Vanguard Emerging Markets ETF (VWO)	5 percent
WisdomTree International SmallCap Dividend Fund (DLS)	4 percent
Fidelity International Real Estate Fund (FIREX)	3 percent

Bonds: 15 percent

Various high quality tax-exempt municipal bonds

Market-neutral funds: 5 percent

Hussman Strategic Growth (HSGFX)	2.5 percent
Merger Fund (MERFX)	2.5 percent

Commodities: 5 percent

iPath Dow Jones-AIG Commodity Index Total Return ETN (DJP)	2.5 percent
streetTRACKS Gold Trust (GLD)	2.5 percent

Taking the safer road: Less oomph, less swing

We financial professional types hate to admit it, but no matter how much we tinker with our investment strategies, no matter how fancy our portfolio software, we can't entirely remove the luck factor. When you invest in anything, there's always a bit of a gamble. (Keep all your money in cash, stuffed under the proverbial mattress, and you're gambling that inflation won't eat it away or that a house fire won't consume it.) As such, sometimes the greatest investment advice ever given probably comes from Kenny Rogers:

> *You got to know when to hold 'em, know when to fold 'em*
>
> *Know when to walk away and know when to run.*

The time to hold 'em is when you have just enough — when you've pretty much met, or have come close to meeting, your financial goals.

I now present Richard and Maria, who are 65 and 58, married, and nearing retirement. Richard, who sank in his chair when I asked about his employment, told me that he was in a job he detests in the ever-changing (and not necessarily changing for the better) newspaper business. Maria was doing part-time public relations work. I added up Richard's Social Security, a small pension from the newspaper, Maria's part-time income, and income from their investments, and I told Richard that he didn't have to stay at a job he hates. There was enough money for him to retire, provided the couple agreed to live somewhat frugally, and provided the investments — $700,000 — could keep up with inflation and not sag too badly in the next bear market.

For a couple like Richard and Maria, portfolio construction is a tricky matter. Go too conservative, and the couple may run out of money before they die. Go too aggressive, and the couple may run out of money tomorrow. It's a delicate balancing act. In this case, I took Richard and Maria's $700,000 and appropriated 25 percent — $175,500 — to a Vanguard immediate fixed annuity, inflation adjusted. (The annuity was put in Richard's name, with 50 percent joint survivorship for Maria.) The rest of the money — $525,000 — I allocated to a portfolio of largely ETFs. Figure 16-3 illustrates the portfolio breakdown, which I detail here.

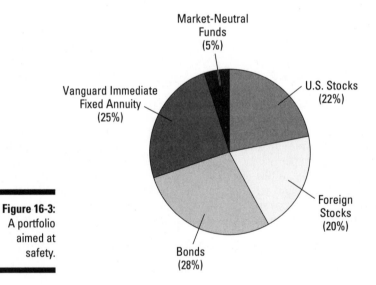

Figure 16-3:
A portfolio aimed at safety.

Market-Neutral Funds (5%)

Vanguard Immediate Fixed Annuity (25%)

U.S. Stocks (22%)

Foreign Stocks (20%)

Bonds (28%)

U.S. stocks: 22 percent

Rydex S&P 500 Equal Weight (RSP)	12 percent
Vanguard Small Cap Value ETF (VBR)	4 percent
Vanguard REIT ETF (VNQ)	4 percent
Vanguard Small Cap Growth ETF (VBK)	2 percent

Foreign stocks: 20 percent

Vanguard European ETF (VGK)	6.5 percent
Vanguard Pacific ETF (VPL)	6.5 percent
BLDRS Emerging Markets 50 ADR (ADRE)	4 percent
WisdomTree International SmallCap Dividend Fund (DLS)	3 percent

Bonds: 28 percent

iShares Lehman Aggregate Bond Fund (AGG)	10 percent
iShares Lehman TIPS Bond Fund (TIP)	10 percent
Vanguard High-Yield Corporate Bond Fund (VWEHX)	8 percent

Vanguard immediate fixed annuity: 25 percent

Inflation adjusted, with 50 percent joint survivorship

Market-neutral funds: 5 percent

Hussman Strategic Growth (HSGFX)	2.5 percent
Merger Fund (MERFX)	2.5 percent

Dividing up the pie either conservatively or aggressively by industry sector

In Chapter 9, I talk about *sector* investing (investing by industry sector), as opposed to *grid* investing (splitting your equity into large/small/value/growth). If you want to use sector investing (I have no major problem with that), know that various sectors fall in different places on the risk/return continuum.

According to the people at State Street Global Advisors (SSgA), purveyors of Select Sector SPDR ETFs, with the help of Ibbotson Associates, the following sector allocations are the most appropriate for the U.S. equity piece of your portfolio.

Conservative portfolio (15 percent U.S. stocks)

Consumer Discretionary Select Sector SPDR (XLY)	5 percent
Consumer Staples Select Sector SPDR (XLP)	16 percent
Energy Select Sector SPDR (XLE)	14 percent
Financial Select Sector SPDR (XLF)	15 percent
Health Care Select Sector SPDR (XLV)	10 percent
Industrial Select Sector SPDR (XLI)	15 percent
Materials Select Sector SPDR (XLB)	10 percent
Technology Select Sector SPDR (XLK)	0 percent
Utilities Select Sector SPDR (XLU)	15 percent

Aggressive portfolio (63 percent U.S. stocks)

Consumer Discretionary Select Sector SPDR (XLY)	15 percent
Consumer Staples Select Sector SPDR (XLP)	8 percent
Energy Select Sector SPDR (XLE)	6 percent
Financial Select Sector SPDR (XLF)	23 percent
Health Care Select Sector SPDR (XLV)	16 percent
Industrial Select Sector SPDR (XLI)	9 percent
Materials Select Sector SPDR (XLB)	5 percent
Technology Select Sector SPDR (XLK)	18 percent
Utilities Select Sector SPDR (XLU)	0 percent

Chapter 17

Buying and Holding: The Key to ETF Investment Success

In This Chapter

▶ Understanding the charts

▶ Peeking into the world of day-trading

▶ Examining "investment pornography"

▶ Making a commitment to be patient

▶ Recounting the story of the tortoise and the hare

*N*ow, dear reader, we get to the part of this book you've been waiting for: How to get rich quick using ETFs! The trick is understanding charting patterns.

Let me explain what I mean.

The chart in Figure 17-1 captures a hypothetical daily pricing pattern for a hypothetical ETF that we will hypothetically give the hypothetical ticker symbol UGH. What you see at point A is a major reversal pattern known to technical analysts as the "Head-and-Shoulders." Notice that as the price dips below the "Neckline" and then rises with simultaneous "Increased Volume" that the "Reversal" of the "Trend" begins to manifest. Time to sell! Within a short time, however, as you can clearly see at point B, a "Minor Top" forms indicating an "Upward Trend" reinforced by the classic "Inverted Triangle." Time to buy! Two minutes later, at point C, where volume increases and the price again rises a point, we see a "Breakaway Gap." Time to sell again!

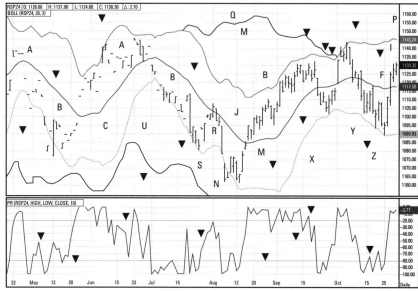

Figure 17-1:
The daily pricing pattern for UGH.

In the next chart (see Figure 17-2), we examine the daily pricing patterns of a hypothetical ETF that we will hypothetically call DUM. You can make millions overnight if you truly understand this charting pattern!

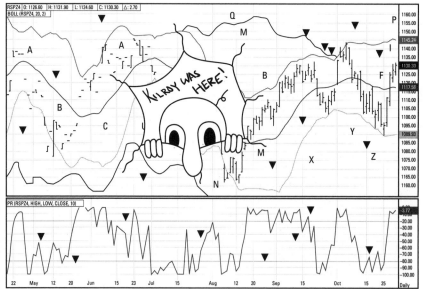

Figure 17-2:
The daily pricing pattern for DUM.

Unless you are totally humor challenged, by now you see that I'm not being entirely serious. Many, if not most, day-traders (who tend to *love* ETFs) believe in something called *technical analysis*: the use of charts and graphs to predict movements in securities. Much of the language I used to explain Figure 17-1, as well as the basic idea behind the charts, comes from a best-selling book on technical analysis.

I once had the honor of interviewing one of the biggest names in technical analysis. This guy writes books, gives seminars, and tells everyone that he makes oodles and oodles of money by following charting patterns and buying and selling securities accordingly. At the time I interviewed him, I had been a journalist for 20 years, writing for many of the top U.S. magazines, covering many topics. If you develop one thing being a journalist for two decades, it is a very well-honed bullshit radar. I can tell you after spending an hour on the phone with this "expert" that he is perhaps making of oodles and oodles of money with his books and seminars, but he is *not* making oodles and oodles of money with his charts. And neither will you.

The key to success in investing isn't to do a lot of trading based on formulas every bit as fruitless as alchemy. The key is to keep your investment costs low (ETFs will do that for you), diversify your portfolio (ETFs can do that, too), and *buy and hold* (that part's up to you).

In this chapter, I present the evidence to back up my contention that buying and holding is the thing to do. You will see that buyers and holders are the true champions of the investing world. And you will discover the difference between hypothetical investing and investing in the real world.

It's huge.

The Tale of the Average Investor (A Tragicomedy in One Act)

I talk a bit in this book about *correlation,* the tendency for two things (such as two ETFs or other investments) to move in the same direction. A correlation of 1.0 indicates a *perfect* correlation: think Lucille Ball in the mirror imitating Harpo Marx. Another perfect correlation is the correlation between stock prices and the public's willingness to purchase those stocks.

For some strange reason, the market for stocks (and stock funds, such as ETFs) does not work the same way as, say, the market for cars or refrigerators. With most products, if the sellers drop the price, the public is likely to increase consumption. With stocks and stock funds, when the price *rises,* the public increases consumption.

For example, after tech stocks had their fabulous run in the 1990s, only then — in the latter part of the decade — did money start pouring into tech stocks. As soon as the bubble burst and tech stocks were selling cheaper than tarnished dirt, people were selling right and left, and no one was buying.

Today, everyone is rushing into small international stocks, commodities, and emerging market stocks. As soon as the bubble bursts, well, it'll be red tag sale day once again.

Returns that fall way short of the indexes

One 2003 study by the investment research group Dalbar found that the average stock mutual fund investor between January 1984 and December 2002 earned just 2.57 percent annually — not even keeping up with inflation. During that same timeframe, the S&P 500 enjoyed an average annual return of 12.22 percent. During the very same period, bond fund investors earned a 4.2 percent annualized return, lagging well behind the 5.5 percent annualized gain for Treasury bills.

How to explain such lackluster returns? In part, the culprit is the average investor's inclination to invest in pricey and poor-performing mutual funds. Another problem is that the average investor jumps ship too often, constantly buying when the market is hot, selling when it chills, and hopping back on board when the market heats up again. He is forever buying high and selling low.

ETFs solve the first part of the problem. They are not pricey. They are not going to underperform the indexes because they by and large mirror the indexes. As for the second problem, however, the jumping in and out of the market, I fear that ETFs can actually *exacerbate* the problem.

ETFs can make failure even easier!

ETFs were first brought to light by marketing people from the Toronto Stock Exchange who saw a way to beef up trading volume. Unlike mutual funds, which can be bought and sold only at day's end, ETFs trade throughout the day. In a flash, you can plunk a million in the stock market. A few seconds later, you can sell it all.

Yipeee!

In other words, the next time Dalbar does a 20-year return study, after ETFs have really caught on with the average investor, I fear that their findings may be even more dismal. Remember: Just because ETFs can be traded through-out the day doesn't mean you *have* to or that you *should*!

The vast majority of ETF trades are done by institutional investors: managers of mutual funds and multibillion-dollar endowments and pension funds. These are highly trained, incredibly well-paid professionals who do nothing all day but study the markets. When you go to buy, say, the ETF QQQQ (rep-resenting the top 100 stocks that trade on the NASDAQ), you are betting that the price is going to go up. If you are day-trading, you are betting that the price will go up that day. If you are selling, you are betting the price will fall that day. Someone, most likely a highly educated financial professional, is on the other end of your transaction. As you sell, he is buying. Or, as you buy, he is selling. Obviously his vision of the next few hours is different than yours. Let me ask you a question: What makes you think you are smarter than he is?

Obviously, lots of ETF traders think they are pretty smart, because ETFs are among the most frequently traded of all securities — see the sidebar "The ten ETFs that day-traders love the most." Also see the sidebar "An author's con-fession (and a few rules if you are going to day-trade)" for an inside view into a repentant day-trader's mind.

The lure of quick riches

If you jump onto the Internet, as I just did, and type in the words "Market timing success," you will see all kinds of Web sites and newsletters offering you all kinds of advice (much of it having to do with reading charts) sure to make you rich. Add the initials "ETF" to your search, and you'll quickly see that an entire cottage industry has formed to sell advice to wannabe ETF day-traders.

According to these Web sites and newsletters, following their advice has yielded phenomenal returns in the past. (They'll give you specific BIG num-bers.) And following their advice in the future (after you've paid your hefty subscription price) will likewise yield phenomenal returns.

If you're wondering, by the way, who regulates investment Web sites and newsletters and the performance figures they publish, wonder no more. No one does. The U.S. Supreme Court decided in 1985 that, just as long as a newsletter is providing general and not personal advice, the publisher is pro-tected by First Amendment rights.

John Rekenthaler, a VP at Morningstar, once told me (and I love how he put this): "Investment newsletter publishers have the same rights as tabloid publishers. There's nothing illegal about a headline that reads 'Martian Baby Born with Three Heads!' and there's nothing illegal about a headline that reads 'We Beat the Market Year In and Year Out!'" Both should be read with equal skepticism.

The Value Line Paradox

Perhaps the most popular purveyor of market-timing and stock-picking advice — though not the worst offender, by far — is Value Line. It's a household name. Not only are the Value Line people now offering advice on picking ETFs as well as stocks, one ETF — the PowerShares Value Line Timeliness Selection (PIV) — actually mirrors the advice given by the famed Value Line newsletter. Although the PowerShares folks don't exactly call the ETF "actively managed," that's pretty much what it is.

Don't jump to buy PIV.

Some things — Robert E. Lee's march into Pennsylvania, the Titanic — look fabulous on paper but, when translated into reality, reveal some rather tremendous flaws.

Paper versus practice

Using a proprietary system more secretly guarded than the recipe for Coke, the Value Line newsletter's performance track record has been nothing short of eye popping. On paper, at least.

From the Value Line Web site:

> A stock portfolio of #1 Ranked stocks for *Timeliness* from ***The Value Line Investment Survey,*** beginning in 1965 and updated at the beginning of each year, would have shown a **gain of 19,715% through December 31, 2004.** This gain would have beaten the **S&P 500 by more than 15 to 1** for the same time span.

These are numbers to kill your mother for, but just how accurately do they reflect the return of real investors in the real world who subscribed to Value Line and put the newsletter's advice into action?

Ah, there's the rub.

As I scroll further down Value Line's Web site, I see that the company offers not only the newsletter but a few mutual funds — *ergo* real investors in the real world. The flagship Value Line mutual fund (VLIFX), which, according to its prospectus, taps into the very same wisdom that guides the newsletter, has not exactly set the world on fire. The fund has beaten the S&P 500 only two out of the last ten years. According to Morningstar Principia, the fund's ten-year annual return as of May 30, 2006 was 5.96, compared to 8.94 for the S&P. Going back 15 years, the fund's return was an annual average of 9.09 compared to 10.90 for the market. Not only would you have earned lackluster returns, but VLIFX's volatility was substantially greater than that of the S&P 500!

The lesson to be learned

How can the mutual fund that tracks the allegedly super-successful newsletter be such a flaming dud? There are a number of possible explanations. One is that the return numbers given by Value Line are a bit, um, off. (In fact, independent research has come up with far, far lower return figures.) Or perhaps the managers of the mutual fund can't follow the advice given in their own newsletter. Perhaps trading costs ate up all profits — and then some. Whatever the explanation, I don't see why the new Value Line ETF should do much better over time than has the long-lived mutual fund.

But my point in sharing the Value Line paradox isn't so much to steer you away from any single ETF. My point is to steer you away from thinking you can trade in and out of ETFs, stocks, bonds, or anything else successfully. It's not nearly as easy as many people (such as the Value Line editors) make it seem.

The ten ETFs that day-traders love the most

They are volatile. They are *liquid* (meaning they trade easily). And they are flipped more often than all other ETFs — and the vast majority of individual stocks. That doesn't necessarily make them bad buy-and-hold investments, however:

- NASDAQ-100 Trust Series 1 (QQQQ)
- SPDR 500 (SPY)
- iShares Russell 2000 (IWM)
- Energy Select Sector SPDR (XLE)
- iShares MSCI Japan Index (EWJ)
- streetTRACKS Gold Trust (GLD)
- Semiconductor HOLDRS (SMH)
- Oil Service HOLDRS (OIH)
- Financial Select Sector SPDR (XLF)
- DIAMONDS Trust Series 1 (DIA)

"Investment Pornography" in Your Mailbox (and Mine)

Investment Web sites and newsletters are part of a phenomenon that financial journalist Jane Bryant Quinn once called "investment pornography." Many newsletters, magazines, newspaper columns, books, and television shows exist to titillate and tease you with the promise of riches. Achieving those riches with ETFs is only the latest gimmick.

On the day I am writing this chapter, a glossy consumer finance magazine just arrived in the mail. I have it sitting in front of me at this moment. An attractive woman is walking along the beach. She holds a purse in her hand. (Why is she carrying a purse on the beach?) I am told by the caption under her left foot that the attractive woman earned 40 percent return in one year.

I turn to page 65 of the magazine, and there she is: a single woman! She earned her 40 percent by investing ("on the advice of a friend") in the Hodges mid cap mutual fund. Mid caps have happened to kick ass in the past 12 months. What the article doesn't tell you is that the Hodges fund has an expense ratio of 2.0 percent and — no big surprise here — a ten-year return that trails the S&P MidCap 400 Index by almost 2.0 percent.

Welcome to the wild, wacky world of investment advice

In 1999, a very popular book entitled *Dow 36,000: The New Strategy for Profiting from the Coming Rise in the Stock Market* gave readers 300 pages of in-depth explanation why the Dow Jones Industrial average, at that time riding around 10,000, was destined to more than triple in value. "The case is compelling that 36,000 is a fair value for the Dow today. And stocks should rise to such heights very quickly," wrote James K. Glassman and co-author Kevin A. Hassett. Of course, as soon as the book came out, advising people to pour money into stocks, the Dow proceeded to tumble to less than 8,000 over a three-year bear market.

Where do you suppose that James K. Glassman is today? Why, he's writing an investment advice column, of course.

Before Glassman, there were the Beardstown Ladies. In 1983, 16 women in Beardstown, Illinois, started an investment club. In 1994, claiming a 23.4 percent annualized ten-year return, they wrote a book called *The Beardstown*

Ladies' Common-Sense Investment Guide. It became a huge bestseller. Oops. It turns out, upon further inspection, that the Beardstown Ladies overstated their returns. Their actual return was 9.1 percent a year, considerably less than the stock market.

What happened to the good Ladies of Beardstown? Why, they went on to write five more investment books, of course.

E caveat emptor: ETF-trading Web sites for suckers

I share investment horror stories so you don't wind up a player in any future ones. One way to make sure you don't is to be on the lookout for ridiculous claims. Market timing services are popping up all over the Internet. Why not? ETFs are hot. They are in the news. They sound so impressive. And there is a sucker born every minute.

Please, please, don't fork over your money assuming that you're going to get the secrets to instant wealth by trading ETFs. It won't happen.

Following are just a few examples of the countless Web sites hoping to lure you in with big promises. I can't possibly list them all, so be wary:

✔ **www.stockmarkettiming.com**

Cost: $279/year for the "Platinum Plan"

Direct from the Web site: *StockMarketTiming.com, LLC is a financial service for investors and traders who want to increase their portfolios in the most non-stressful and effective way possible in both bullish and bearish markets! We have developed a market timing system that uses technical analysis for trading the popular Exchange Traded Funds (ETFs) — DIA, SPY, and QQQQ, which has produced outstanding gains!*

Russell says: Outstands gains for whom? The Webmaster, no doubt.

We are the home of the most honest, concise, credible (unbiased and zero-hype), low-risk, and one of the most effective financial Web sites on the Internet today!

Russell says: I'm glad that the hype is unbiased. I hate biased hype.

✔ **www.marketpolygraph.com**

Cost: $72.25/month

Direct from the Web site: *Marketpolygraph provides proprietary market timing research to private and professional investors who receive decisive trading signals for specific exchange traded funds (ETFs). Our simple and direct market timing research entails only minutes of follow-up effort every month and represents the singular requirement for realizing exceptional investment returns.*

Russell says: Only minutes a month, eh? It takes me longer than that just to boot up my computer. And just where does the name *Marketpolygraph* come from?

✔ **www.kt-timing.com**

Cost (from the Web site): *The yearly subscription fee is USD 150 for each of the OPEN or CLOSE model signals. If you opt for both the OPEN and the CLOSE signals, both services are available for USD 200.*

Russell says: Don't ask me what this means; I have no idea.

Direct from the Web site: *In March 2005 we completed development of what appears to be a very strong additional sub-module for the short term QQQ-a trading system. This should hopefully lead to improved and more consistent results from this point onwards. The core filtering algorithm was also reviewed and the final result, when employing the complete set of revised rules, was an astonishingly smooth and linear curve representing some 100-fold compounding of an investment made in August 2000.*

Russell says: Such impressive big words! My favorite word is "hopefully." Indeed.

Patience Pays

The flip side of flipping ETFs is buying and holding them, which is almost guaranteed, in the long run, to bring results far superior to market timing. It's the corollary to choosing ETFs over stocks. Study after study shows that the markets are by and large very *efficient*. What does that mean? So many smart players are constantly buying and selling securities, always on the lookout for any good deals, that your chances of beating the indexes, whether by market timing or stock picking, are very slim.

One of the more recent studies on the subject, "The Difficulty of Selecting Superior Mutual Fund Performance" by Thomas P. McGuigan, appeared in the February 2006 issue of *Journal of Financial Planning*. McGuigan found that only 10 to 11 percent of actively managed mutual funds outperform index funds over a 20-year period. (*Active managers* are professionals who try to pick stocks and time the market.)

We can probably safely assume that the professionals do better than the amateurs, and even the professionals fail to beat the market over 90 percent of the time!

Talk about unpredictability

Timing doesn't work because markets are largely random. The unpredictability in the stock market (or bond market) never ceases to amaze me. Just when things seem certain to take off, they sink. Just when things seem certain to sink, they fly.

I recently had a client, a 52-year-old allergist in Allentown, PA, who read up on avian flu and became so concerned with what a pandemic might do to the stock market that he urged me to take his $500,000 portfolio and put everything in cash. We set up a meeting in his office, and I was able to temper his desire to cash out. (However, we did move his portfolio to a somewhat more conservative position.)

Prior to our meeting, I sent the client the following e-mail, which I would like to share with you:

> *Dear Tom,*
>
> *Since your initial e-mail on this topic, I've done a fair amount of reading, and you have reason, for sure, to be concerned. I am, too. (Author's note: I was being truthful here, although my concern is more a health concern than a financial one.)*
>
> *Holding some cash and gold wouldn't be a bad idea. (If we had a real economic crisis, you would want small gold coins . . . 1/10 ounce.)*
>
> *But don't assume that pandemics, or any other crisis, necessarily result in stock market crashes.*
>
> *Keep in mind that 1918, the year of the worst pandemic in world history, was a good year for stocks:* `http://www.econ.yale.edu/~shiller/data/chapt26.html`.
>
> *1962 (Cuban Missile Crisis) was a very good year. 1942 (Japan attacked Pearl Harbor; Hitler marched across Europe) wasn't too bad, either.*
>
> *In contrast, let's look at the worst years of the stock market. In 1929, nothing catastrophic was going on. Ditto for 1987. Ditto for 2000.*
>
> *I can't explain the incredible unpredictability of the markets. I can only share these historical truths.*
>
> *Yours,*
>
> *Russell*

A short history of the market's resiliency

The Dow fell 200 points today. Nearly all my ETFs lost money. Some of the more volatile ones, such as the iShares Russell Microcap Index (IWC), lost a bundle. Am I happy? No, of course not. Am I panicking? Nope.

The Dow is now at roughly 11,000, so a 200-point fall represents a loss of about 1.8 percent. Recent history has seen much, much bigger losses, and somehow, the market keeps coming back.

Remember September 11, 2001? Following the destruction of the World Trade Center towers, the Dow immediately dropped 7.13 percent. Six months later, the Dow was up by 10.47 percent. Years prior to that, on September 24, 1955, President Eisenhower's heart attack led to a one-day drop of 6.54 percent. Six months later, the Dow was up 12.48 percent. I could give example after example.

That's not to say that the market will *always* come back. One of these days . . . well, even Rome eventually fell. But history shows that the stock market is a mighty resilient beast. I suggest that you build a portfolio of ETFs — including stock and bond ETFs — and hang tight. Sooner or later (barring some truly major economic upheaval), you will very likely be rewarded.

The author's confession (and a few rules if you are going to day-trade)

Um . . . er . . . I don't know quite how to say this, but, despite all my talk in this chapter and throughout this book about buying and holding, and the futility of day-trading, yes — YES! YES! — I've done it. I admit it! I've bought and sold ETFs within the same day in the hope of making a quick gain! I've done it with the QQQQ (an ETF that tracks the NASDAQ) and with EEM (an emerging markets ETF).

What can I say? Gambling (and that is what such short-term forays into the market are) can be fun. Not only that, but the odds of making money by gambling on an ETF are much greater than they are by, say, playing the horses or shooting craps. After all, the "house" takes only a small cut when you play the markets. And time is on your side.

Have I made any short-terms gains? Sure. I've also lost some money. On balance, over the years, I've probably just about broken even . . . or maybe earned ten cents an hour for all my efforts. But it has been fun!

I am sharing this with you because I know that some of you are going to occasionally have that feeling in your gut that you "know" some security is going to go up (or down, if you're into short selling), and you may take a stab.

Okay, go ahead if you must; I'll just ask you to play by a few rules.

Rule #1

Separate investing from gambling; have a fixed (small) amount of money with which you gamble on the market. Take it from cash. Don't sell your buy-and-hold investments to support your gambling.

Rule #2

If you find that you are getting fixated on your wins or losses, quit. If it isn't fun, don't do it. If you find that you are spending an inordinate amount of time playing the markets, quit. There is more to life.

Rule #3

Don't buy on margin. If you are borrowing money from the brokerage house to trade, that could spell big trouble. Margin money usually costs much more than you think. I hold Fidelity Investments in high regard, but I really don't like their recent full-page magazine advertisements offering low rates for margin borrowing. If you read the very small print at the bottom of the page, it explains that the advertised rate pertains only to margin loans over $500,000. Small players — like you and me — pay much more.

Rule #4

Ask yourself what you're going to do if you get stuck. Have an exit plan. What if you buy EEM on an exceptionally volatile day, and you expect it to rise 3 percent, but instead it falls 4 percent? Are you going to hold it until it climbs back up? Are you going to cash out and take the hit?

Rule #5

I doubt that you do, but even if you find that you have a superhuman ability to time the markets, ask yourself if that is really what you want to do for a living. Day-trading isn't exactly a career that benefits the community or grows your consciousness. I've known a good number of day-traders; most seem like shallow, unhappy people.

Chapter 18

Exceptions to the Rule (Ain't There Always)

In This Chapter

▶ Rebalancing your ETF portfolio once a year

▶ Harvesting tax losses

▶ Understanding the IRS's wash rule

▶ Revamping your portfolio with life changes

▶ Playing (or not playing) the ETF options game

*W*hen I was a kid, long before online banking, I would often pedal my metallic blue three-speed Schwinn bicycle to one of the local savings banks on Long Island to deposit my allowance money. In those days, if you opened a new account, you were often given a free gift: a toaster, clock radio, leather wallet, crystal candlesticks, or such. This was a great encouragement to switch banks, and I did so with some regularity.

Today, I don't generally take my bicycle to the bank. I don't think they even make three-speeds anymore. And most neighborhood banks no longer give away toasters or clock radios. Times change! Still, however, it sometimes makes sense to switch your investments around.

In the previous chapter, I talk of the virtues of a buy-and-hold approach to ETF investing. But that doesn't mean you purchase a bunch of ETFs and *never* touch them. Switching from one ETF to another won't get you a clock radio or a leather wallet, but there can be other benefits, for sure.

In this chapter, I discuss certain circumstances where it makes sense to trade ETFs, rather than buy and hold. For example, you need to rebalance your portfolio on an annual basis to keep risk in check, and on occasion you may want to swap ETFs to harvest taxes at year end. I also discuss the ways in which life changes may warrant tweaking a portfolio. And finally, I introduce you to the world of ETF options, where frequent trading is a way of life.

Rebalancing to Keep Your Portfolio Fit

I have a client whom I'll call Jonathan. A 55-year-old chemical engineer, divorced for several years, Jonathan got clobbered during the three-year bear market of 2000–2002. Part of Jonathan's problem, and a problem for so many other investors back at the turn of century, was that he forgot to rebalance. Jonathan jumped onto the tech-stock gravy train in November 1997 with the purchase of two high-flying tech mutual funds. He invested $60,000 in each for a total of $120,000, which, at the time, was about half the balance of his 401(k).

By March 2000, Jonathan's investment in information technology had grown from $120,000 to just about $400,000. Meanwhile, the other half of his nest egg, invested in less glamorous bonds and non-tech stocks, grew from $120,000 to a mere $130,000 during the same two-and-a-half year span. His total 401(k) portfolio, by March 2000, was a very handsome $530,000. But instead of having a portfolio of 50 percent tech stocks, he then had a portfolio of more than three-quarters tech stocks.

In April 2000, the gravy train came to a screeching halt. Jonathan decided to grit his teeth and hold onto his two mutual funds. By the end of the year, they lost 45 percent. One year later, by the end of 2001, they had lost another 30 percent. And by the end of 2002, they dropped yet *another* 38 percent. Jonathan's tech stock mutual funds were now worth only $95,480. His entire portfolio, which had a balance of $240,000 in 1997, was now, five years later, worth barely over $200,000.

To add insult to injury, both mutual funds experienced heavy turnover, and even though Jonathan lost a bundle, he still had to pay the IRS a small capital gains tax. That really hurt.

When I finally met him in 2003, Jonathan needed to see his portfolio grow 265 percent to get back to where it was at its peak.

How rebalancing works

I put Jonathan into a well-diversified portfolio of largely ETFs, and despite a number of very good years, he's still not quite back to where he started before his exciting ride to riches and back.

What happened to Jonathan can be avoided! How? The answer is fairly simple: Don't allow any one slice of your portfolio to overtake the rest. Periodically pull your portfolio back into balance.

To illustrate, I'll use a very simple middle-of-the-road ETF portfolio that I introduce in Chapter 16. At the start of the year, the portfolio is just where you want it to be: 70 percent diversified stocks, 30 percent bonds. But it turns out to be a banner year for stocks, and especially for small cap U.S. stocks. At the end of the year, as you can see in Table 18-1, the portfolio looks quite different than it did at the beginning.

Table 18-1	A Shifting Portfolio Balance
Beginning of year one (in balance)	
ETF	**Percent of portfolio**
PowerShares FTSE RAFI U.S. 1000 (PRF)	30
Vanguard Small Cap ETF (VB)	10
iShares MSCI EAFE (EFA)	25
Vanguard Emerging Markets ETF (VWO)	5
iShares Lehman Aggregate Bond Fund (AGG)	30
End of year one (out of balance)	
ETF	**Percent of portfolio**
PowerShares FTSE RAFI U.S. 1000 (PRF)	33
Vanguard Small Cap ETF (VB)	14
iShares MSCI EAFE (EFA)	22
Vanguard Emerging Markets ETF (VWO)	5
iShares Lehman Aggregate Bond Fund (AGG)	26

What to do? Bring things back into balance, starting with the bond position. That's because the split between stocks and bonds has the greatest impact on portfolio risk. In this example, you need to increase the bond allocation from 26 percent back up to 30 percent. If you have a year-end portfolio of $100,000, that means you'll buy $4,000 of AGG to bring it up 4 percentage points.

Where will the $4,000 come from? That depends. You could sell off part of your stock position, if necessary. Or, you could take the money from your cash position. Since you must pay a commission to trade an ETF, the fewer trades you make, the better. Therefore, I prefer to allow the cash position to build up — either with fresh deposits or with dividends and interest earned — and use that cash for rebalancing.

How often to rebalance

The question of how often to rebalance has been studied and restudied, and most financial professionals agree that once a year is a good timeframe. Anything less, and you increase your risk as positions get out of whack. Anything more, and you may lower your returns by interrupting rallies too often.

Ah, but ETFs involve trading costs, and sometimes you may have to weigh the cost of trading into the rebalancing decision. Tweaking a portfolio by several dollars here and there to achieve "perfect" balance may not make financial sense.

A rule I give myself is to never pay more than one-half of 1 percent to make a trade for rebalancing purposes. In the example in the previous section, a trade of $4,000 of AGG is going to cost you $15, so you are forking out only 0.37 percent of $4,000; make the trade.

If, however, your bond allocation had dipped to only 28 percent, necessitating a purchase of $2,000 to get it in balance, I don't think I'd opt to spend the $15 to make the trade. Rather, I'd wait another year (or perhaps less if I sensed that a major shift had occurred) to make the rebalance.

Harvesting Tax Losses, and the IRS's Oh-So-Tricky "Wash Rule"

So you had a bad year on a particular investment? You had a bad year on *many* of your investments? Allow Uncle Sam to share your pain. You only need to sell the investment(s) by December 31st, and you can use the loss to offset any capital gains. Or, if you've had no capital gains, you can deduct the loss from your taxable ordinary income for the year, up to $3,000.

But there's a problem. Because of the IRS's "wash rule," you can't sell an investment on December 31st and claim a loss if you buy back that same investment or any "substantially identical" investment within 30 days of the sale. You may simply want to leave your takings in cash. That way, you save on any transaction costs and avoid the hassle of trading.

On the other hand, January is historically a very good time for stocks. You may not want to be out of the market that month. What to do?

ETFs to the rescue!

What the heck is "substantially identical" anyway?

The IRS rules are a bit hazy when it comes to identifying "substantially identical" investments. Clearly, you can't sell and then buy back the same stock. But if you sell $10,000 of Exxon Mobil Corp. stock, you *can* buy $10,000 of an ETF that covers the energy industry, such as the Energy Select Sector SPDR (XLE) or the Vanguard Energy ETF (VDE). Not the same thing, for sure, but either one will give you some exposure to Exxon Mobil Corp. (and its competitors as well) for the 30 days that you must live without your stock.

I, of course, would prefer that you keep most of your portfolio in ETFs. If you follow my advice, and one year turns out to be an especially bad year for, say, large cap value stocks, no problem. If you are holding the iShares S&P 500 Value Index (IVE) and you sell for a loss, you can buy the Vanguard Value ETF (VTV), hold it for a month, and then switch back to what you had if you wish.

Two ETFs that track similar indexes are going to be very, very similar, but not "substantially identical." At least the IRS *so far* has not deemed them substantially identical. But the IRS changes its rules often, and what constitutes "substantially identical" could change tomorrow or the next day. It's a good idea to consult with a tax professional (which I am not) before proceeding with any tax harvesting plans.

As always, consider cost

I'll remind you again that trading an ETF requires you to pay a trading commission to a brokerage house. To harvest a tax loss generally requires four trades. (Sell the original holding, buy the replacement, sell the replacement, buy back the original holding.) If you're paying $15 a trade, that adds up to

$60. Plus, you lose a bit of money on each trade with the *spread* (the difference between the ask and bid price on a security). If you are in the 25 percent tax bracket, that tells me your loss on a particular investment should be *at least* $300 or so before you bother with tax harvesting in an ETF portfolio.

Revamping Your Portfolio with Life Changes: Marriage, Divorce, and Babies

Rebalancing to bring your portfolio back to its original position isn't the only occasion to buy and sell your ETFs. Just as you may need a new suit if you lose or gain weight, sometimes you need to tailor your portfolio in response to changes in your life.

As I discuss in Chapter 16, the prime consideration in portfolio construction is whether you can take risk in the hope of garnering high return or whether you must limit your risk with the understanding that your returns will likely be modest. (Diversification can certainly help to reduce investment risk, but it can't eliminate it.) Certain events may occur in your life that warrant a reassessment of where you belong on the risk/return continuum.

A single woman (or man), walks into my office and asks me to help build a portfolio, and one of the first questions I ask is, "How's your love life?" A married couple walks into my office, and one of the first things I take note of is how close they sit together. And if the woman has a swollen belly, I really take notice.

No, I'm not being nosy. Marriage, divorce, and the arrival of babies are major life changes and need to be weighed heavily in any investment decisions. So too are the death of a spouse or parent, a child's decision to attend college, any major career changes, or a big purchase such as a new car.

Betsy and Mark: A fairly typical couple

Betsy and Mark are engaged to be married. They don't have a lot of money. But both are young (early 30s), in good health, gainfully employed, and without debt. They plan to merge their savings of roughly $33,500 and ask me to help them invest it for the long haul.

The first thing we do is decide how much money to take out for emergency coverage. Given their monthly expenses of roughly $3,500, we decide to earmark five months' of living expenses — $17,500 — and plunk that into a money market account. That leaves us with $16,000 to spare.

Normally, I wouldn't look at an ETF portfolio for $16,000, but this is money they tell me they aren't going to touch until retirement. I urge them to each open a Roth IRA. (Any money you put into a Roth IRA grows tax-free for as long as you wish; more on retirement accounts in the next chapter.) I ask them to divide the $16,000 into the two accounts. Since they can both contribute $4,000 for each year, I have them both make double contributions — one for the past year (for example, you can make your 2007 contribution until April 15, 2008), and one for the present year.

To save on transaction costs, I limit the number of investments and give each partner a "partial" portfolio. Neither account alone is well-diversified, but together, they are.

Betsy's Roth IRA

Vanguard Total Stock Market ETF (VTI)	$5,000
iShares Lehman Aggregate Bond Fund (AGG)	$3,000

Mark's Roth IRA

iShares Morningstar Small Core (JKJ)	$4,000
iShares MSCI EAFE (EFA)	$4,000

As Betsy and Mark's portfolio grows, I would plan to add other asset classes (real estate investment trusts, foreign small cap stocks, high-yield bonds, and so on) and other accounts.

One year later

Betsy is pregnant with twins! The couple is saving up for their first home, with a goal of making that purchase within 18 months. Although the Roth IRA is normally not to be touched (without stiff penalty) before age 59½, an exception is made for first-time home purchases. Betsy and Mark could take out as much as $10,000 without penalty.

I'd rather they leave their Roth IRA money untouched, but the couple inform me that they think the money may need to be tapped. By this point, the money in the Roth IRA has grown from $16,000 to $18,000 (for illustration purposes, I'm pretending that each investment grew by an equal amount), and the couple can each contribute another $4,000, bringing the total of both accounts to $26,000. Since there is a possibility that $10,000 will need to be yanked in one year, I earmark any fresh money to a non-volatile short-term bond ETF.

Betsy's Roth IRA

Vanguard Total Stock Market ETF (VTI)	$5,500
iShares Lehman Aggregate Bond Fund (AGG)	$3,500
iShares Lehman 1–3 Year Treasury Bond Fund (SHY)	$4,000

Mark's Roth IRA

iShares Morningstar Small Core (JKJ)	$4,500
iShares MSCI EAFE (EFA)	$4,500
iShares Lehman 1–3 Year Treasury Bond Fund (SHY)	$4,000

Yet one year later

The twins (Tyler and Tucker) have arrived! Much to their surprise, Betsy's parents have gifted the couple $10,000 for the purchase of the home. The Roth IRA money needn't be touched. At this point, I would sell the short-term bond fund and add to their existing positions. Also, provided the couple had another $4,000 each to contribute, I'd begin adding asset classes to the mix, perhaps starting with Vanguard Emerging Markets ETF (VWO), the Vanguard REIT ETF (VNQ), and the PowerShares WilderHill Clean Energy Fund (PBW).

Hopefully, Betsy and Mark (and Tyler and Tucker) will have many happy years together. And with each major life event, I would urge them to adjust their growing portfolio appropriately.

Are Options An Option for You?

Beyond the world of exchange-traded funds, an entirely different universe is filled with things called *exchange-traded derivatives*. A *derivative* is a financial instrument that has no real value in and of itself; rather, its value is directly tied to some underlying item of value, be that a commodity, a stock, a currency, or an ETF.

The most popular derivative is called an *option*. Think of an option as sort of a movie ticket. You give the cashier $7.50 to see the movie, not to hold some dumb little piece of cardboard. Certainly the ticket itself has no intrinsic value. But the ticket gives access (the option) to see the movie.

Most options in the investment world give you the right to either buy or sell a security at a certain price (*the strike price*) up to a certain specified date (*the expiration date*). Options are a prime example of a *leveraged* investment. In other words, you can leverage a little bit of money to win big money — or (unfortunately) lose big money.

Lately, options on ETFs have been hot, hot, hot . . . and growing hotter. Options on certain ETFs, most notably the QQQQ (which represents the 100 largest company stocks traded on the NASDAQ), typically trade just as many shares on an average day as the ETF itself. (See the sidebar "QQQQ, SPY, and IWM are the options champs.") On most days, options on ETFs like the QQQQ and SPY (representing the S&P 500) trade more shares than any other kind of options, including options on individual stocks, commodities pools, and such.

You see, ETFs provide traders with the opportunity to trade the entire stock market, or large pieces of it, rather than merely individual securities. In the past, this was doable but difficult. You cannot trade a mutual fund on the options market as you do an ETF.

Much of this often frenetic trading in ETF options is being done by speculators, not investors. If you have an itch to take huge amounts of risk and gamble in the hopes of hitting it big, options may be for you. In that case, I'll refer you to *Futures & Options For Dummies* by Joe Duarte, M.D. (Wiley). Dr. Duarte will warn you, as I am warning you, that successful option trading takes an iron gut, a lot of capital, and a lot of expertise. And even if you have all that, you may still lose your shirt!

Understanding puts and calls

All kinds of options exist, including (sort of) options on options. The derivatives market almost seems infinite — as do the number of ways you can play with derivatives. But the two most basic kinds of options, and the two most popular by far, are *put options* and *call options,* otherwise known simply as *puts* and *calls.* I'm going to take just a moment to describe how these babies work.

QQQQ, SPY, and IWM are the options champs

"ETFs are a *huge* part of the options market," says Jim Binder, spokesperson for the Options Clearing Corporation, the world's largest clearing organization for options. According to Binder, of the top six most commonly traded options on U.S. exchanges, three are ETFs. (These are subject to change, of course.) Here are the top six:

Security	Ticker symbol	Type
NASDAQ-100	QQQQ	ETF
S&P Index	SPX	An index option created and managed by the Chicago Board Options Exchange
SPDR 500	SPY	ETF
Google	GOOG	Individual stock
iShares Russell 2000	IWM	ETF
Altria	MO	Individual stock

Puts: Options to sell

With a put option in hand, you may, for example, have bought yourself the right to sell 100 shares of the QQQQ (currently trading at $40) at $35 (the strike price) a share at any point between now and December 15th (the expiration date). By December 15th, if the QQQQ has fallen to any price under $35, you will likely choose to sell. If the QQQQ is trading above $35, you'd be a fool to sell. Your option will simply expire, unused.

Calls: Options to buy

With a call option in hand, you may, for example, have bought yourself the right to buy 100 shares of the QQQQ (currently trading at $40) at $45 (the strike price) a share at any point between now and, say, December 18th (the expiration date). If the QQQQ rises above $45, you would, of course, take the option and buy the 100 shares at $45. After all, you can then turn around and sell them immediately on the open market for a nifty profit. If, however, the price of the QQQQ does not rise to $45 or above, you are not going to exercise your option. Why in the world would you? You can buy the stock cheaper on the market. In that case, your option expires worthless.

Using options to make gains without risk

Those people who use calls as an investment (as opposed to gambling) strategy are assuming (as do most investors) that the market is going to continue its historical upward trajectory. But instead of banking perhaps 60 or 70 percent of their portfolio on stocks, as many of us do, they take a much smaller percentage of their money and buy calls. If the stock market goes up, they may collect many times what they invested. If the stock market doesn't go up, they lose it all — but only a modest amount. Meanwhile, the bulk of their money can be invested in something much less volatile than the stock market, such as bonds.

Zvi Bodie, Professor of Finance and Economics at Boston University School of Management, wrote a book with Michael J. Clowes entitled *Worry-Free Investing: A Safe Approach to Achieving Your Lifetime Financial Goals* (Prentice Hall) in which he suggests an investment strategy using long-term stock options and Treasury Inflation-Protected Securities (TIPS). If you have $100,000 to invest, says Bodie, you might consider putting roughly 90 percent of it into TIPS. (A very convenient way to do that would be to purchase the iShares Lehman TIPS Bond Fund ETF.) That way, he asserts, your principal is protected.

To shoot for growth, says Bodie, take the other 10 percent or so and invest it in long-term call options (otherwise know as *Long-Term Anticipation Securities* or *LEAPS*), going about three years out. If the market soars, you take home the bacon. If, however, the market sinks, your call options merely expire, and you still have your TIPS, which by this point, three years later, have grown to match your original $100,000.

It's an intriguing strategy that just may make sense, especially for older investors tapping into their savings who can't wait for the stock market to come back after a serious bear market.

Interestingly, a similar kind of "worry-free investing" may be achieved by owning *all* stocks (or close to it) but using put options to protect yourself from the downside.

Insuring yourself against big, bad bears

The put option is an option to sell. This investment strategy allows you to have money in the stock market (all of it, if you so desire), but you carry insurance in the form of puts. If the market tumbles, you're covered.

Suppose you want to invest everything in the NASDAQ index through the ETF QQQQ. Normally, an investor would have to be insane to bet everything on such a volatile asset. But with the right put options in place, you can actually enjoy any explosive growth but limit your losses to whatever you wish: 5 percent, 10 percent, 15 percent.

With a pocketful of puts, you can laugh a bear market in the face. If the QQQQ drops by, say, 50 percent in the next week, you will have checked out long before, smiling as you hold your cash.

Seeming almost too good to be true

So options allow you to capture the gains of the stock market with very limited risk. They allow you to invest in the market and not have to worry about downturns. What's not to love about options?

Whoaaa. Not so fast! You need to know a couple little things about options:

- **They are expensive.** Every time you buy either a put or a call, you pay. The price can vary enormously depending on the strike price, the expiration date you choose, and the volatility of the ETF the option is based on. But in no case are options cheap. And the *vast majority* of options reach their expiration date and simply expire.

  So, yes, options can save you in a bear market, and they can help you to capture a bull market, but either way, you're going to pay. Free lunches are very hard to come by!

- **If you happen to make a gain on an option, the income will usually be considered a short-term gain by the IRS.** As such, you may pay twice the tax on it that you would on the long-term appreciation of a stock.

Weighing options strategies against the diversified ETF portfolio

Don't misunderstand me. I'm not saying that the price you pay for options isn't worth it — even with taxes included. Options do provide a viable strategy for investing. The real question, though, is whether using puts and calls makes any more sense than investing in a well-diversified portfolio of low-cost ETFs. Most financial professionals I know are skeptical. And that includes several who have traded heavily in options only to learn the hard way that it is very tricky business.

To be sure, if I knew a bear market was coming, I would definitely buy myself a slew of put options. If I knew a bull market was coming, I would certainly buy a fistful of call options. But here's the problem: I don't know which way the market is going. And if I buy both puts and calls on a regular basis, I'm going to be forever bleeding cash.

Not only that, if the market stagnates, then both my puts and calls will prove worthless. In that case, I'm really going to be one unhappy camper.

So here's the way I look at it: The chances of success with a steady call strategy are one in three: I win if there's a bull market; I lose if there's a bear market; I lose if the market stagnates. Ditto for a put option strategy: I win if there's a bear market; I lose if there's a bull market; I lose if the market stagnates.

With a well-diversified portfolio of low-cost ETFs — stock, bond, REIT, and commodity ETFs — I reckon my chances of success are more like two in three: I lose if there's a bear market; I win if there's a bull market; in the case of a stagnant stock market, *something* in my portfolio will likely continue to make me money anyway.

You may recall I said earlier in the chapter that the derivatives market almost seems infinite, as do the number of ways you can play with derivatives. If you wish, ETF options strategies exist that allow you to make money in a stagnant market, too. The most common such strategy is called alternatively a *buy-write strategy* or *selling a covered call*. I explain how that strategy works (but don't necessarily advocate it) in the sidebar "How to profit with ETF options in a stagnant market."

Factoring in time and hassle

One final (but fairly large) consideration: Options trading generally requires much more time and effort than does buy-and-hold investing in a diversified portfolio. Let me ask you this: Would you rather be tinkering with your investments on weekends, spending hours at your computer, or would you rather be sailing?

How to profit with ETF options in a stagnant market

Selling a covered call is a traditional way that many people get started in the world of options, says Jim Bittman, an instructor with the Chicago Board Options Exchange's Options Institute. "You can take a non-dividend paying ETF and turn it into an income-generating asset," he says.

Here is how selling a covered call, otherwise known as a *buy-write strategy,* works:

You buy, say, 1,000 shares of the NASDAQ-100 (QQQQ). Let's assume that the current price is $38 a share. You've just spent $38,000 (plus a small trading commission of perhaps $15 or so, which, for simplicity's sake, we'll ignore for the moment).

Now you sell your covered call. In other words, through a brokerage house, you offer someone else the right to purchase your shares at a certain price in the future. You may, for example, offer the right to purchase your 1,000 shares at $40 (the strike price) within 90 days (the expiration date). For selling this right, you get paid. In this scenario, you may get paid something in the ballpark of 75 cents a share for a total of $750 (roughly 2 percent of your original investment).

If, in the next 90 days, the QQQQ stays between $38 and $40 (the market is relatively flat), your covered call expires. You walk away with your $750, and life is good. (However, you will have to pay the IRS a short-term capital gains tax on that money. The short-term capital gains tax is usually the same as your marginal income tax rate. In many cases, that will be about twice as high as the tax you would pay cashing out on a long-term investment.)

But now suppose that the market tanks: You are left holding 1,000 shares of the QQQQ that may be worth much less than $38,000. And suppose the market soars: You just lost out, too. The QQQQ may be selling at $60 a share, but the guy who bought your contract can buy them from you (and certainly *will* buy them from you) at the agreed-upon price of $40 a share. In that case, you've just suffered an opportunity loss of $20,000.

And there's the catch. I've known a good number of investors who *rave* about their experiences with covered calls . . . as long as the markets are relatively stagnant. As soon as there is major movement either up or down, they stop raving and start ranting.

Chapter 19

Using ETFs to Fund Your Golden Years

I have this imaginary script that often runs in my head when a client asks me to look at his or her 401(k) plan. In this make-believe play, the benefits manager at my client's place of employment is speaking with a representative of an investment company that runs retirement plans.

> *Benefits manager:* Our employees work hard, and we really don't ever want to lose them.

> *Investment company rep:* No problemo! We offer a retirement plan so incredibly bad that those employees of yours will *never* be able to retire! Just take a look at this array of some of the most expensive and poorly performing mutual funds available on the market today. That's what we offer!

> *Benefits manager:* Good. Good. And what about portfolio diversification?

> *Investment company rep:* None. Four of the nine mutual funds under our umbrella are large U.S. growth funds. We offer no small cap. No international anything. Just large U.S. growth, a few ridiculously expensive and volatile bond funds, and a lifestyle fund similarly overpriced with wholly inappropriate allocations for employees of all ages.

> *Benefits manager:* Excellent! Will the fees wipe out any potential gains?

Investment company rep: Absolutely! Each mutual fund in the plan charges at least a 5 percent load, a good chunk of cash each year beyond that in operating fees, and then we slap on yet *another* high fee on top of it all! And did I mention that several of the mutual fund companies we use have recently been involved in legal scandals? I can almost guarantee you that your employees' investments won't earn squat, and they'll be working for you forever.

Benefits manager: You're hired!

Okay, maybe this is a paranoid fantasy on my part, but I'm not so sure. Many of the 401(k) plans I see — and I see many — are so manifestly terrible, so ridiculously designed and priced, and so poorly managed that you can't help but imagine that someone set out to make them as horrible as possible.

And that makes me sad. The traditional company pension — grandpa's retirement plan that provided him with a steady paycheck from the day he retired till the day he died — is disappearing from the land. Social Security typically provides a modest income, and no more, and even that is at risk. That leaves the omnipresent 401(k) plan (and the lottery ticket) as many working people's last hope for a comfortable retirement.

My advice? Read this chapter. It's about . . . you guessed it . . . ETFs, potential financial knights in white armor.

ETFs alone are not going to allow everyone everywhere to retire to the golf course or the home in the mountains. But they could take you a very long way in that direction. In this chapter, I discuss how you should be using your ETFs in tax-advantaged retirement accounts to get the most bang for your investment buck. I offer advice for those of you stuck with crappy 401(k) plans at work. (Hint: Corner that benefits manager by the water cooler and hand him this book.) And I escort you into your retirement years to see how an ETF portfolio may provide you with the income you need to replace your current paycheck.

Setting the Stage for Economic Self-Sufficiency

I've got all the money I'll ever need — if I die by four o'clock this afternoon.

Henny Youngman

How much you need in your portfolio to call yourself economically self-sufficient ("retired," if you prefer to call it that) starts off with a very simple formula: $A \times B = \$\$\$\$$.

A is the amount of money you need to live on for one year. *B* is the number of years you plan to live without a paycheck. $$$$ is the amount you should have before bidding the boss adieu. There you have it.

Of course, that is waaay oversimplified. You also need to factor in such things as return on your future portfolio, inflation, Social Security, and, for the very lucky, any potential inheritances. For a more detailed reckoning of how much money you should be looking to save, I'll refer you to some fairly decent online retirement calculators; see the sidebar "How much is enough?"

TIP

How much is enough?

A reasonable accumulation goal for most families is 20 times the amount you spend in a year. To reach that goal, most families have to put away a minimum of 15 percent of their salaries for a minimum of two to three decades. For more accurate (but still ballpark) numbers, I can refer you to a number of retirement calculators on the Web.

Good (and *very* quick!):

✔ www.moneychimp.com/calculator/
   retirement_calculator.htm

Better:

✔ www.dinkytown.net/java/
   RetirementIncome.html

✔ https://flagship4.vanguard.
   com/VGApp/hnw/Retirement
   Savings

Best (but not perfect):

✔ www.fireseeker.com

Note: If you use any of the first three calculators, be realistic about your expected rate of return. (Fireseeker will help figure out a realistic rate of return for you.)

If you do use fireseeker (*fire* stands for "financial independence/retire early"), please take note:

Although I love this guy's free Web site (please contribute a few dollars to it as I have), I disagree *strongly* with his assertion that all you will need to live on in retirement is "30 – 50% of current gross." I understand the man's reasoning. And maybe that 30 to 50 percent of gross would hold true for Canadians and Brits, but most people in the United States are likely going to be shelling out small fortunes on healthcare in their older years. (According to a recent study from Fidelity Investments, a 65-year-old couple retiring today should have at least $190,000 saved just to cover out-of-pocket medical expenses during the retirement years. For people ages 60, 55, and 50 planning to leave the workforce at 65, the numbers jump to $260,000, $370,000, and $530,000, respectively.) That makes it very likely that your current expenses are not going to decrease, or decrease by much.

One more bit of advice for getting the most out of the fireseeker calculator: When the program asks you for the total annual investment expenses (as a percentage of total value), type in *1.67* percent if you currently have most of your money in mutual funds. If you intend to follow my advice in this book and move to a portfolio of ETFs, you can lower that to, oh, let's say *0.30* percent. Note how much of a difference that alone can make in your retirement projections!

Taking the basic steps

Whatever the amount you set as your goal, you need to do three basic things to achieve it:

✔ Perhaps obvious, although most people prefer to ignore it, you have to *save* and save some more. A retirement portfolio doesn't just pop up out of nowhere and grow like Jack's beanstalk. You need to feed it. Regularly.

✔ You need to invest your money wisely. That's where a well-diversified portfolio of ETFs comes in.

✔ It behooves you to take maximum advantage of retirement plans such as your company 401(k) plan — even if it's sub par — IRAs, and (my favorite) Roth IRAs. If your 401(k) plan offers only pitiful options, you need to do the best you can. I provide some specific advice on that situation later in this chapter.

Choosing the right vessels

If you will, try to think of your retirement plans — your 401(k), your IRA — as separate vessels of money. How much your nest egg grows depends on not just how much you put into it and which investments you choose, but also which vessels you have.

There are three basic kinds of vessels. (I'm big into three's all of a sudden.)

✔ First are your basic vanilla retirement plans, such as the company 401(k), the IRA, or, for the self-employed, the SEP-IRA or Individual 401(k). These are all *tax-deferred* vehicles: You don't pay taxes on the money in the year you earn it; rather, you pay taxes at whatever point you withdraw money from your account, typically only after you retire.

✔ Next are the Roth IRA and the 529 college plans. Those are *tax free:* As long as you play by certain rules (discuss them with your accountant), anything you plunk into these two vehicles (money you've generally already paid tax on) can double, triple, or (oh please!) quadruple, and you'll never owe the IRS a cent.

✔ Third is your non-retirement brokerage or savings bank account. Except for certain select investments, such as municipal bonds ("munis"), all earnings on your holdings are taxable.

Why your choice of vessels matters — a whole lot

How much can your choice of vessel affect the ultimate condition of your nest egg? *Lots.* Even in a portfolio of all ETFs.

True, ETFs are marvelously tax-efficient instruments. Often, in the case of stock ETFs, they eliminate the need to pay any capital gains tax (as you would with most mutual funds) for as long as you hold the ETF. Still, there may be taxes to pay at the end of the game when you finally cash out. And in the case of certain ETFs (such as any of the bond ETFs) that pay either interest or high dividends, you will certainly pay taxes along the way.

Suppose you're an average middle-class guy or gal with a marginal income tax rate of 30 percent (federal + state + local). Next, suppose that you have $50,000 that you've already paid tax on, and you're ready to squirrel it away for the future. You invest this money in the iShares GS $ InvesTop Corporate Bond Fund (LQD), which yields (hypothetically) 6 percent over the life of the investment, and you keep it for the next 15 years. Now, if that ETF is held in your regular brokerage account, and you have to pay taxes on the interest every year, at the end of 15 years you'd have a pot worth $92,680. Not too shabby. But if you hold that very same $50,000 bond ETF in your Roth IRA and pay no taxes each year nor any taxes at the end, after 15 years you'd have $119,828 — an extra *$27,148.*

Unfortunately, the amount of money you can put into retirement accounts is limited, although the law has allowed the sum to grow in recent years. For example, as I write this book, the maximum annual contribution amount in the most commonly used retirement accounts for the self-employed, the IRA and the Roth IRA, is $4,000 if you're under 50 and $5,000 if you're above 50. (The amount is subject to change each year.) Other retirement plans, such as the 401(k), SIMPLE plan, or Keogh, may have higher limits, but there is always a cap. (You need to talk to your accountant about these plan limits; the formulas can get terribly complicated.)

What should go where?

Given these investment limitations, which ETFs and other investments should get utmost priority and go first into your retirement accounts, and which are best left out? Follow these four (yeah, I've given up on three's) primary principles, and you can't go too wrong:

- ✔ **Any investment that generates a lot of taxable income, you want in your retirement account; any investment that throws off little or no taxable income, you don't.** Any of the bond ETFs, the REIT ETFs, or the high-dividend ETFs are probably best held in your retirement account.

- ✔ **Keep your emergency funds out of your IRA.** Any money you think you may need to withdraw in a hurry should be kept out of your retirement accounts. Withdrawing money from a retirement account can often be tricky, possibly involving penalties if before age 59½, and often triggering taxation. You don't want to have to worry about such things when you need money by noon tomorrow.

✔ **House those investments with the greatest potential for growth in your tax-free Roth IRA.** This may include your small-value ETF, micro cap ETF, or emerging markets ETF. Roth IRA money won't ever be taxed (assuming no change in the law), so why not try to get the most bang for your ETF buck?

✔ **Foreign stock ETFs are perhaps best kept in your taxable account.** That's because the U.S. government will reimburse you for any taxes your fund paid out to foreign governments, but only if you have that fund in a taxable account. Over the long-run, this "rebate" can add about half a percentage point a year to your returns; it doesn't sound like a lot, but that amount can add up over time.

Before you decide where to plunk your investments, refer to the following two sections for the basic rules.

Caveat: Tax laws change all the time. For example, the lower rates on capital gains and dividends, unless Congress steps in to intervene, will revert in 2009 to pre-2003 levels. Because of the constant change, I advise you to review your portfolio every year or two to make sure you have your assets in the right "containers."

Retirement accounts

First are ETFs and other investments generally best kept in a retirement account:

✔ **Bond ETFs.** Examples include

  • iShares Lehman Aggregate Bond Fund (AGG)

  • iShares Lehman 7–10 Treasury Bond Fund (IEF)

  • iShares Lehman TIPS Bond Fund (TIP)

✔ **ETFs that invest in real estate investment trusts (REITS).** Examples include

  • Vanguard REIT ETF (VNQ)

  • iShares Cohen & Steers Realty Majors Index Fund (ICF)

  • streetTRACKS Wilshire REIT Index Fund (RWR)

✔ **High-dividend ETFs.** Examples include

  • PowerShares High Yield Equity Dividend Achievers Portfolio (PEY)

  • SPDR Dividend (SDY)

  • iShares Dow Jones Dividend Index (DVY)

✔ **Actively managed mutual funds.**

Taxable accounts

Next are ETFs and other investments generally best kept in a taxable account:

✔ **Cash reserve for emergencies.**

✔ **Stock ETFs, except for the highest dividend-paying funds.** Examples include

- Fidelity NASDAQ Composite (ONEQ)

- iShares Morningstar Large Growth (JKE)

- streetTRACKS Dow Jones U.S. Small Cap Growth (DSG)

✔ **Foreign stock ETFs.** Examples include

- iShares S&P Europe 350 (IEV)

- Vanguard Pacific (VPL)

- BLDRS Emerging Markets 50 ADR (ADRE)

✔ **Municipal bonds.**

Curing a Seemingly Incurable Case of the 401 (k) Blues

Got one of those plans at work that I describe in the intro to this chapter, certain to eat you up alive in fees, about as well-diversified as a lunar landscape? Don't despair. All is not lost. Here is what I suggest:

✔ **Take the boss's money with a smile.** Make a big effort to shovel in at least the minimum you need to contribute to get your full company match (which will differ company to company). If you do not contribute enough to receive your employer's full matching contribution, you are, in essence, leaving free money on the table. Even if the investment options are horrible, you'll likely wind up well ahead of the game if your employer is kicking in an extra 25 or 50 percent.

✔ **Invest the best you can.** Among the horrible choices, pick the least horrible. Choose those that will give you exposure to different asset classes. Choose index funds if available. Strongly favor whichever funds are least expensive. Avoid *load* (fat commission up front) funds!

If you need help understanding the different offerings in your 401(k) plan, ask someone in the human resources department, or the plan administrator, to help you. If you can't get a clear answer (you very well may not), you may wish to hire a financial planner for at least a short consult.

✔ **Argue for better options.** Tell the human resources people (diplomatically, of course) that their plan is a dog. They should look for another plan that includes either ETFs or (sometimes just as good) low-cost index funds. Not sure what to say or where to send them? Specific advice is coming in the next section.

✔ **Check your statements.** It doesn't happen often, thank goodness, but yes, sometimes employers steal from their employees' retirement funds. Check your statements with some regularity, and make certain that the money you are contributing is being registered in your account.

✔ **Plan your rollover.** If you leave your job, you may have the option of keeping your 401(k) plan right where it is. HA! Ninety percent of the time, you will do much better by rolling your 401(k) into an IRA and then building yourself a well-diversified ETF portfolio.

One important caveat: You can't withdraw IRA money without penalty until you are 59½, whereas some (but not all) 401(k) plans allow you to withdraw your money penalty-free at 55 if you decide to retire at that point. Don't be too quick to initiate a rollover if you think you may need to tap your funds in the years between 55 and 59½.

If you do initiate a rollover, and you have your own company's stock in your 401(k), you may want to leave just that part behind. You'll get a nice tax break at retirement.

Lobbying the benefits manager at the office

Okay, you have a 401(k) plan. The plan is so bad you want to cry. Your first job is to educate the benefits manager as to why. Don't assume that the people in HR have any more knowledge of personal finance than you do. If you have a lousy 401(k) plan, chances are they don't have a clue. Chances are good that they were bamboozled into accepting a high priced, poorly constructed plan by a fast talking sales rep from a financial institution (often a large financial institution with a well-known name) that specializes in milking the public.

I started this chapter with a hypothetical dialogue between the benefits manager of your company and a representative from a financial institution looking to sell its crappy retirement plan. Here I present a hypothetical dialogue between *you* and your benefits manager:

You: Hey, Joe!

Benefits manager: Hey, _____! What's that black and yellow thing in your hand, a copy of *Goldbricking For Dummies*? (Har har har.)

You: Actually, Joe, this is a book called *Exchange-Traded Funds For Dummies,* and I've been meaning to share it with you.

Benefits manager: Whoa! Exchange-traded whaa?

You: Exchange-Traded Funds For Dummies. It's all about exchange-traded funds — they're the hottest thing on Wall Street. They're basically like index mutual funds that trade like stocks, and they are very inexpensive and have many other benefits for the investor. In fact, I've done a little bit of calculation, and I believe that we could slash the expenses on our company's 401(k) plan by as much as three-quarters, while giving participants an opportunity to build much better diversified portfolios than they can under the present plan.

Benefits manager: [Mouth open wide, bit of coffee dribbling down the side of his chin.]

You: Here, take this, Joe. [You pass him this book.] I want you to read especially Chapter 19, and particularly the sidebar "ETFs and 401(k) plans," where the author gives specific advice for where really sharp and industrious HR managers like you can turn for more information. Oh, see the sidebar "What a 401(k) plan *can* look like," too.

Introducing the Roth 401(k)

On January 1, 2006, a new kid on the retirement block came into being: the Roth 401(k). While you're chatting with your benefits manager, you may want to bring this subject up, too.

ETFs and 401(k) plans

Not many companies offer 401(k) retirement plans with ETF offerings, but the market is "exploding" according to one industry insider. You'd think that would make me — great lover of ETFs that I am — jump for joy.

I'm not jumping.

The problem with ETFs in 401(k) plans isn't what you may think. Even though you may be making weekly contributions, the trading fees can easily be overcome in an employee retirement plan. By making all the employee's trades together, the plan sponsor can actually cut the trading costs down to almost nothing.

No, the problem is that from what I've seen, many 401(k) plan sponsors are packing their ETFs into nonsensical allocations and slapping on charges (as high as 2 percentage points!) that pretty much outweigh the benefits of the ETFs.

Why do they do that? Because ETFs are hot, and they make for a good sales presentation, but the plan sponsor's bottom line may be making money for itself — not for you.

There are exceptions, however. One company called Invest n Retire, LLC, based in Portland, Oregon (www.investnretire.com) puts together ETF-based 401(k) plans with decent allocations and a total cost to the participant of less than one-half of 1 percent. Tell your human resources people to contact this company! The number is 503-419-2894. The address is 506 SW 6th Avenue, Suite 1200, Portland, OR 97204.

What A 401(k) plan *can* look like

Most of the 401(k) plans I see are horrible: high expenses, hidden expenses, impossible to properly diversify. A few companies, however, have begun to offer excellent 401(k) plans built of ETFs.

Invest n Retire, LLC of Portland, Oregon uses mostly ETFs to build its 401(k) plans. Following is a sample of such a 401(k) plan. The asset allocations here, designed by Darwin Abrahamson, a personal financial planner and CEO of Invest n Retire, represent both a conservative portfolio and a "growth" (higher risk/higher potential return) portfolio.

The total fees for the actual ETFs run 0.23 percent for the conservative allocation portfolio and 0.31 percent for the growth portfolio. The total costs to the employee for such a plan

(depending on the employer) would typically run about 0.57 percent. In contrast, the average 401(k) plan charges 1.6 percent, with some fees running 3.0 percent.

What's the difference between a retirement plan that charges you 0.57 in management fees and a plan that charges you 3.0 percent? Start with $10,000, then invest $6,000 a year more for 15 years in a plan with the lower expense ratio, and, assuming an 8 percent return on your investments, you'll have a pre-retirement 401(k) worth $185,164. Invest the same amount for the same period of time in a plan that charges the higher (3.0 percent) expense ratio, and you'll be left with $150,261. That's a difference in the size of your nest egg of $34,903.

Conservative Asset Allocation Model

Investment	Allocation of investment to portfolio
Near cash	**30 percent**
Stable Value Fund	30 percent
Fixed income	**44 percent**
iShares Lehman 7–10 Year Treasury Bond Fund (IEF)	22 percent
iShares Lehman 1–3 Year Treasury Bond Fund (SHY)	22 percent
U.S. large cap	**11 percent**
iShares S&P 500 Value Index (IVE)	6 percent
iShares S&P 500 Growth Index (IVW)	5 percent
U.S. small and mid cap	**15 percent**
iShares S&P 600 Value Index (IJS)	5 percent
iShares Dow Jones U.S. Real Estate Index Fund (IYR)	10 percent
Total management fees	**0.23 percent**

Growth Asset Allocation Model

Investment	Allocation of investment to portfolio
Fixed income	**20 percent**
iShares Lehman 7–10 Year Treasury Bond Fund (IEF)	10 percent
iShares Lehman 1–3 Year Treasury Bond Fund (SHY)	10 percent
International stocks	**25 percent**
iShares MSCI Emerging Market (EEM)	10 percent
iShares MSCI EAFE (EFA)	15 percent
U.S. large cap	**25 percent**
iShares S&P 500 Value Index (IVE)	15 percent
iShares S&P 500 Growth Index (IVW)	10 percent
U.S. small and mid cap	**30 percent**
iShares S&P 600 Value Index (IJS)	10 percent
iShares S&P 600 Growth Index (IJT)	10 percent
iShares Dow Jones U.S. Real Estate Index Fund (IYR)	10 percent
Total management fees	**0.31 percent**

To date, a minority of companies (but a growing minority) has started to offer Roth 401(k) plans to employees. This type of plan is similar to the existing Roth IRA in that the money you put in is *after-tax* money. In other words, you won't get a tax deduction up front, as you do with your existing 401(k).

So why do it? There are two main reasons:

✔ First, you aren't going to have to pay any income tax when you withdraw the money in retirement, as you will with your existing 401(k).

✔ Second, you aren't going to have to sweat about taking minimum required distributions starting at age 70½ like you do now with a 401(k). You can keep the money in the Roth as long as you wish. Or you can leave it as an inheritance to your heirs, tax-free.

If you are currently in a low tax bracket, I'd say the Roth 401(k) will prove to be the better long-term option. (My own personal bias may be coming out here. I feel that with the federal deficit as huge as it is and growing, sooner or later, the government will have to raise tax rates. At that point, even though you are retired and living off a fixed income, you may be paying a higher rate than you do today.)

On the other hand, if you are currently in a high tax bracket and expect to be in a lower tax bracket in the future, the Roth may not make sense. If you are single and make over $75,000 a year, or if you and your spouse together make over $100,000, I suggest talking to your financial planner or accountant to find out which plan is best for you.

Unfortunately, as with many 401(k) plans, your investment options may not be the best. If you leave the company, I suggest that you take your 401(k) Roth and roll it into a Roth IRA.

Strategies for the Self-Employed

Although the self-employed have several retirement plan options, the two most popular, by far, are the traditional IRA and the Roth IRA. (Company employees can also contribute to these plans, but few do, and the deductibility of an IRA becomes a complicated matter if you have a retirement plan at work.) Let me compare the two different IRA options.

The traditional IRA versus the Roth IRA

The traditional IRA currently allows you to sock away $4,000 a year if you're under 50 and $5,000 if you're over 50. The money you put into a traditional IRA is generally tax-deductible. You can't touch that money without paying a penalty until you turn 59½. At that point, you can start to withdraw it, but you'll need to pay income tax on both the principal and any growth in the account.

The Roth IRA is available to people with an adjusted gross income (AGI) of less than $110,000 a year. It allows you to sock away the very same amount as the traditional IRA, but the Roth allows your money to grow *tax-free*. You will never have to pay taxes on any of the money you put into your Roth or on any of the gains. You don't, however, get any deductions on the money you contribute to the Roth.

If your income is very low, like under $25,000, you may qualify for a tax credit of up to $1,000 regardless of whether you choose the traditional or the Roth IRA.

Taxes now or taxes later?

So . . . do you want to pay your taxes on the money now and not have to worry about taxes when you retire? (You want a Roth.) Or do you want to hold off paying the taxes now and pay them after you retire? (You want a traditional IRA.)

Which is the better option depends on a few things, but foremost is the size of your income and your income expectations for whenever you plan to withdraw the funds. If you expect that your income will be less in retirement (presumably moving you into a lower tax bracket, although tax brackets can certainly change), you are likely better off with the traditional IRA; take the deduction now. If you are currently in a low income tax bracket and think (or pray) that you may be in a higher bracket in years to come, go with the Roth.

If it seems like a toss-up, choose the Roth. That's because the Roth offers certain non-tax advantages. With a traditional IRA, for example, you need to start withdrawing the money at age 70½. But with a Roth, you'll be able to keep your money growing tax-free for as long as you are still breathing.

Ushering Your Portfolio into Retirement Readiness

A fellow fee-only financial planner and member of NAPFA, William P. Bengen, CFP, wrote a book for financial planners called *Conserving Client Portfolios During Retirement* (FPA Press). Bengen did an enormous amount of number crunching, reviewing historical return figures going back to 1926. He and his computer played out scenario after scenario: If you retired in year X, and you took out $Y for Z years . . . that sort of fun analysis. His conclusion: The conventional wisdom is both right and wrong. Right, stocks drive a portfolio. Wrong, once you retire, you should live off bonds.

15+ years and counting

If you have 15 years or more to go until retirement, the money in your retirement account should — if history is our guide — be all stock, or pretty close to it. Looking back over the many years, your odds of coming out ahead in any 15-year period are pretty close to a certainty. Forget the bonds. (Of course, the future may *not* be like the past, so maybe put a little bit into bonds, just in case.)

Less than 15 years to retirement

For each year less than 15 years to retirement, says Bengen, you may want to shave 2 percentage points off your stock investments and allocate the difference to bonds. So if you have, say, 10 years till retirement, you may want 90 percent stock and 10 percent bonds. At 5 years till retirement, you may be looking at 80 percent stock and 20 percent bonds.

After you get to retirement, assuming you're looking at a 30-year lifespan or so at that point, you should be thinking not about the conventional mostly-bonds retirement portfolio but, rather, ballpark 60 percent stocks and 40 percent bonds. With that mix, your portfolio has the best chance of being around as long as you are.

Throughout his book (as I do throughout this book), Bengen urges investors not to be "wooden" and not to adhere to any strict formulas. The percentages I note here can, and should, bend with circumstance.

I also urge you to think of *stocks* and *bonds* in the broadest sense of "growth investments" and "security investments." Growth investments may include commodities or real estate as well as stocks. Security investments may include a fixed annuity or a market-neutral mutual fund (with a proven track record), as well as government and corporate bonds. Of course, both your stock and bond positions can — and likely should — be held in ETFs.

Withdrawing Funds to Replace Your Paycheck

How much can you withdraw from your retirement funds each year and have a good chance of not running out of money? That, of course, is one of the biggest financial questions retirees have. According to Bengen, the answer is somewhere around 4 to 5 percent of your portfolio, depending on your age, your investment choices, market conditions, the rate of inflation, your tax hit, and how much you want to leave behind for those rotten children of yours who never come to visit anymore.

I say, go with Bengen's rough estimate of 4 to 5 percent and use some of the retirement calculators I mention in the sidebar "How much is enough?" to smooth out the estimate a bit, but do plan to sit down with a financial planner at least once to get some better idea of where you stand. You don't want to run out of money!

As far as withdrawing funds from an ETF portfolio, in the following section, I offer a few special words of advice.

Don't obsess about maintaining principal or drawing from dividends

I'm not quite sure where it got started, this absurd division of the nest egg into *principal* and *interest*. It's a form of almost mass hysteria that began many years ago.

Listen: If you have an account with, say, $100,000, and you withdraw $5,000, how much do you have left? The answer is **$95,000.** The answer will *always* be $95,000. It doesn't matter in the slightest whether that $5,000 comes from principal or whether you took it out of recently received dividends or interest. (There may be a tax difference in a nonretirement brokerage account, but in a retirement account, there is absolutely no difference.)

So what does this mean in terms of withdrawing funds to live on in retirement?

The best way to achieve that end is to rebalance your portfolio with some regularity (perhaps once every six months), tapping into whichever funds have done the best and creating your own "artificial dividend."

For example, say you have an IRA with a balance of $100,000. The money is invested (for simplicity's sake) into three ETFs and a cash position. It looks like this:

- Cash: $5,000 (5 percent)
- Vanguard Total Stock Market ETF (VTI): $25,000 (25 percent)
- iShares MSCI EAFE (EFA): $25,000 (25 percent)
- iShares Lehman Aggregate Bond Fund (AGG): $45,000 (45 percent)

You determine that you will need to withdraw the $5,000 in cash plus another $5,000 over the next 12 months. Your portfolio master plan calls for only 40 percent bonds, and (because it has been a horrible year for stocks and an okay year for bonds) your bond allocation is now 45 percent. The source for your $5,000 is clear: Take it out of the bond ETF. Doing so will not only generate the cash you need but will also bring your portfolio into balance at the same time.

Fast-forward to one year later . . .

Stocks have suddenly been on a tear, and the "principal" you now have invested in stocks has grown, thanks to capital appreciation, considerably. Your Aggregate Bond fund has also grown (from its starting position of $40,000), due mostly to earned interest, which has been reinvested into the ETF. Your bond fund is back where it started the year, with $45,000.

Your portfolio, even though you withdrew $10,000 in cash during the year, is now worth $125,000. It now looks like this:

- ✔ Cash: $0
- ✔ Vanguard Total Stock Market ETF (VTI): $40,000 (32 percent)
- ✔ iShares MSCI EAFE (EFA): $40,000 (32 percent)
- ✔ iShares Lehman Aggregate Bond Fund (AGG): $45,000 (36 percent)

Nothing has really changed in your life (except that you are now a year older and a year grayer), so you determine that you don't need to shake up your original target portfolio allocation: 40 percent AGG, 30 percent VTI, and 30 percent EFA. You figure that you are going to need another $10,000 for the coming year. Do you take it out of the bond fund because the growth is due to interest rather than growth of principal, as was the case with the stock funds? Many people would, yes. Mass hysteria, as I said. That makes no sense.

In this case, I would ask you to take the money from your two stock ETFs: $5,000 from each. That leaves you with a portfolio of $115,000, invested as follows:

- ✔ Vanguard Total Stock Market ETF (VTI): $35,000 (30.4 percent)
- ✔ iShares MSCI EAFE (EFA): $35,000 (30.4 percent)
- ✔ iShares Lehman Aggregate Bond Fund (AGG): $45,000 (39.1 percent)

You have provided yourself with the $10,000 you need, *and* you've brought your portfolio back into near-perfect balance.

As always, watch the fees

In the scenario in the previous section, to withdraw your $10,000 cash need, you sold off bits of two ETFs. That means paying two commissions. That means (if you trade online, which you certainly should do) a total trading cost of perhaps $30. (If you're paying more than $15 a trade, you are with the wrong brokerage house.) In my eyes, that's perfectly acceptable. If you are withdrawing only several hundred dollars at a time, or even just a couple grand, however, you may want to be in no-load, transaction-free, indexed mutual funds rather than ETFs. You'll need to work the numbers.

In general, I'd say you never want to spend more than one-half of 1 percent on a trade, and — on the other side of the equation — you never want to let your portfolio get too out of balance. Another rule: If your biggest allocation factor — stocks versus bonds — is out of whack more than 5 percentage points (bonds should be 40 percent, but instead they've dipped to 35 percent or risen to 45 percent), you need to make a move.

Make your minimum required distributions

After you turn 59½, you can start taking money out of your 401(k) or traditional IRA. (You can do so before that age, but you usually pay a stiff penalty or have to go through a lot of song and dance with the IRS.) When you turn 70½, you *must* start taking money out of your 401(k) or traditional IRA (but not your Roth IRA). If you don't take out at least the minimum required distribution (MRD), you pay a very nasty penalty. The MRD is based on your portfolio total and your age. There are MRD calculators all over the Web; simply Google the words "minimum required distribution calculator," and you'll have many to choose from. Unlike some other calculators, the MRD calculators are all essentially the same.

IRA, 401(k), or regular (taxable) brokerage account: Which to tap first?

For those of you over 70½, your cash needs will come first from Social Security, any pension you may have, and the minimum required distribution on your traditional IRA or 401(k). Beyond that, you may have a choice as to which account to pull the money from. For those of you over 59½ but not yet 70½, the choice is all yours. Most money managers suggest pulling money from your taxable accounts first, and then and only then from your tax-advantaged accounts. I dunno.

Sure, keeping your money as long as possible in a tax-deferred account will keep this year's taxes to a minimum. But if you care about what you're leaving behind to heirs, the IRA is going to be a pain for them to inherit, for they will have to pay income taxes on the money. For most families, it may make the most sense to pull more or less equally from both accounts: tax-deferred and taxable. But there are so many factors involved, it would be worth your while to discuss the matter with your financial planner, accountant, and estate attorney.

Caveat: From my experience, accountants sometimes tend to focus a wee bit too much on your present taxes; estate attorneys focus a tad too much on your inheritance. These are justifiable biases; just be aware of them.

Part V
The Part of Tens

In this part . . .

Time now to wrap up this book with some practical tips (just in case I haven't provided you with enough in previous chapters). I begin by answering the ten most common questions I get about ETFs. That is followed by a discussion of the ten mistakes that most investors — yes, even smart ETF investors! — often make. And finally, I could hardly call myself a financial professional unless I (like seemingly all other financial professionals) made some predictions! And so, I end Part V by pulling out my crystal ball and making ten forecasts about the future of ETFs. Only time will tell if I am right.

Chapter 20

Ten Most Commonly Asked Questions about ETFs

- -

In This Chapter

▶ Assessing risk

▶ Considering professional help

▶ Figuring out which ETFs make sense for you

- -

*O*h, it's been fun writing a book about exchange-traded funds! Every time someone asks me what I'm working on, and I say, *"Exchange-Traded Funds For Dummies,"* I see the eyes glaze over, and then, inevitably, I'm asked what the heck an ETF is. And so I explain (essentially reading them, from memory, a few lines from this book's Introduction). The *next* question I'm asked is invariably one of the following.

Are ETFs Appropriate for Individual Investors?

You bet they are. Although the name *exchange-traded funds* sounds highly technical and maybe a little bit scary, ETFs are essentially friendly index mutual funds with a few spicy perks. They are *more* than appropriate for individual investors. In fact, given their low expense ratios, high tax efficiency, and the ease with which you can use them to construct a diversified portfolio, ETFs form the perfect building blocks for just about any individual investor's portfolio.

Are ETFs Risky?

That all depends.

Some ETFs are way riskier than others. It's a question of what kind of ETF we're talking about. Most ETFs track stock indexes, and some of those stock indexes — such as individual sectors of the U.S. economy, like technology stocks, or the stock markets of emerging-market nations — can be extremely volatile. Others track broader segments of the U.S. stock market, such as the S&P 500. Those can be volatile, too, but less so. And yet others track bond indexes. Those tend to be less volatile (and less potentially rewarding). One ETF (ticker symbol SHY) tracks short-term Treasury bonds, and as such is only a little bit more volatile than a money market.

Always remember when putting together a portfolio that a diversity of investments can temper risk. Although it seems freakily paradoxical, you can sometimes add a risky ETF to a portfolio (such as an ETF that tracks the price of a basket of commodities, or the stocks of foreign small companies) and lower your overall risk! How so? If the value of your newly added ETF tends to rise as your other investments fall, that will lower the volatility of your entire portfolio. (Financial professionals refer to this strange but sweet phenomenon as *modern portfolio theory*.)

Do I Need a Financial Professional to Set Up and Monitor an ETF Portfolio?

Do you need an auto mechanic to service your car? I don't know. It depends on both your particular skills and your inclination to spend a Sunday afternoon getting greasy under the hood. Setting up a decent ETF portfolio, with the aid of this book, is very much doable. You can certainly monitor such a portfolio, as well. A professional, however, has special tools and (I hope) objectivity to help you understand investment risk and construct a portfolio that fits you like a glove, or at least a sock. A financial planner can also help you properly estimate your retirement needs and plan your savings accordingly.

Do be aware that many investment "advisors" out there are nothing more than salespeople in disguise. Don't be at all surprised if you bump into a few who express their disgust of ETFs! ETFs make no money for those salespeople who make a living hawking expensive (often inferior) investment products. Your best bet for good advice is to find a *fee-only* (takes no commissions) financial planner. If you are more or less a do-it-yourselfer but simply wish for a little guidance, try to find a fee-only who will work with you on an hourly basis.

How Much Money Do I Need to Invest in ETFs?

You can buy one share of any number of ETFs for as low as the price of a share. But since you pay a commission to trade (I'd say the average trading commission is about $15), buying one $20 share (and thus paying a 75 percent commission) would hardly make good sense. Starting at about $3,000 perhaps, it may be worth investing in ETFs, but only if you plan to keep that money invested for at least several years. Smaller amounts of money are best invested in mutual funds (preferably low-cost index mutual funds), money markets, or other instruments that incur no trading costs.

With Hundreds of ETFs to Choose From, Where Do I Start?

The answer depends on your objective. If you are looking to round out an existing portfolio of stocks or mutual funds, your ETF should complement what already exists. Your goal is always to have a well-diversified collection of investments. If you are starting to build a portfolio, you want to make sure to include stocks and bonds and to diversify as much as is practical within each of those two broad asset classes.

There is not much in the world of stocks that can't be satisfied with ETFs. Try to have both U.S. and international stock ETFs. And within the U.S. stock arena, shoot to have large cap growth, small cap growth, large cap value, and small cap value. (I explain these grid terms in Chapters 5 through 8.) You can also diversify your ETFs by industry sector: consumer staples, energy, financials, and so on. (See Chapter 9 for a discussion of sector diversification.) Generally, I wouldn't attempt to do both grid diversification and sector diversification. That would call for an unwieldy number of holdings.

Although all ETFs are somewhat reasonably priced, some are more reasonably priced than others. If you are going to pay 0.60 percent a year in operating expenses for a certain ETF, you should have a good reason for doing so. Many ETFs are available for under 0.30 percent, some for even less than 0.10 percent.

On the bond side of your portfolio, you can fill most of your needs with Barclays iShares fixed-income ETFs. For certain kinds of bonds, such as tax-free munis and international bonds, you have to go with mutual funds or individual securities — at least for now. I'm sure those ETFs will eventually hit the market, too.

Where Is the Best Place for Me to Buy ETFs?

I suggest setting up an account with a financial supermarket, such as Fidelity, Vanguard, T. Rowe Price, Charles Schwab, or TD AMERITRADE. Each of these allows you to hold ETFs, along with other investments — such as mutual funds or individual stocks or bonds — in one account.

Different financial supermarkets offer different services and charge different prices depending on how much you have to invest, how often you trade, and whether you do everything online or by phone. You need to do some shopping to find the brokerage house that works best for you. I provide more suggestions for shopping financial supermarkets in Chapter 3. You'll find contact information there; you'll also see a listing of Web sites in Appendix B.

Is There an Especially Good or Bad Time to Buy ETFs?

Nope, not really. Studies show rather conclusively that the stock and bond markets (or any segment of the stock or bond markets) is just about as likely to go up after a good day as it is after a bad day (week, month, year, or any other piece of the calendar). Trying to time the market tends to be a fool's game — or, just as often, a game that some like to play with other people's money.

Do ETFs Have Any Disadvantages?

Because most ETFs follow an index, you probably won't see your ETF (or any of your index mutual funds) wind up number one on *Wise Money* magazine's list of Top Funds for the Year. (But you probably won't find any of your ETFs on the bottom of such a list, either.) The bigger disadvantage of ETFs is the cost of trading them, although that cost should be minimal.

Building a well-diversified portfolio of ETFs — stocks, bonds, large cap, small cap, U.S., international — may also seem to have the disadvantage that in any year, some of your ETFs are going to do poorly. Just remember that *next* year those particular investments, the ones that look so disgustingly dull right now, may be the shiniest things in your portfolio.

Does It Matter Which Exchange My ETF Is Traded On?

No. The vast majority of ETFs are traded either on the American Stock Exchange or the NASDAQ. It doesn't matter in the slightest to you, the individual investor. The cost of your trade is determined by the brokerage house you do business with. The *spread* (the difference between the ask and buy price) is determined by the volume of the ETF being traded. Regardless of which exchange the ETF is being traded on, if the volume is small (such as would be the case for, say, the iShares MSCI South Korea Fund), you may want to place a *limit order* rather than a *market order*. I explain the different kinds of orders in a sidebar in Chapter 2.

Which ETFs Are Best in My IRA, and Which Are Best in My Taxable Account?

Generally, those investments that generate income — either interest or dividends — are best kept in a tax-advantaged retirement account, such as your IRA or 401(k) plan. That would include any bond, REIT, or high-dividend paying ETF. You'll eventually need to pay income tax on any money you withdraw from those accounts, but it is generally better to pay later than sooner. In the case of a Roth IRA, which is often the best case of all, you will never have to pay taxes on the earnings, the principal, what is in the account, or what you withdraw. Try to put your ETFs that have the greatest potential for growth into your Roth IRA.

Since retirement accounts generally require you to keep your money put until age 59½, anyone younger than that would want to keep all emergency money in a non-retirement account.

Chapter 21

Ten Mistakes Most Investors (Even Smart Ones) Make

In This Chapter

▶ Paying and risking too much

▶ Selling too frequently

▶ Saving too little and expecting too much from the market

▶ Ignoring inflation and IRS rules

*R*emember that personal investing course you took in high school?

Of course you don't! Your high school never offered such a course. Chances are that you've never taken such a course. Few have. And that lack of education — combined with a surfeit of cheesy and oft-advertised investment industry products, plus an irresponsible and lazy financial press — leads many investors to make some very costly mistakes.

Paying Too Much Money for an Investment Product

Most investors pay way, way too much to middlemen who suck the lifeblood out of portfolios, leaving many investors with little to show for their investments. By investing primarily in ETFs, you spare yourself and your family this tragic fate. The typical ETF costs a fraction of what you would pay in yearly management fees to a mutual fund company. You never pay any *loads* (high commissions). And trading fees, as long as you're not dealing in dribs and drabs, should be minimal.

Failing to Properly Diversify

Thou shalt not put all thy eggs in one basket is perhaps the first commandment of investing, but it is astonishing how many sinners there are among us. ETFs allow for easy and effective diversification. By investing in ETFs rather than individual securities, you have already made a great step in the right direction. Don't blow it by pouring all your money into one ETF that represents a single hot sector! To the extent possible, invest in the *entire* market: value, growth, small cap, large cap, U.S., and international (see Part II). ETFs make such diversification easy.

Taking on Inappropriate Risks

Some people take way too much risk, investing perhaps everything in highly volatile technology or biotech stocks. But many people don't take enough risk, leaving their money to sit in secure but low-yielding money market funds or, worse, in the vault of their local savings and loan. If you want your money to grow, you may have to stomach some volatility. In general, the longer you can tie your money up, the more volatile (risky) your portfolio can be. A portfolio of ETFs can be amazingly fine-tuned to match your particular appropriate level of risk and return.

Selling Out When the Going Gets Rough

It can be a scary thing, for sure, when your portfolio value drops 10 or 20 percent. But if you invest in stock ETFs, that scenario is going to happen. It has happened many times in the past; it will happen many times in the future. That's just the nature of the beast. If you sell when the going gets rough (as many investors do), you lose the game. The stock market is resilient. Hang tough. Bears are followed by bulls. Your portfolio — as long as you are well diversified — will bounce back, given enough time.

Paying Too Much Attention to Recent Performance

Many investors make a habit of bailing out of whatever market segment has recently taken a dive. Conversely, they often look for whatever market segment has recently shot through the roof, and that's the one they buy. Then, when *that* market segment tanks, they sell once again. By forever buying high and selling low, their portfolios dwindle over time to nothing.

When you build your portfolio, don't overload it with last year's ETF superstars. You don't know what will happen next year. Stay cool. You may notice that in this book, I do not include performance figures for any of the ETFs discussed (except in one or two circumstances to make a specific point). That omission was intentional. Most of the ETFs I discuss are only a few years old, and a few years' returns tell you *nothing*. On the other hand, the indexes tracked by certain ETFs go back decades. In those cases, I do provide performance figures.

Not Saving Enough for Retirement

As opposed to spending, saving isn't a whole lot of joy. But you can't build a portfolio out of thin air. If your goal is to one day be financially independent, to retire with dignity, you probably need to build a nest egg equal to about 20 times your yearly budget. (More on that subject in Chapter 19.) Doing so won't be easy. It may mean saving 15 percent of your paycheck for several decades. The earlier you start, the easier it will be.

Savings comes from the difference between what you earn and what you spend. Remember that both are adjustable figures. One great way to save is to contribute at least enough to your 401(k) plan at work to get your employer's full match. Do it! Another is to remember that material goodies do not buy happiness. Honest. Psychologists have studied the matter, and their findings are rather conclusive.

Having Unrealistic Expectations of Market Returns

One reason many people don't save enough is that they have unrealistic expectations; they believe fervently that they are going to win the lottery or (next best thing) earn 25 percent a year on their investments. The truth: The stock market, over the past 75 years, has returned about 10 percent a year before inflation and 7 percent a year after inflation. Bonds have returned about half as much. A well-balanced portfolio, therefore, may have returned 7 or 8 percent before inflation and maybe 5 percent or so after inflation.

Five percent growth after inflation — with interest compounded every year — isn't too shabby. In 20 years time, an investment of $10,000 growing at 5 percent will turn to $26,530 in constant dollars. With a very well-diversified portfolio, leaning toward higher-yielding asset classes (see Part II), you may be able to do a tad better. If you want to earn 25 percent a year, however, you are going to have to take inordinate risk. And even then, I wouldn't bank on it.

Discounting the Damaging Effect of Inflation

No, a dollar certainly doesn't buy what it used to. Think of what a candy bar cost when you were a kid. Think of what you earned on your first job. Remember when gas was 32 cents a gallon? Now look into the future, and realize that your nest egg, unless wisely invested, will shrivel and shrink. Historically, certain investments do a better job of keeping up with inflation than others. Those investments, which include stocks, tend to be somewhat volatile. It's a price you need to pay, however, to keep the inflation monster at bay. The world of ETFs includes many ways to invest in stocks. You may also consider a position in Treasury Inflation-Protected Securities (TIPS). The iShares Lehman TIPS Bond Fund (TIP) tracks an index of TIPS. You can read about TIPS in Chapter 12.

Not Following the IRS Rules

When they leave their jobs, many employees cash out their 401(k) accounts, thereupon paying the IRS a stiff penalty and immediately losing the great benefit of tax deferral. The government allows certain tax breaks for special kinds of accounts, and you really need to play by the rules or you can wind up worse off than had you never invested in the first place.

People over 70½ must be especially careful to take the Minimum Required Distributions from their IRAs or 401(k) plans. Calculators are available online; simply type "MRD calculator" into your favorite search engine. Unlike a retirement calculator, based on all kinds of assumptions, the MRD is a straightforward equation. Any online calculator can take you there. Or ask your accountant.

Failing to Incorporate Investments into a Broader Financial Plan

Have you paid off all your high-interest credit card debt? Do you have proper disability insurance? Do you have enough life insurance so that, if necessary, your co-parent and children could survive without you? A finely manicured portfolio is only part of a larger picture that includes issues such as debt management, insurance, and estate planning. Don't spend too much time tinkering with your ETF portfolio and ignore these other very important financial issues.

Chapter 22

Ten Forecasts about the Future of ETFs and Personal Investing

I try not to watch any of the investment shows on television. Stock "Expert" Number One gives his prediction of the future. Then "Expert" Number Two gives her (often contradictory) opinion. Viewers may be amused by the heated debate but never know what to do in the end.

I also usually try not to make predictions about the future, but I'll ask you to please indulge me now. I can't resist. It just seems like sooo much fun!

Here are my predictions, for whatever they are worth, about the world of ETFs.

ETFs Will Grow for Another Couple Years

Most people should be investing most of their money in index mutual funds or ETFs, but I don't see that happening — not now, not ever. The recent popularity of ETFs is due largely to the interest of educated institutional investors and a minority of savvy individual investors, like you.

The vast majority of investors will *never, never* give up their belief that they can beat the market. They'll try any which way they can. They will attend pricey workshops that promise to teach them how to double their money overnight. They will subscribe to newsletters and magazines telling them which stocks or mutual funds to buy this week for sure-fire rapid appreciation. They will buy high-priced mutual funds and will actually pay a fat commission for the honor of doing so.

That's their problem, not yours.

More Players Will Enter the Field, But Only a Few

Barclays, State Street, and Vanguard got the jump on ETFs, with others, like PowerShares, Rydex, and WisdomTree, riding close behind. Other investment houses will offer ETFs in time. Unlike the world of mutual funds, however, the profit margin on ETFs is small, so I don't think we'll see hundreds of issuers of ETFs, as we do mutual funds.

Investors Will Have More, and Better, Options

There are currently black holes in the ETF universe: entire asset classes unrepresented. I'm quite eager to see those holes filled, and I'm certain that will happen before long.

By the time I write the second edition of this book, I suspect that we will see an ETF for tax-free municipal bonds; several *market-neutral* ETFs (meaning that, like hedge funds, they have little to no correlation to the broad stock market, even though they may invest in stocks); at least a handful of small cap international ETFs; international bond ETFs; a few more commodity ETFs; and, in time, perhaps some asset classes that don't even exist yet. (Shuttlecraft and warp-drive production ETFs?)

Investors Will Get Suckered into Buying More Bad Products

Alas, good ETFs can be turned into bad financial products. It's already happening with some of the ETF offerings in 401(k) plans. In that case, perfectly good ETFs are packaged in such a way that the investor (trapped like a fly in a bowl of milk in his company's plan) is paying as much as 3 percent in management fees. I'm sure that good ETFs will similarly pop up in crappy annuity plans, 529 college plans, and other investments where someone somewhere stands to make a big buck off the small investor.

Brokers Will Find a Way to Slap Loads on ETFs

They've tried before (with PowerShares), and they'll try again. There's nothing as succulent to a broker as a fat upfront commission. The financial world will not allow this juicy source of revenue to dry up as more people invest in ETFs.

The Markets Will (Unfortunately) See Greater Correlation

As the world continues to become a smaller place, and the economies of nations become yet more interdependent, so too will stock and bond markets around the world tend to move up and down in unison. This is not a good thing for investors because it lessens the power of diversification to mollify risk. Investors will find a growing need to tap into alternative investments, such as market-neutral funds. An expanded menu of ETFs will become an important part of an alternative investment strategy.

Asset Class Returns Will Revert Toward Their Historic Means

Astronomical rises in the price of energy (and oil company stocks), certain commodities (silver, copper, gold), and residential real estate (San Francisco, Long Island) cannot and will not continue. Neither will the seemingly permanent leveling off in the sad price of large U.S. growth stocks. Or the pitiful recent performance of long-term bonds. Large growth stocks will rise, and commodities and energy stocks will fall, as we see these asset class returns revert to their historical norms.

In terms of an ETF portfolio, this may be a good time to slightly underweight energy and commodities and overweight large growth stocks. (Tilt your portfolio oh-so-slightly because these are only one man's predictions!) By the time this book appears in print, of course, anything could have happened.

Taxes Will Rise

Let's see . . . The United States has a raging federal deficit; an aging population; a medical "system" (if you can even call it that) that has left millions unable to pay for their doctor, dentist, and hospital bills; a sagging Social Security system; and a seriously challenged public school system. Despite huge tax cuts (mostly for the wealthy), these problems persist and worsen. Sooner or later, *something* has to give.

I believe that future administrations will have no option but to raise taxes on everyone. I advocate squirreling as much of your ETF portfolio into a tax-free Roth IRA as you can. (And then pray that Congress doesn't change the rules on Roths.)

Inflation Will Remain Tame

Although I'm certainly concerned about inflation and recognize that it can devastate a paycheck or a portfolio, I'm not too worried about a return to the double-digit inflation of the 1980s. There is a reason that we saw double-digit inflation back then: The United States decided to abandon the gold standard in the 1970s, and the new monetary system was walking on its baby legs. I anticipate that inflation in the next decade or two will be similar to what it has been in the past decade or two: somewhere in the ballpark of 3 percent. Protect yourself with a good helping of stock ETFs (stocks have a pretty good track record of keeping up with inflation) and a position in the iShares Lehman TIPS Bond Fund (TIP), which tracks an index of U.S. Treasury Inflation-Protected Securities.

The Shelves of Bookstores Will See More Books on ETFs!

Of all my predictions, this is the one I'd put money on.

I'm already seeing magazine articles with headings such as "Build Instant Wealth and Retire Early with ETFs!" It's only a matter of time before someone decides to spin off one of these articles into a book. I suspect titles such as, "Beat the Market with ETFs!" and "You Can Make a Killing in ETFs!" One of them may become a bestseller, which means that it will make a lot of money for someone — but not for the readers.

Part VI
Appendixes

The 5th Wave   By Rich Tennant

That's the Harrisons. Never have I seen an investment portfolio start so strong and go south so quickly.

In this part . . .

In this part, you get some handy reference info: a complete list of ETFs (as of this writing — by the time you're reading these words, it is quite possible that more will have appeared on the market), a list of Web sites to check whenever you're craving even more ETF info, and a glossary that can help you navigate this book and any other ETF resource.

Appendix A

A Complete Listing of ETFs

The following listing of ETFs available as of this writing comes from www.etfguide.com (© 2004–06 Enforte Financial Services, LLC All Rights Reserved). New ETFs are being created all the time, so for the most up-to-date listing, please visit the Web site.

Broad Market Indexes	Ticker Symbol	Expense Ratio	Exchange
iShares Dow Jones U.S. Total Market	IYY	0.20%	Amex
iShares Russell 3000	IWV	0.20%	Amex
iShares Russell 3000 Growth	IWZ	0.25%	Amex
iShares Russell 3000 Value	IWW	0.25%	Amex
iShares S&P 1500	ISI	0.20%	NYSE
iShares NYSE Composite	NYC	0.25%	NYSE
Fidelity NASDAQ Composite	ONEQ	0.30%	NASDAQ
First Trust NASDAQ-100 Equal Weight	QQEW	0.60%	NASDAQ
NASDAQ-100 Trust Series 1	QQQQ	0.20%	NASDAQ
PowerShares Dividend Achievers Portfolio	PFM	0.50%	Amex
PowerShares Dynamic OTC Portfolio	PWO	0.60%	Amex
PowerShares Dynamic Market Portfolio	PWC	0.60%	Amex
PowerShares FTSE RAFI U.S. 1000	PRF	0.60%	NYSE
PowerShares High Yield Equity Dividend Achievers Portfolio	PEY	0.50%	Amex
PowerShares High Growth Rate Dividend Achievers Portfolio	PHJ	0.50%	Amex
PowerShares Value Line Timeliness Selection	PIV	0.60%	Amex
streetTRACKS Total Market	TMW	0.20%	Amex
Vanguard Total Stock Market ETF	VTI	0.07%	Amex
Vanguard Extended Market ETF	VXF	0.08%	Amex
WisdomTree Total Dividend Fund	DTD	0.28%	NYSE
WisdomTree High-Yield Equity Fund	DHS	0.38%	NYSE
Expense Ratio Category Average		**0.35%**	

Large Cap Indexes	Ticker Symbol	Expense Ratio	Exchange
DIAMONDS Trust Series 1	DIA	0.18%	Amex
SPDR 500	SPY	0.10%	Amex
First Trust Morningstar Dividend Leaders Index Fund	FDL	0.45%	Amex
First Trust DB Strategic Value Index	FDV	0.65%	Amex
iShares Dow Jones Select Dividend Index Fund	DVY	0.40%	NYSE
iShares KLD Select Social Index	KLD	0.50%	NYSE
iShares Morningstar Large Core	JKD	0.20%	NYSE
iShares Morningstar Large Growth	JKE	0.25%	NYSE
iShares Morningstar Large Value	JKF	0.25%	NYSE
iShares Russell 1000	IWB	0.15%	Amex
iShares Russell 1000 Growth	IWF	0.20%	Amex
iShares Russell 1000 Value	IWD	0.20%	Amex
iShares S&P 100	OEF	0.20%	Amex
iShares S&P 500	IVV	0.09%	NYSE
iShares S&P 500 Growth	IVW	0.18%	NYSE
iShares S&P 500 Value	IVE	0.18%	NYSE
iShares NYSE 100 Index	NY	0.20%	NYSE
PowerShares Dynamic Large Cap Growth Portfolio	PWB	0.60%	Amex
PowerShares Dynamic Large Cap Value Portfolio	PWV	0.60%	Amex
Rydex S&P 500 Equal Weight	RSP	0.40%	Amex
Rydex S&P 500 Pure Growth	RPG	0.35%	Amex
Rydex S&P 500 Pure Value	RPV	0.35%	Amex
Rydex Russell Top 50 Index	XLG	0.20%	Amex
SPDR Dividend	SDY	0.30%	Amex
streetTRACKS Dow Jones Wilshire Large Cap	ELR	0.20%	Amex
streetTRACKS Dow Jones U.S. Large Cap Growth	ELG	0.20%	Amex
streetTRACKS Dow Jones U.S. Large Cap Value	ELV	0.20%	Amex
streetTRACKS SPDR O-Strip	OOO	0.35%	Amex

Large Cap Indexes	Ticker Symbol	Expense Ratio	Exchange
Vanguard Dividend Appreciation ETF	VIG	0.28%	Amex
Vanguard Large Cap ETF	VV	0.07%	Amex
Vanguard Growth ETF	VUG	0.11%	Amex
Vanguard Value ETF	VTV	0.11%	Amex
WisdomTree LargeCap Dividend Fund	DLN	0.28%	NYSE
WisdomTree Dividend Top 100 Fund	DON	0.38%	NYSE
Expense Ratio Category Average		**0.28%**	

Mid Cap Indexes	Ticker Symbol	Expense Ratio	Exchange
SPDR 400	MDY	0.25%	Amex
iShares Morningstar Mid Core	JKG	0.25%	NYSE
iShares Morningstar Mid Growth	JKH	0.30%	NYSE
iShares Morningstar Mid Value	JKI	0.30%	NYSE
iShares Russell Mid Cap	IWR	0.20%	Amex
iShares Russell Mid Cap Growth	IWP	0.25%	Amex
iShares Russell Mid Cap Value	IWS	0.25%	Amex
iShares S&P 400 Mid Cap	IJH	0.20%	NYSE
iShares S&P 400 Growth	IJK	0.25%	NYSE
iShares S&P 400 Value	IJJ	0.20%	NYSE
PowerShares Dynamic Mid Cap Growth Portfolio	PWJ	0.60%	Amex
PowerShares Dynamic Mid Cap Value Portfolio	PWP	0.60%	Amex
Rydex S&P 400 Mid Cap Pure Growth	RFG	0.35%	Amex
Rydex S&P 400 Mid Cap Pure Value	RFV	0.35%	Amex
streetTRACKS Dow Jones Wilshire Mid Cap	EMM	0.25%	Amex
streetTRACKS Dow Jones Wilshire Mid Cap Growth	EMG	0.25%	Amex
streetTRACKS Dow Jones Wilshire Mid Cap Value	EMV	0.25%	Amex
Vanguard Mid Cap ETF	VO	0.13%	Amex
WisdomTree MidCap Dividend Fund	DES	0.38%	NYSE
Expense Ratio Category Average		**0.30%**	

Small Cap Indexes	Ticker Symbol	Expense Ratio	Exchange
iShares Morningstar Small Core	JKJ	0.25%	NYSE
iShares Morningstar Small Growth	JKK	0.30%	NYSE
iShares Morningstar Small Value	JKL	0.30%	NYSE
iShares Russell 2000	IWM	0.20%	Amex
iShares Russell 2000 Growth	IWO	0.25%	Amex
iShares Russell 2000 Value	IWN	0.25%	Amex
iShares Russell Microcap Index	IWC	0.60%	NYSE
iShares S&P Small Cap 600	IJR	0.20%	NYSE
iShares S&P Small Cap 600 Growth	IJT	0.25%	NYSE
iShares S&P Small Cap 600 Value	IJS	0.25%	NYSE
PowerShares Dynamic Small Cap Growth Portfolio	PWT	0.60%	Amex
PowerShares Dynamic Small Cap Value Portfolio	PWY	0.60%	Amex
PowerShares Zacks Microcap Index	PZI	0.60%	Amex
PowerShares Zacks Small Cap Portfolio	PZJ	0.60%	Amex
Rydex S&P 600 Small Cap Pure Growth	RZG	0.35%	Amex
Rydex S&P 600 Small Cap Pure Value	RZV	0.35%	Amex
streetTRACKS Dow Jones Wilshire Small Cap	DSC	0.25%	Amex
streetTRACKS Dow Jones U.S. Small Cap Growth	DSG	0.25%	Amex
streetTRACKS Dow Jones U.S. Small Cap Value	DSV	0.25%	Amex
Vanguard Small Cap ETF	VB	0.10%	Amex
Vanguard Small Cap Growth ETF	VBK	0.12%	Amex
Vanguard Small Cap Value ETF	VBR	0.12%	Amex
First Trust Dow Jones Select Microcap Index	FDM	0.60%	Amex
WisdomTree SmallCap Dividend Fund	DTN	0.38%	NYSE
Expense Ratio Category Average		**0.33%**	

Industry & Sector Indexes	Ticker Symbol	Expense Ratio	Exchange
iShares Dow Jones U.S. Basic Materials	IYM	0.48%	NYSE
iShares Dow Jones U.S. Consumer Services	IYC	0.48%	NYSE
iShares Dow Jones U.S. Consumer Goods	IYK	0.48%	NYSE

Industry & Sector Indexes	Ticker Symbol	Expense Ratio	Exchange
iShares Dow Jones U.S. Energy Index	IYE	0.48%	NYSE
iShares Dow Jones U.S. Financial Index	IYF	0.48%	NYSE
iShares Dow Jones U.S. Financial Services Index	IYG	0.48%	NYSE
iShares Dow Jones U.S. Healthcare Index	IYH	0.48%	NYSE
iShares Dow Jones U.S. Industrial Index	IYJ	0.48%	NYSE
iShares Dow Jones U.S. Real Estate Index	IYR	0.48%	NYSE
iShares Dow Jones U.S. Technology Index	IYW	0.48%	NYSE
iShares Dow Jones U.S. Telecommunications Index	IYZ	0.48%	NYSE
iShares Dow Jones U.S. Transportation Index	IYT	0.48%	NYSE
iShares Dow Jones U.S. Utilities Index	IDU	0.48%	Amex
iShares Dow Jones U.S. Oil & Gas Exploration/Production	IEO	0.48%	NYSE
iShares Dow Jones U.S. Oil Equipment & Services	IEZ	0.48%	NYSE
iShares Dow Jones U.S. Pharmaceuticals	IHE	0.48%	NYSE
iShares Dow Jones U.S. Healthcare Providers	IHF	0.48%	NYSE
iShares Dow Jones U.S. Medical Devices	IHI	0.48%	NYSE
iShares Dow Jones U.S. Broker/ Dealers	IAI	0.48%	NYSE
iShares Dow Jones U.S. Insurance	IAK	0.48%	NYSE
iShares Dow Jones U.S. Regional Banks	IAT	0.48%	NYSE
iShares Dow Jones U.S. Aerospace & Defense	ITA	0.48%	NYSE
iShares Dow Jones U.S. Home Construction	ITB	0.48%	NYSE
iShares Cohen & Steers Realty Majors Index	ICF	0.35%	Amex
iShares NASDAQ Biotechnology Index	IBB	0.48%	Amex
iShares Goldman Sachs Natural Resources Index	IGE	0.50%	Amex
iShares Goldman Sachs Networking Index	IGN	0.48%	Amex
iShares Goldman Sachs Semi-conductor Index	IGW	0.48%	Amex
iShares Goldman Sachs Software Index	IGV	0.48%	Amex

(continued)

Industry & Sector Indexes	Ticker Symbol	Expense Ratio	Exchange
iShares Goldman Sachs Technology Index	IGM	0.48%	Amex
First Trust Amex Biotechnology Index	FBT	0.60%	Amex
First Trust Dow Jones Internet Index	FDN	0.60%	Amex
First Trust NASDAQ-100 Technology	QTEC	0.60%	NASDAQ
Market Vectors Gold Miners	GDX	0.55%	Amex
PowerShares Dynamic Pharmaceuticals	PJP	0.60%	Amex
PowerShares Dynamic Biotechnology & Genome	PBE	0.60%	Amex
PowerShares Dynamic Food & Beverage	PBJ	0.60%	Amex
PowerShares Dynamic Leisure & Entertainment	PEJ	0.60%	Amex
PowerShares Dynamic Media	PBS	0.60%	Amex
PowerShares Dynamic Networking	PXQ	0.60%	Amex
PowerShares Dynamic Semiconductor	PSI	0.60%	Amex
PowerShares Dynamic Software	PSJ	0.60%	Amex
PowerShares LUX Nanotech	PXN	0.60%	Amex
PowerShares Aerospace & Defense	PPA	0.60%	Amex
PowerShares Dynamic Building & Construction	PKB	0.60%	Amex
PowerShares Dynamic Energy & Exploration	PXE	0.60%	Amex
PowerShares Dynamic Hardware & Consumer Electronics	PHW	0.60%	Amex
PowerShares Dynamic Insurance	PIC	0.60%	Amex
PowerShares Dynamic Retail	PMR	0.60%	Amex
PowerShares Dynamic Oil & Gas	PXJ	0.60%	Amex
PowerShares Dynamic Telecommunications & Wireless	PTE	0.60%	Amex
PowerShares Dynamic Utilities	PUI	0.60%	Amex
PowerShares WilderHill Clean Energy Fund	PBW	0.60%	Amex
PowerShares Water Resources	PHO	0.60%	Amex
Consumer Staples Select Sector SPDR	XLP	0.25%	Amex
Consumer Discretionary Select Sector SPDR	XLY	0.25%	Amex
Energy Select Sector SPDR	XLE	0.24%	Amex

Industry & Sector Indexes	Ticker Symbol	Expense Ratio	Exchange
Financial Select Sector SPDR	XLF	0.25%	Amex
Healthcare Select Sector SPDR	XLV	0.24%	Amex
Industrial Select Sector SPDR	XLI	0.24%	Amex
Materials Select Sector SPDR	XLB	0.25%	Amex
Technology Select Sector SPDR	XLK	0.25%	Amex
Utilities Select Sector SPDR	XLU	0.25%	Amex
SPDR Biotech	XBI	0.35%	Amex
SPDR Homebuilders	XHB	0.35%	Amex
SPDR Metals & Mining	XME	0.35%	Amex
SPDR Pharmaceuticals	XPH	0.35%	Amex
SPDR Retail	XRT	0.35%	Amex
SPDR Semiconductor	XSD	0.35%	Amex
SPDR Oil & Gas Equipment & Services	XES	0.35%	Amex
SPDR Oil & Gas Exploration & Production	XOP	0.35%	Amex
streetTRACKS KBW Bank	KBE	0.35%	Amex
streetTRACKS KBW Regional Bank	KRE	0.35%	Amex
streetTRACKS KBW Capital Markets	KCE	0.35%	Amex
streetTRACKS KBW Insurance	KIE	0.35%	Amex
streetTRACKS Morgan Stanley Technology Index	MTK	0.50%	Amex
streetTRACKS Wilshire REIT Index	RWR	0.25%	Amex
Vanguard Consumer Discretionary ETF	VCR	0.25%	Amex
Vanguard Consumer Staples ETF	VDC	0.25%	Amex
Vanguard Energy ETF	VDE	0.25%	Amex
Vanguard Financials ETF	VFH	0.25%	Amex
Vanguard Health Care ETF	VHT	0.25%	Amex
Vanguard Industrials ETF	VIS	0.25%	Amex
Vanguard Information Technology ETF	VGT	0.25%	Amex
Vanguard Materials ETF	VAW	0.25%	Amex
Vanguard REIT ETF	VNQ	0.12%	Amex
Vanguard Telecommunications ETF	VOX	0.25%	Amex
Vanguard Utilities ETF	VPU	0.25%	Amex
Expense Ratio Category Average		**0.44%**	

Global & International Developed Market Indexes	Ticker Symbol	Expense Ratio	Exchange
BLDRs Developed Markets 100 ADR	ADRD	0.30%	NASDAQ
BLDRs Europe 100 ADR	ADRU	0.30%	NASDAQ
BLDRs Asia 50 ADR	ADRA	0.30%	NASDAQ
iShares MSCI EMU	EZU	0.59%	Amex
iShares MSCI EAFE	EFA	0.35%	Amex
iShares MSCI EAFE Value Index	EFV	0.40%	NYSE
iShares MSCI EAFE Growth Index	EFG	0.40%	NYSE
iShares MSCI Pacific ex-Japan	EPP	0.50%	Amex
iShares S&P Europe 350	IEV	0.60%	NYSE
iShares S&P Latin America 40	ILF	0.50%	Amex
iShares S&P TOPIX 150	ITF	0.50%	Amex
iShares S&P Global 100	IOO	0.40%	NYSE
iShares S&P Global Energy Index	IXC	0.48%	Amex
iShares S&P Global Financials Index	IXG	0.48%	Amex
iShares S&P Global Healthcare Index	IXJ	0.48%	Amex
iShares S&P Global Technology Index	IXN	0.48%	Amex
iShares S&P Global Telecommunications Index	IXP	0.48%	Amex
iShares MSCI Australia	EWA	0.59%	Amex
iShares MSCI Austria	EWO	0.59%	Amex
iShares MSCI Belgium	EWK	0.59%	NYSE
iShares MSCI Canada	EWC	0.59%	Amex
iShares MSCI France	EWQ	0.59%	NYSE
iShares MSCI Germany	EWG	0.59%	Amex
iShares MSCI Hong Kong	EWH	0.59%	NYSE
iShares MSCI Italy	EWI	0.59%	NYSE
iShares MSCI Japan	EWJ	0.59%	NYSE
iShares MSCI Netherlands	EWN	0.59%	NYSE
iShares MSCI Singapore	EWS	0.59%	NYSE
iShares MSCI Spain	EWP	0.59%	NYSE
iShares MSCI Sweden	EWD	0.59%	NYSE
iShares MSCI Switzerland	EWL	0.59%	NYSE
iShares MSCI United Kingdom	EWU	0.59%	NYSE
iShares FTSE/Xinhua China 25 Index	FXI	0.74%	NYSE

Global & International Developed Market Indexes	Ticker Symbol	Expense Ratio	Exchange
PowerShares Golden Dragon Halter USX China	PGJ	0.60%	Amex
PowerShares International Dividend Achievers Portfolio	PID	0.50%	Amex
streetTRACKS Dow Jones EURO	FEZ	0.33%	NYSE
streetTRACKS Dow Jones STOXX 50	FEU	0.33%	NYSE
streetTRACKS Dow Jones Global Titans	DGT	0.50%	Amex
Vanguard European ETF	VGK	0.18%	Amex
Vanguard Pacific ETF	VPL	0.18%	Amex
WisdomTree DIEFA Fund	DWM	0.48%	NYSE
WisdomTree DIEFA High Yielding Equity Fund	DTH	0.58%	NYSE
WisdomTree Europe Total Dividend Fund	DEB	0.48%	NYSE
WisdomTree Europe High Yielding Equity Fund	DEW	0.58%	NYSE
WisdomTree Europe SmallCap Dividend Fund	DFE	0.58%	NYSE
WisdomTree Japan Total Dividend Fund	DXJ	0.48%	NYSE
WisdomTree Japan High-Yielding Equity Fund	DNL	0.58%	NYSE
WisdomTree Japan SmallCap Dividend Fund	DFJ	0.58%	NYSE
WisdomTree Pacific ex-Japan Total Dividend	DND	0.48%	NYSE
WisdomTree Pacific ex-Japan High-Yielding Equity	DNH	0.58%	NYSE
WisdomTree International Large Cap Dividend Fund	DOL	0.48%	NYSE
WisdomTree International Dividend Top 100 Fund	DOO	0.58%	NYSE
WisdomTree International MidCap Dividend Fund	DIM	0.58%	NYSE
WisdomTree International SmallCap Dividend Fund	DLS	0.58%	NYSE
Expense Ratio Category Average		**0.51%**	

Emerging Market Indexes	Ticker Symbol	Expense Ratio	Exchange
BLDRS Emerging Markets 50 ADR	ADRE	0.30%	NASDAQ
iShares MSCI Emerging Markets	EEM	0.75%	Amex
iShares MSCI Brazil	EWZ	0.74%	NYSE
iShares MSCI Malaysia	EWM	0.59%	NYSE
iShares MSCI Mexico	EWW	0.59%	Amex
iShares MSCI South Africa	EZA	0.74%	Amex
iShares MSCI South Korea	EWY	0.74%	NYSE
iShares MSCI Taiwan	EWT	0.74%	NYSE
Vanguard Emerging Markets ETF	VWO	0.30%	Amex
Expense Ratio Category Average		**0.61%**	

Fixed Income Indexes	Ticker Symbol	Expense Ratio	Exchange
iShares Lehman Aggregate Bond Fund	AGG	0.20%	Amex
iShares Lehman 1–3 Year Treasury Bond Fund	SHY	0.15%	Amex
iShares Lehman 7–10 Year Treasury Bond Fund	IEF	0.15%	Amex
iShares Lehman 20+ Year Treasury Bond	TLT	0.15%	Amex
iShares Lehman TIPS Bond Fund	TIP	0.20%	Amex
iShares GS $ InvesTop Corporate Bond Fund	LQD	0.15%	Amex
Expense Ratio Category Average		**0.17%**	

Commodities (including ETFs and Exchange-traded Notes)	Ticker Symbol	Expense Ratio	Exchange
DB Commodity Index Tracking Fund	DBC	0.83%	Amex
iShares COMEX Gold Trust	IAU	0.40%	Amex
streetTRACKS Gold Trust	GLD	0.40%	NYSE
United States Oil Fund	USO	0.50%	Amex
iShares Silver Trust	SLV	0.50%	Amex
iPath Dow Jones-AIG Commodity Index Total Return ETN	DJP	0.75%	NYSE
iPath GSCI Total Return Index ETN	GSP	0.75%	NYSE
Expense Ratio Category Average		**0.59%**	

Currencies	*Ticker Symbol*	*Expense Ratio*	*Exchange*
CurrencyShares Australian Dollar Trust	FXA	0.40%	NYSE
CurrencyShares British Pound Sterling Trust	FXB	0.40%	NYSE
CurrencyShares Canadian Dollar Trust	FXC	0.40%	NYSE
CurrencyShares Mexican Peso Trust	FXM	0.40%	NYSE
CurrencyShares Swedish Krona Trust	FXS	0.40%	NYSE
CurrencyShares Swiss Franc Trust	FXF	0.40%	NYSE
Euro Currency Trust	FXE	0.40%	NYSE
Expense Ratio Category Average		**0.40%**	

Specialty ETFs	*Ticker Symbol*	*Expense Ratio*	*Exchange*
First Trust IPOX-100 Index Fund	FPX	0.60%	Amex
Short QQQ ProShares	PSQ	0.95%	Amex
Ultra QQQ ProShares	QLD	0.95%	Amex
UltraShort QQQ ProShares	QID	0.95%	Amex
Short S&P500 ProShares	SH	0.95%	Amex
Short Dow30 ProShares	DOG	0.95%	Amex
Ultra S&P500 ProShares	SSO	0.95%	Amex
Ultra Dow30 ProShares	DDM	0.95%	Amex
UltraShort S&P500 ProShares	SDS	0.95%	Amex
UltraShort Dow30 ProShares	DXD	0.95%	Amex
Short MidCap S&P400 ProShares	MYY	0.95%	Amex
Ultra MidCap S&P400 ProShares	MVV	0.95%	Amex
UltraShort MidCap S&P400 ProShares	MZZ	0.95%	Amex
Expense Ratio Category Average		**0.92%**	

*Unmanaged Indexes**	*Ticker Symbol*	*Expense Ratio*	*Exchange*
Biotech HOLDRS	BBH	*See Footnote	Amex
Broadband HOLDRS	BDH	*See Footnote	Amex
B2B HOLDRS	BHH	*See Footnote	Amex
Europe HOLDRS	EKH	*See Footnote	Amex
Internet HOLDRS	HHH	*See Footnote	Amex
Internet Architecture HOLDRS	IAH	*See Footnote	Amex

(continued)

Unmanaged Indexes*	Ticker Symbol	Expense Ratio	Exchange
Internet Infrastructure HOLDRS	IIH	*See Footnote	Amex
Market 2000+ HOLDRS	MKH	*See Footnote	Amex
Oil Service HOLDRS	OIH	*See Footnote	Amex
Pharmaceutical HOLDRS	PPH	*See Footnote	Amex
Regional Bank HOLDRS	RKH	*See Footnote	Amex
Retail HOLDRS	RTH	*See Footnote	Amex
Semiconductor HOLDRS	SMH	*See Footnote	Amex
Software HOLDRS	SWH	*See Footnote	Amex
Telecom HOLDRS	TTH	*See Footnote	Amex
Utilities HOLDRS	UTH	*See Footnote	Amex
Wireless HOLDRS	WMH	*See Footnote	Amex

*HOLDRS can be purchased only in 100 round-lot share increments. Each round-lot is subject to an $8 annual custodial fee.

Appendix B

Great Web Resources to Help You Invest in ETFs

You can find anything on the Web: gob and gobs of information — and misinformation. And in the world of finance, there is more misinformation than information. If you pressed me, I'd put the ratio at 7:2. Following are some Web sites you can trust to keep you informed about ETFs and other investment issues.

Independent ETF-Specific Web Sites

www.etfconnect.com: Quotes, yields, and ETF nuts-n-bolts information (expense ratios, performance records). A search function allows you to rummage through the world of ETFs to find one that fits whatever criteria.

www.etfguide.com: A good, quick summary of the entire ETF world. Contains a complete listing of all ETFs available, along with ticker symbols. (The same list appears in Appendix A, although, naturally, the Web site's will be more up-to-date.)

www.etftrends.com: A gossip column of sorts for ETF enthusiasts. There's chit chat about new ETFs on the market, ETFs pending approval of the SEC, behind-the-scenes industry workings, and rumors.

http://finance.yahoo.com/etf: Features a search function with intimate details on individual funds, an ETF glossary, and regularly updated news and commentary.

www.indexuniverse.com: See "Breaking News" for the most up-to-date information on ETFs and index mutual funds. See the "Data" section to help screen for ETFs of your liking.

`www.morningstar.com` **(Click the ETF icon on blue bar at top of screen):** Thorough information on individual funds, along with Morningstar's trademarked rating system. (One star is bad, five stars is grand.)

`www.nasd.com`: The National Association of Securities Dealers. "Mutual Fund Expense Analyzer" is a great tool that allows you to see the impact of operating fees on a fund's total return over time.

Web Sites of ETF Providers

Ninety-nine percent of all ETFs come from one of the following ten product lines.

The biggies

`www.ishares.com`: Barclays iShares. The British-based company dominates the ETF market, especially in the international stock and fixed-income arenas.

`www.spdrindex.com`: The SPDRs are issued by State Street Global Advisors (SSgA) and track broad indexes as well as industry sector indexes.

`www.streettracks.com`: SSgA's sister ETFs.

`www.vanguard.com`: The King of Indexing produces some of the lowest-cost ETFs.

Smaller players

`www.bldrsfunds.com`: Inexpensive, straight, and simple international offerings.

`www.holdrs.com`: Industry sectors galore.

`www.powershares.com`: A host of unusual indexes, for better or worse.

`www.proshares.com`: ETFs for a wild ride.

`www.rydexfunds.com`: ETFs for nonconformists.

`www.wisdomtree.com`: You say you like dividends?

Best Retirement Calculator

How large a portfolio are you going to need to retire in style? How much are you going to have to sock away, and what kind of rate of return do you need to get there?

www.fireseeker.com: *Fire* stands for *financial independence/retire early.* If you didn't realize it, there is an entire movement out there devoted to financial independence. Use this Web site as your entry point. You find what is arguably the best retirement calculator on the Web, along with an Early Retirement Forum where other *Fire* fans passionately discuss their strategies.

Financial Supermarkets

Otherwise known as large brokerage houses, here are some places where you can buy, sell, and house your ETFs — as well as other investments, such as mutual funds and individual stocks and bonds.

www.fidelity.com: Or telephone Fidelity at 1-800-544-8888.

www.schwab.com: Or telephone Charles Schwab at 1-866-232-9890.

www.tdameritrade.com: Or telephone TD AMERITRADE at 1-800-454-9272.

www.troweprice.com: Or telephone T. Rowe Price at 1-800-638-5660.

www.vanguard.com: Or telephone Vanguard at 1-800-662-7447.

Stock Exchanges

www.amex.com: Almost half of all ETFs are listed on the American Stock Exchange (AMEX). It's a bland Web site, but it provides all the ETF basics.

www.nasdaq.com: Despite the fact that not many ETFs are listed on the NASDAQ, the Web site has some very cool ETF-related things. Check out especially the "ETF Dynamic Heatmap."

www.nyse.com: Those ETFS that aren't listed on the AMEX are by and large traded on the New York Stock Exchange. Surprisingly, there isn't a lot of ETF information on the Web site, but there is a wealth of general information about the world of finance.

Specialty Web Sites

www.cboe.com: The Chicago Board Options Exchange. If options trading is your kind of thing.

www.investinginbonds.org: The National Bond Marketing Association. Get a quickie education on bond investing.

www.investinreits.org: Everything you could want to know about real estate investment trusts (REITs), including REIT ETFs.

www.investnretire.com: A company that sets up ETF-based retirement plans for employers. Let it serve as a model to others.

www.nareit.org: The National Association of REITs. Very rah-rah.

www.socialinvest.org: A wealth of information on socially responsible investing.

Where to Find a Financial Planner

www.cambridgeadvisors.com: A national network of fee-onlies (financial people who work for a straight fee rather than commissions) who are eager to work with middle-class folk.

www.cfainstitute.org: CFA Institute is where you want to go to find a Chartered Financial Analyst (CFA), which is not as well-known but very similar to a Certified Financial Planner (CFP).

www.cfp.net: The Certified Financial Planning Board of Standards. Lists Certified Financial Planners (CFPs) nationwide. The CFP designation assures that the person has a fair amount of education and experience, and passed a wicked 10-hour exam.

www.fpanet.org: Financial Planning Association. The nation's largest organization of financial planners. It doesn't take much to join.

www.garrettplanningnetwork.com: A network of 250 financial advisors who charge for services on an hourly, as-needed basis.

www.napfa.org: National Association of Personal Financial Advisors. This is the association for *fee-onlies:* financial people who don't take commissions but, rather, work for a straight fee. About four out of ten financial planners are fee-onlies.

Regulatory Agency

www.sec.gov: The United States Securities and Exchange Commission. Click on "check out brokers and advisors" to make sure a financial planner is fully licensed. You'll also find out if your candidate has any disciplinary history for unethical conduct.

The People Who Create the Indexes

Dow Jones, Morgan Stanley, Russell, and Standard and Poors create the indexes that the majority of ETFs track. Just in case you're interested:

- ✔ www.djindexes.com
- ✔ www.msci.com
- ✔ www.russell.com
- ✔ www.standardandpoors.com

Good Places to Go for General Financial News, Advice, and Education

www.bloomberg.com: Hardcore financial data.

www.cnnfn.com: Get your daily fix of everything money related.

http://finance.yahoo.com: Extensive information and analysis, all for free.

www.moneychimp.com: For the more advanced investor.

www.morningstar.com: Anything and everything about stocks, mutual funds, and ETFs.

www.sensible-investor.com: A gateway to other financial Web sites, including the most esoteric (gay and lesbian investors, black investors, Christian investors . . .).

Yours Truly

www.globalportfolios.net or **www.russellwild.com:** Both URLs will take you to the same place: the author's own rock 'em sock 'em Web site.

Appendix C

Glossary

· ·

*I*f you're going to be an ETF investor, you need to know the lingo. If you're not going to be an ETF investor, you can still use the following phrases to impress at cocktail parties and Republican fundraising events. Please note that any word in *italics* (except for the word *italics*) appears as its own entry elsewhere in the glossary.

Active investing. Ah, to beat the market. Isn't it every investor's dream? Through stock picking or market timing, or both strategies, active investing offers hope of market-beating returns. Alas, it sounds a lot easier than it really is. Compare to *passive investing*.

Alpha. Given a certain level of risk, you should expect a certain rate of return. If your stock/fund/portfolio return exceeds that expectation, congratulations! — you've just achieved what people in the finance world call "positive Alpha." Pass the caviar. If your stock/fund/portfolio return falls shy of that expectation, you are in the dark and depressing land of "negative Alpha." Pass the herring.

Ask price. It's the rock-bottom price that any stock or ETF seller is willing to accept. If any buyer is willing to fork over that amount, a sale is made. If no buyers are willing to match the ask price, gravity will eventually start to drag down the price of the stock. Compare to *bid price* and *spread*.

Asset class. To build a diversified portfolio (meaning not have all your eggs in one flimsy straw basket), you want to have your investments spread out among different asset classes. An asset class is any group of similar investments. Examples may include small value stocks, utility stocks, high-yield bonds, Japanese small company stocks, or Rembrandts (paintings, not the toothpaste).

Beta. A common measurement of the volatility of an investment. If your ETF has a beta of 1.5, it tends to move up 15 percent whenever the market as a whole (usually represented, somewhat clumsily, by the S&P 500 Index) goes up 10 percent. If the market as a whole goes down 10 percent, your ETF will fall 15 percent. Note that beta is a relative measure of risk, while *standard deviation* (a generally more useful tool) is an absolute measure of risk.

Bid price. The highest price that any buyer is willing to spend to purchase shares of a stock or ETF. Compare to *ask price* and *spread*.

Cap size. A less fancy way of saying "market capitalization." It refers to the size of a company as measured by the total number of stock outstanding times the market price of each share. In general, stocks are classified as either large cap (over $5 billion), small cap (under $1 billion), or mid cap (anything in between).

Closet index fund. A mutual fund may call itself actively managed and may charge you a boatload of money, but it may be, in essence, an index fund. Shhhhhh. The manager doesn't want to come out of the closet, lest he lose his excuse for charging you what he charges you and be forced to surrender the keys to the Mercedes.

Correlation. The degree to which two investments — such as two ETFs — move up and down at the same time. A correlation of 1 means that the two investments move up and down together, like the Rockettes. A correlation of –1 means that when one goes up, the other goes down, like two pistons. A correlation of 0 means that there is no correlation between the two, like the price of bananas and the Philadelphia Eagles.

Diversification. It means dividing your investments into different *asset classes* with limited *correlation*. Diversification is good. Very good. ETFs make it easy. Did I already mention that diversification is good?

EAFE index. EAFE stands for Europe, Australia, and Far East. This index is often used (incorrectly) to represent foreign stocks. What it really tracks are large cap stocks of developed foreign nations.

Emerging markets. This is a common euphemism for "countries where most people live on rice and corn." People who invest in emerging markets hope that these nations (mostly in Africa, South America, and Asia) are, in fact, emerging. No one knows. The fortunes of emerging market stocks are closely tied to the markets for natural resources. Emerging market ETFs tend to be rather volatile, but offer excellent return possibilities.

Expense ratio. Sometimes referred to as the "management fee," this is a yearly bill you pay to a mutual fund or ETF. The money is taken directly out of your account. The expense ratio for ETFs is usually much, much less than that of mutual funds. If the expense ratio for your entire portfolio is more than 1 percent, you're paying too much.

Fundamental analysis. If you're going to be picking stocks, it makes sense, I suppose, to do some fundamental analysis: an analysis of the company's profitability both present and future. Just know that fundamental analysis is an awfully fuzzy science. And, ironically, the strongest, fastest-growing companies don't always make for the most profitable stocks. See *value premium*.

Growth fund. A fund that invests in stocks of companies that have been fast-growing and are expected (by fundamental analysts) to continue to be fast-growing. In its day, Enron was a growth stock. You never know . . .

Indexing. This term is synonymous with *passive investing.* Index investing has been around for a good while; ETFs simply make it easier, less expensive, and more *tax efficient.*

iShares. This is the brand name for ETFs issued by Barclays, the largest purveyor of ETFs in the world. Roughly half the money invested in ETFs is invested in iShares.

Liquidity. A liquid asset can readily be turned into cash. Examples include money market funds and very short-term bond funds. *Ill*iquid assets are trickier things to turn into cash. The classic example of an illiquid asset is the family home.

Load. A wad of cash that you need to fork over in order to purchase certain mutual funds. Study after study shows that load funds perform no better than no-load funds, yet people are willing to pay rather huge loads. Go figure. ETFs never charge loads. Gotta love that about them.

Modern Portfolio Theory. It says that a portfolio doesn't have to be excessively risky, even if its separate components are riskier than skydiving without a parachute. The trick is to fill your portfolio with investments that have low *correlation* to one another. When one crashes, another soars — or at least hovers.

Passive investing. You buy an index of stocks (preferably through an ETF), and you hold them. And you hold them. And you hold them. It's as boring as a game of bingo in which none of the letters called are the ones you need. And yet passive investors beat the pants off most active investors, year in and year out.

Price/earnings ratio (P/E). Take a company's total earnings over the past 12 months and divide that by the number of shares of stock outstanding. The resulting number represents earnings, the lower number in the equation. Price — the upper number — refers to the market price of the stock. The P/E is the most common way in which stocks are identified as either value stocks or growth stocks. High P/E = growth. Low P/E = value.

Qubes. A nickname for the QQQ, an index that tracks the top 100 companies listed on the NASDAQ stock exchange. QQQQ is the *ticker* for the most popular ETF that tracks the QQQ. Why QQQQ and not QQQ? I don't knowww.

REIT stock/fund. A stock or fund that invests in a company or companies that make their money in real estate — most often commercial real estate, such as office buildings and shopping malls. REIT funds tend to be interest-rate sensitive and often have limited *correlation* to other funds.

Risk. When we investment types talk of risk, we generally mean but one thing: *volatility,* or the unpredictability of an investment. The higher the risk, the greater the potential return.

R squared. This measurement shows how tightly an investment hugs a certain index. An R squared of .90 means that 90 percent of a fund's movement is attributable to movement in the index to which it is most similar. For an index fund or ETF, an R squared of 1.00 is usually the goal. For an allegedly actively managed fund, an R squared of 1.00 (or anything higher than .85 or so) means that you have a *closet index fund,* and you are being ripped off.

Sector investing. If you break up your stock portfolio into different industry sectors — energy, consumer staples, financials — then you are a sector investor, as opposed to a *style investor.*

Sharpe ratio. A risk-adjusted measure of fund performance. In other words, it measures a fund's average historical return per unit of risk. The higher the number, the happier you should be.

Sophisticated investor. Often mistaken for someone who trades every day and is constantly checking his account balance. Or someone who uses charts and graphs and tries to time the markets. In the real world, such "sophisticated" investors rarely do as well as the "dummy" who builds a well-diversified portfolio of low-cost index funds (such as ETFs) and lets it sit undisturbed.

SPDRs. This is the nickname for most of the ETFs issued by State Street Global Advisors (SSgA), the second-largest purveyor of ETFs after Barclays. (SSgA also issues streetTRACKS ETFs.)

Spread. The difference between the *ask price* and *bid price* for a stock or ETF.

Standard deviation. The most used measure of volatility in the world of investments. The formula is long and complicated with lots of Greek symbols. Suffice to say this: A standard deviation of 5 means that roughly two-thirds of the time, your investment returns will fall within 5 percentage points of the mean. So if your ETF has an historical mean return of 10 percent, two-thirds of the time you can expect to see your returns fall somewhere between 5 percent and 15 percent. If your ETF has an historical mean return of 5 percent, two-thirds of the time you can expect your return to be somewhere between 0 percent and 10 percent.

streetTRACKS. The name of one of two lineups of ETFs issued by State Street Global Advisors. (The other is _SPDRs._)

Style investing. If you divvy up your stock investments into large, small, value, and growth, you are a style investor, as opposed to a _sector investor._ Which is better? Hard to say.

Style drift. It's 11 p.m. Do you know where your investments are? A manager of an active mutual fund tells you that her fund is, say, a large growth fund. And perhaps it once was. But lately, this gal has been loading up on large value companies. Is she a growth investor or a value investor? Only she knows for sure. Investors, meanwhile, get stuck with her style drift and aren't sure exactly what they are holding. See _transparency._

Tax efficiency. ETFs are often praised for their tax efficiency. That means the funds generate little in the way of capital gains, so you pay only taxes on dividends until such time as you actually cash out. With many mutual funds, you can wind up paying taxes at the most inopportune moments.

Tax-loss harvesting. Late in the year (most often), you can sell off a losing investment in order to claim a loss on your taxes. You can usually use tax losses to wipe out capital gains of the same amount. If your losses exceed your gains, you can generally take the loss to wipe out ordinary income, up to $3,000. In effect, Uncle Sam is helping to share the burden of your woes.

Technical analysis. The use of charts and graphs to try to predict the stock market. Some people take it very, very seriously — despite a lack of any evidence that it works.

Ticker. The two- to five-letter symbol used for a stock, mutual fund, or ETF. Examples include SPY, QQQQ, and EWJ. Heck, there's even one called DOG (but none yet with the ticker GOD).

Transparency. ETFs are beautifully transparent, which means that you know exactly what stocks or bonds your ETF holds. The same is not always true with mutual funds, hedge funds, or your spouse's safe deposit box.

Turnover. The degree to which a fund changes its investments over the course of a year. A turnover rate of 100 means that the fund starts and ends the year with a completely different set of stocks. Turnover generally creates unpleasant tax liabilities for investors. Turnover, almost always, also involves hidden trading costs.

Value fund. A mutual fund or ETF that invests in companies whose recent growth may be less than eye-popping, but whose stock prices are believed to be cheap in comparison to the prices of stocks of other like companies.

Value premium. Over the past century or so, ever since the birth of organized stock markets, value stocks have performed much better than growth
stocks, with relatively the same degree of *risk*. Theories abound. But to date,
economists can't seem to agree why this apparent value premium exists, or
whether it is likely to continue.

Volatility. Whoooeee. What goes up fast often comes down just as fast. A
stock or ETF that gained 40 percent last year can lose 40 percent this year. It
is volatile. It is risky. It can bring you great joy or great misery. Hope for the
former, but be prepared for the latter.

Yield. This term is most often used to mean the income derived from an
investment over the past 12 months, as a percentage of the total investment.
Income may come from dividends (most often the case with stocks or stock
ETFs) or interest (from a bond or bond ETF). If you sink $10,000 into an ETF
and it generates $500 in yearly income, your yield is 5 percent. If it generates
$600, your yield is 6 percent, and so on.

YTD. Year-to-date return, or the total return (dividends plus any rise in the
price of the stock or ETF) from January 1 of the present year until today —
whatever day today is.

Index

BUSINESS, CAREERS & PERSONAL FINANCE

0-7645-5307-0

0-7645-5331-3 *†

Also available:
- Accounting For Dummies †
  0-7645-5314-3
- Business Plans Kit For Dummies †
  0-7645-5365-8
- Cover Letters For Dummies
  0-7645-5224-4
- Frugal Living For Dummies
  0-7645-5403-4
- Leadership For Dummies
  0-7645-5176-0
- Managing For Dummies
  0-7645-1771-6

- Marketing For Dummies
  0-7645-5600-2
- Personal Finance For Dummies *
  0-7645-2590-5
- Project Management For Dummies
  0-7645-5283-X
- Resumes For Dummies †
  0-7645-5471-9
- Selling For Dummies
  0-7645-5363-1
- Small Business Kit For Dummies *†
  0-7645-5093-4

HOME & BUSINESS COMPUTER BASICS

0-7645-4074-2

0-7645-3758-X

Also available:
- ACT! 6 For Dummies
  0-7645-2645-6
- iLife '04 All-in-One Desk Reference
  For Dummies
  0-7645-7347-0
- iPAQ For Dummies
  0-7645-6769-1
- Mac OS X Panther Timesaving
  Techniques For Dummies
  0-7645-5812-9
- Macs For Dummies
  0-7645-5656-8

- Microsoft Money 2004 For Dummies
  0-7645-4195-1
- Office 2003 All-in-One Desk Reference
  For Dummies
  0-7645-3883-7
- Outlook 2003 For Dummies
  0-7645-3759-8
- PCs For Dummies
  0-7645-4074-2
- TiVo For Dummies
  0-7645-6923-6
- Upgrading and Fixing PCs For Dummies
  0-7645-1665-5
- Windows XP Timesaving Techniques
  For Dummies
  0-7645-3748-2

FOOD, HOME, GARDEN, HOBBIES, MUSIC & PETS

0-7645-5295-3

0-7645-5232-5

Also available:
- Bass Guitar For Dummies
  0-7645-2487-9
- Diabetes Cookbook For Dummies
  0-7645-5230-9
- Gardening For Dummies *
  0-7645-5130-2
- Guitar For Dummies
  0-7645-5106-X
- Holiday Decorating For Dummies
  0-7645-2570-0
- Home Improvement All-in-One
  For Dummies
  0-7645-5680-0

- Knitting For Dummies
  0-7645-5395-X
- Piano For Dummies
  0-7645-5105-1
- Puppies For Dummies
  0-7645-5255-4
- Scrapbooking For Dummies
  0-7645-7208-3
- Senior Dogs For Dummies
  0-7645-5818-8
- Singing For Dummies
  0-7645-2475-5
- 30-Minute Meals For Dummies
  0-7645-2589-1

INTERNET & DIGITAL MEDIA

0-7645-1664-7

0-7645-6924-4

Also available:
- 2005 Online Shopping Directory
  For Dummies
  0-7645-7495-7
- CD & DVD Recording For Dummies
  0-7645-5956-7
- eBay For Dummies
  0-7645-5654-1
- Fighting Spam For Dummies
  0-7645-5965-6
- Genealogy Online For Dummies
  0-7645-5964-8
- Google For Dummies
  0-7645-4420-9

- Home Recording For Musicians
  For Dummies
  0-7645-1634-5
- The Internet For Dummies
  0-7645-4173-0
- iPod & iTunes For Dummies
  0-7645-7772-7
- Preventing Identity Theft For Dummies
  0-7645-7336-5
- Pro Tools All-in-One Desk Reference
  For Dummies
  0-7645-5714-9
- Roxio Easy Media Creator For Dummies
  0-7645-7131-1

* Separate Canadian edition also available
† Separate U.K. edition also available

Available wherever books are sold. For more information or to order direct: U.S. customers visit www.dummies.com or call 1-877-762-2974.
U.K. customers visit www.wileyeurope.com or call 0800 243407. Canadian customers visit www.wiley.ca or call 1-800-567-4797.

SPORTS, FITNESS, PARENTING, RELIGION & SPIRITUALITY

0-7645-5146-9

0-7645-5418-2

Also available:

Adoption For Dummies
0-7645-5488-3

Basketball For Dummies
0-7645-5248-1

The Bible For Dummies
0-7645-5296-1

Buddhism For Dummies
0-7645-5359-3

Catholicism For Dummies
0-7645-5391-7

Hockey For Dummies
0-7645-5228-7

Judaism For Dummies
0-7645-5299-6

Martial Arts For Dummies
0-7645-5358-5

Pilates For Dummies
0-7645-5397-6

Religion For Dummies
0-7645-5264-3

Teaching Kids to Read For Dummies
0-7645-4043-2

Weight Training For Dummies
0-7645-5168-X

Yoga For Dummies
0-7645-5117-5

TRAVEL

0-7645-5438-7

0-7645-5453-0

Also available:

Alaska For Dummies
0-7645-1761-9

Arizona For Dummies
0-7645-6938-4

Cancún and the Yucatán For Dummies
0-7645-2437-2

Cruise Vacations For Dummies
0-7645-6941-4

Europe For Dummies
0-7645-5456-5

Ireland For Dummies
0-7645-5455-7

Las Vegas For Dummies
0-7645-5448-4

London For Dummies
0-7645-4277-X

New York City For Dummies
0-7645-6945-7

Paris For Dummies
0-7645-5494-8

RV Vacations For Dummies
0-7645-5443-3

Walt Disney World & Orlando For Dummies
0-7645-6943-0

GRAPHICS, DESIGN & WEB DEVELOPMENT

0-7645-4345-8

0-7645-5589-8

Also available:

Adobe Acrobat 6 PDF For Dummies
0-7645-3760-1

Building a Web Site For Dummies
0-7645-7144-3

Dreamweaver MX 2004 For Dummies
0-7645-4342-3

FrontPage 2003 For Dummies
0-7645-3882-9

HTML 4 For Dummies
0-7645-1995-6

Illustrator CS For Dummies
0-7645-4084-X

Macromedia Flash MX 2004 For Dummies
0-7645-4358-X

Photoshop 7 All-in-One Desk
Reference For Dummies
0-7645-1667-1

Photoshop CS Timesaving Techniques
For Dummies
0-7645-6782-9

PHP 5 For Dummies
0-7645-4166-8

PowerPoint 2003 For Dummies
0-7645-3908-6

QuarkXPress 6 For Dummies
0-7645-2593-X

NETWORKING, SECURITY, PROGRAMMING & DATABASES

0-7645-6852-3

0-7645-5784-X

Also available:

A+ Certification For Dummies
0-7645-4187-0

Access 2003 All-in-One Desk
Reference For Dummies
0-7645-3988-4

Beginning Programming For Dummies
0-7645-4997-9

C For Dummies
0-7645-7068-4

Firewalls For Dummies
0-7645-4048-3

Home Networking For Dummies
0-7645-42796

Network Security For Dummies
0-7645-1679-5

Networking For Dummies
0-7645-1677-9

TCP/IP For Dummies
0-7645-1760-0

VBA For Dummies
0-7645-3989-2

Wireless All In-One Desk Reference
For Dummies
0-7645-7496-5

Wireless Home Networking For Dummies
0-7645-3910-8

HEALTH & SELF-HELP

0-7645-6820-5 *†

0-7645-2566-2

Also available:

- Alzheimer's For Dummies
  0-7645-3899-3
- Asthma For Dummies
  0-7645-4233-8
- Controlling Cholesterol For Dummies
  0-7645-5440-9
- Depression For Dummies
  0-7645-3900-0
- Dieting For Dummies
  0-7645-4149-8
- Fertility For Dummies
  0-7645-2549-2

- Fibromyalgia For Dummies
  0-7645-5441-7
- Improving Your Memory For Dummies
  0-7645-5435-2
- Pregnancy For Dummies †
  0-7645-4483-7
- Quitting Smoking For Dummies
  0-7645-2629-4
- Relationships For Dummies
  0-7645-5384-4
- Thyroid For Dummies
  0-7645-5385-2

EDUCATION, HISTORY, REFERENCE & TEST PREPARATION

0-7645-5194-9

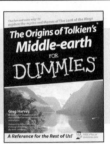

0-7645-4186-2

Also available:

- Algebra For Dummies
  0-7645-5325-9
- British History For Dummies
  0-7645-7021-8
- Calculus For Dummies
  0-7645-2498-4
- English Grammar For Dummies
  0-7645-5322-4
- Forensics For Dummies
  0-7645-5580-4
- The GMAT For Dummies
  0-7645-5251-1
- Inglés Para Dummies
  0-7645-5427-1

- Italian For Dummies
  0-7645-5196-5
- Latin For Dummies
  0-7645-5431-X
- Lewis & Clark For Dummies
  0-7645-2545-X
- Research Papers For Dummies
  0-7645-5426-3
- The SAT I For Dummies
  0-7645-7193-1
- Science Fair Projects For Dummies
  0-7645-5460-3
- U.S. History For Dummies
  0-7645-5249-X

Get smart @ dummies.com®

- **Find a full list of Dummies titles**
- **Look into loads of FREE on-site articles**
- **Sign up for FREE eTips e-mailed to you weekly**
- **See what other products carry the Dummies name**
- **Shop directly from the Dummies bookstore**
- **Enter to win new prizes every month!**

Separate Canadian edition also available
Separate U.K. edition also available

Available wherever books are sold. For more information or to order direct: U.S. customers visit www.dummies.com or call 1-877-762-2974.
U.K. customers visit www.wileyeurope.com or call 0800 243407. Canadian customers visit www.wiley.ca or call 1-800-567-4797.

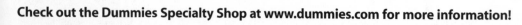